Understanding Combustion

Second Edition

H S Mukunda

Combustion, Gasification and Propulsion Laboratory
Indian Institute of Science, Bangalore

Universities Press

Universities Press (India) Private Limited

Registered Office
3-6-747/1/A & 3-6-754/1, Himayatnagar,
Hyderabad 500 029 (A.P.), India
e-mail: info@universitiespress.com

Distributed by
Orient Blackswan Private Limited

Registered Office
3-6-752, Himayatnagar, Hyderabad 500 029 (A.P.), India

Other Offices
Bangalore / Bhopal / Bhubaneshwar / Chennai / Ernakulam / Guwahati
Hyderabad / Jaipur / Kolkata / Lucknow / Mumbai / New Delhi / Patna

First published by MacMillan India Ltd., 1989
Reprinted 1992
Second edition 2009 (First Universities Press impression)
Reprinted 2013

Cover and book design

ISBN: 978 81 7371 685 0

Set in Times New Roman 10.6/12.6 *by*
OSDATA, Hyderabad 500 029

Printed in India at
Bluebells Secure Prints
Hyderabad 500 072

Published by
Universities Press (India) Private Limited
3-6-747/1/A & 3-6-754/1, Himayatnagar, Hyderabad 500 029 (A.P), India

Contents

Preface to the Second Edition

This is the second edition of the book *Understanding Combustion*. The first book was written in the 1986–1987 time frame. When this book was first published, it was not clear what the response of the readers would be. Fortunately, there has been positive feedback on the readability of the book from several unexpected quarters, both academic and industrial. This has been the motivation to amend chapters and add new chapters for a slightly more comprehensive book which aims to give the reader the essence of the subject before launching into other books written in greater detail meant more for a professional.

Even though the essentials have remained the same, much has happened in the subject in the intervening period—the rising cost of fossil fuels has been a serious issue arising out of the peaking of liquid fossil fuel availability across the world. We have burnt up much more than we can sustainably produce. Mining has been excessive. Solid fuels like coal do not belong to this category yet. Efforts to develop and use renewable liquid fuels like biofuels and other solid fuels including the urban solid waste brought up by indiscriminate urbanisation should be on the rise. Hence, there is no escape from combustion either at home, workplace or in travel, be it via ground, air or outer space. Conservation of fuels with better combustion efficiency and limiting the emission of undesirable intermediate chemical components have become a compelling necessity.

Three new chapters have been added to this book on gasification of solid fuels, emission of pollutants, and explosion and detonation. The developments in gasification in the last twenty years have been the primary motivation for including the topic of gasification. It is anticipated that the technique will come into vogue in all parts of world, particularly the developing world, in the coming two decades in very significant way. The other two subjects which were missed out in the earlier edition have been included now to ensure greater awareness on these among readers.

It is useful to point out that this book is meant for armchair reading. A student would require to sit at a table and look up at hard data only when there is a need to make some calculations. It was thought that a general reader does not need to know where a specific knowledge originated from;

it is sufficient to know that the logic for a certain train of thought is based on experiments or a certain theory more complex than can be set out in a small volume like this. It is for this reasons that a detailed referencing of original papers is not carried out. A list of books and sources for original papers is provided at the end. The Internet can greatly enhance the information base on the subject.

The present effort to update the book is due largely to the prodding of Dr C S Bhaskar Dixit, my former student. Not only did he persuade, he put in effort for getting the book to this shape in many ways. Mrs Uma Dixit helped in drawing the figures in the new format. Mrs Neesa Sharma converted the original book into a soft copy for carrying out the modifications and additions.

H S Mukunda
Indian Institute of Science
Bangalore

Preface to the First Edition

This book discusses combustion. Combustion is a field which involves fluid mechanics, heat transfer and energy addition and absorption by chemistry. Mathematics is essential for establishing inter-relationships between observed phenomena and the control parameters like ambient pressure, temperature and geometry through solution of simple or complex equations.

This book has been written to provoke a perceptive student, a working engineer or a scientist to obtain a glimpse of the way combustion problems are understood and tackled. The motivation for this book comes from the fact that most books on combustion are meant only for serious students of combustion and that many important but less sophisticated aspects are not treated in the currently available books. The word understanding used here has two implications. The first one is at a qualitative level and the level of seeing relationships—seeing the important elements affecting the phenomena. The next level is one of examining the detailed features of phenomena through the solution of conservation equations and specifically designed experiments. The present work addresses only the first part.

The first five chapters, particularly chapters 3, 4 and 5, lay the foundation for understanding combustion phenomena. These consist of stoichiometry, adiabatic flame temperature and composition and rates of reactions. Rest of the chapters is devoted to the study of the two limits of combustion phenomena—premixed and diffusion, ignition and steady propagation. The attempt in the treatment of the subject is to emphasize the physical features, establish mathematical relationships and derive physically relevant conclusions.

Fire has been an object of worship from Vedic times. Several thousand verses in cryptic Sanskrit have been set out more than five thousand years ago providing some insight into the importance of fire in the life of those times. "Agnihrudaya" (the heart of fire) refers to the root of fire whose understanding implies mastery over the workings of fire. The quotations from *Rig Veda* given in this book and the English translation are taken from "Hymns on the Mystic Fire" by Sri Aurobindo.

I will feel gratified if the readers' understanding of combustion is improved by a study of this book.

It is a pleasure to record that Dr. B.N. Raghunandan has carefully scrutinized the manuscript and made some incisive comments for improvement and Dr. P. J. Paul has contributed ideas concerning quali¬tative explanations. Mr. S. Satish has taken the trouble of setting the manuscript on the computer meticulously. Mr. N.K.S. Rajan has helped in several aspects of the computer interface. Mr. D. Venkatesh and S. Manjunath have contributed in getting the figures and copies ready. Many thanks are due to them.

H S Mukunda
Indian Institute of Science
Bangalore

Symbols

A_b	Burning area (m^2)
A_f	Frequency factor
A/F	Air-to-fuel ratio
f_s and s	Stoichiometric fuel-to-air ratio and air-to-fuel ratio
B_v and B_c	Transfer number for evaporation and combustion
c^*	Characteristic velocity (m/s)
c_p and c_v	Specific heats at constant pressure and volume (J/mole K or J/kg K)
d	Characteristic dimension–diameter of a droplet, jet, etc (m)
D_1	Damkholer number = τ_f/τ_{ch}
D_{12}	Mass diffusivity (m^2/s)
$e.r$	Equivalence ratio = (F/A)/f_s
Gr	Grashoff number (= $\rho^2 d^3 g(T_f - T_0)/(\mu^2 T_0)$
g	Acceleration due to gravity (= 9.81 m^2/s)
g_i	Gibbs free energy of species i (kJ/mole)
h_g	Heat transfer coefficient (W/m^2 K)
h_{si} and h_{fi}	Sensible enthalpy and heat of formation of species i (kJ/mole)
H_c	Heat of combustion (MJ/kg)
k, k_g	Thermal conductivity (W/m K)
$K_p(T)$	Equilibrium constant, a function of temperature T
k_f and k_b	Forward and backward rate constants
K_v and K_c	Droplet evaporation and combustion constant (m^2/s)
L	Latent heat of phase transformation (J/kg)
L_e	Size of explosive
n_i, m_i and $\mathcal{M}_i$	Moles, mass and molecular weight of species i
$\dot{m}$, $\dot{m}''$	Mass flow rate (kg/s), mass flux (kg/m^2 s)
Nu	Nusselt number = $h_g d/k_g$
p, v, and T	Pressure (atm) and volume (m^3) and temperature (K)
$\dot{q}''$	Heat flux (W/m^2)
Re, Pr	Reynolds number = $\rho U d/\mu$, Prandtl number = $\mu c_p/k$
$\dot{r}$	Burn rate, also regression rate (mm/s)
$\mathcal{R}$	Universal gas constant (J/mole K)
S_u and S_T	Laminar and turbulent flame speeds (m/s)
T_0 and T_f	Ambient and flame temperatures (K)
X_i, Y_i	Mole and mass fractions = n_i/n, m_i/m respectively
U, V and M	Velocities (m/s) and Mach number
$\dot{w}_i'''$	Reaction rate of species i (kg/m^3s)

γ	Ratio of specific heats = c_p/c_v
μ	Viscosity (kg m/s)
ρ, ρ_p	Density and density of liquid or solid (kg/m^3)
τ_{ch}, τ_f	Characteristic chemical kinetic and fluid flow times (s)

Abbreviations

amp	Ampere
atm	Atmosphere
AP	Ammonium perchlorate
CTPB	Carboxy terminated polybutadiene
e.r	Equivalence ratio
g/nm^3	Grams per normal cubic meter
g/MJ	Grams per Mega Joule
HMX	Cyclotetramethylene tetranitramine
HSD	High speed diesel
HTPB	Hydroxy terminated polybutadiene
kg	Kilogram
kWth	Kilowatt thermal
kWe	Kilowatt electric
LDO	Light diesel oil
LPG	Liquified petroleum gas
NC	Nitrocellulose
MPa	Mega Pascals
mm	Millimeter
ms	Milliseconds
m/s	Meters per second
rpm	Revolutions per minute
NG	Nitroglycerine
ppm	Parts per million
PS	Polystyrene
PVC	Polyvinyl chloride
RDX	Cyclotrimethylene trinitramine
TNT	Trinitrotolulene
UHC	Unburnt hydrocarbons

1 Why Should One Attempt to Understand Combustion?

कविं केतुं धासिं भनुमद्रेर्हिन्वन्ति शं राज्यं रोदस्योः।
पुरंदस्य गोर्भिरा विवासेएनेर्न्वतानि पूर्व्या महानि ।।२।।

Him they send, the seer, the ray of intuition, the foundation. the light on the hill, the kingdom of peace in earth and heaven; I illumine with the words of Indra the great and ancient laws of working of Fire who rends the cities.

Rig Veda

Combustion has a million years of history. In nature, fire must have been caused due to wind-swayed dry branches of trees rubbing against one another or by lava from an active volcano igniting wood or dry grass in its path. The primitive human witnessing these must have felt awed by the heat and light of the fire and may have run away from it at first and later, perhaps, bowed before it in respect. That was, probably, how the fire God, *Agni Bhagavan*, was born.

Combustion, to a large class of users of firewood for cooking, means putting together solid pieces of fuel wood and igniting it with the modern equivalent of the flint stone, the match stick. A bit of kerosene is sometimes sprinkled on the wood to get the fire going quickly. The flame is then maintained by adding fuel pieces or rearranging the pieces already introduced. The smoke produced is tolerated if the design does not have a chimney to draw away the burnt gases. More than five hundred million homes in the world depend on solid bio-fuels for cooking.

Another class of users, largely urban, uses liquefied petroleum gas. Lighting of a gas stove is a far simple process—one just opens the valve in the gas stove and uses a spark igniter or sometimes, a matchstick. The spark igniter may not always ignite the mixture if not sparked at the right time. If it sparks a little later and a little away from the burner, a sudden large flame may result. But a steady flame is sustained afterwards.

The use of fire is not confined to cooking alone; humans have found a plethora of uses for it, especially after the industrial revolution. In creating new materials, for instance, heat generated by fire is used to melt ores or create new alloys from metals. Coal, the natural product arising out of a million years of compression of plant material under the earth, is the mainstay of combustion in such cases.

Natural gas, another fuel available in some parts of the earth, for example Assam and Gujarat in India, is used as a fuel in engines to generate motive or stationary power and in some instances, for high temperature chemical processes. Oils like diesel or gasoline are burnt in reciprocating engines of the compression-ignition kind or the spark-ignition kind to generate power for stationary applications as well as for the purpose of traction. Fuel oil or furnace oil, the crudest of the liquid distillates, is largely used in furnaces as well as large reciprocating engines for generating electricity.

The aviation industry, which has developed at a fantastic pace in the last hundred years, uses kerosene oil in its engines, mostly gas turbine engines, which burn kerosene oil along with air taken from the atmosphere at high pressure. The hot gases expand in the turbine to generate power which is used for compressing the incoming air; the residual power runs a propeller to provide the propulsive power to the airplane. There are other classes of engines that expand the hot high-pressure gases by letting it out through a nozzle into the atmosphere to create high speed jets; this process generates thrust.

During the last forty years, the use of rockets to go beyond earth's atmosphere has become a reality. These rockets burn exotic chemicals at high pressure in a small chamber. The resulting hot gases are expanded into the atmosphere via nozzles as high velocity jets, which generates the thrust necessary for propelling the vehicles into space.

The understanding required to build a good combustion system is far more complex than the impression that one may get, say while witnessing biomass cooking stoves at work. Even a kerosene wick stove has many nuances that may be missed because they are too common to merit observation. To light a kerosene stove, the outer perforated sheet around the wicks is first removed and the wicks are lighted. The flames at this stage are all tall and sooty yellow around each wick. If now, the outer perforated sheet is replaced, a nice bluish flame becomes stabilised in the annular region, occasionally with bluish buttons of flames around the holes in the perforated sheet. Such an elegant and simple combustion device that a stove is, a question arises as to whether alternate strategies for burning kerosene in a stove can be conceived? It might be tempting to think that one can obtain other designs, but in fact, there have not been many. The only other design is that of a pressure stove which heats up kerosene in the flame zone itself and issues it out as a gas jet. The jet of kerosene vapour entrains the surrounding air and burns up in a near-blue turbulent flame. It may be difficult to appreciate that in order to design such a system the geometric parameters must be chosen carefully so as to ensure that the duct carrying the kerosene does not burn up or that the resulting flame is not from the trickling drops.

The gas turbine engine combustion chamber that burns kerosene is even more complex. The requirement is to burn the fuel and the oxidiser under lean conditions (fuel fraction less than the correct proportion for combustion to be complete) at high pressure to provide a relatively uniform high temperature profile at the exit cross-section of the combustion chamber and limit the emissions of undesirable products of combustion, namely, unburnt hydrocarbons, carbon monoxide and oxides of nitrogen. Minimising the volume and weight of the system constitute the additional demands. That all these requirements have been met with in the last four decades with increasing index of performance is an evidence to progress in the understanding of the processes and the use of all the advanced design tools.

Liquid fuels, in some situations, vaporise and combust with air as in kerosene stoves. In some others, like in a furnace or gas turbine combustor, the liquid fuel is sprayed through injectors and the fine droplets burn up in an oxidiser-rich environment. In solid propellants, wherein the oxidiser and the fuel are in close proximity, combustion takes place at a high pressure. The propellant components react in condensed phase (solid/liquid), vaporise and react exothermally in gas phase, and transfer the heat back to the condensed phase to sustain the combustion process.

At the very root of these processes is the fact that a flame is produced because the flowing system has the fuel vapour and oxidiser mixing in the right proportions, chemically reacting in the released heat, which becomes the sustaining element for continued reactions. In some instances the fuel and the oxidiser are mixed before the reactions take place. These are termed 'premixed flames' (e.g., kerosene wick stove). In others, the fuel and the oxidiser are unmixed until combustion takes place at the flame. These are diffusion flames (e.g., candle flame). The entire range of flames is essentially either of the above two extremes or a combination of them. There is, therefore, a need to understand the interaction between the fluid flow and the chemical reaction under various conditions of temperature and pressure and the ways of mixing the fuel and the oxidiser in order to appreciate the design of various devices—wood stove, a reciprocating engine combustion system, a gas turbine combustor, or a rocket engine combustor.

The motivation for understanding combustion to design combustion systems arises from two considerations: (i) the systems are too complex to be understood easily and trial and error techniques of design simply do not work and (ii) the systems are so large that trial and error techniques are far too expensive to practice.

One important approach to understanding processes is dimensionless analysis. Much has been said about dimensionless numbers in engineering literature. Dimensionless analysis is a powerful and simple tool for understanding, explaining and predicting the behaviour of engineering systems, including chemical systems.

There are more powerful methods which involve conservation equations of mass, momentum, energy and species the solutions of which lead to accurate prediction of the behaviour of chemical-engineering systems. However, useful information in many cases can be extracted from dimensional analysis referred to above.

A better understanding does not always imply generation of a design procedure. It gives an insight into the way things work and hence significantly reduces the dependence on trial and error techniques.

1.1 Overview

Fuels and oxidisers can be in gaseous, liquid or solid form. They undergo exothermic reactions under a variety of conditions including those at near-ambient pressure to very high pressures to result in high temperature gases that travel at either low speeds (called deflagrations) or very high speeds (called detonations).

The main aim of engineering combustion is to release the energy of the fuels by reacting them with suitable oxidisers to release sensible heat such that the efficiency of combustion is as high as possible (close to 100 % in many instances) and to keep undesirable emissions at a minimum. The broad spectrum of conditions under which combustion is performed calls for a fundamental understanding of the various effects associated with combustion. In this endeavour, an understanding of both fluid mechanics and chemical thermodynamics is called for. To signify this, the field of combustion is sometimes referred to as aero-thermochemistry.

To achieve an understanding of the subject of combustion, experimental data and analytical tools of varying complexity are needed. This book adopts the simplest of approaches to understand the phenomena.

2 What Do We Burn and Why?

We burn fuels for two major purposes: (i) for generating heat for say, cooking, melting metals, heat treatment, etc., and (ii) for generating power, like an internal combustion reciprocating and rotating machinery, or for generating work or force like an air breathing and rocket engines.

The sensitivity of systems to the nature of fuel is much more in those cases where power/ work /force (like in case (ii)) is demanded than those where the requirement is for heat (as in case (i)). Unfortunately, this fact is not greatly appreciated and one comes across several instances where fuels meant for engines are used for heating purposes as well.

Fuels can be classified into gaseous, liquid and solid forms. Some of the fuels are listed in Table 2.1.

2.1 Gaseous fuels

Liquefied petroleum gas (LPG), the first of the fuels in Table 2.1, is a product of petroleum refining. It is used as cooking gas in most urban areas in India. It is also used as a transport fuel in three- and four-wheelers. The name, LPG, is a bit strange in that it starts with 'liquid' and ends in 'gas'. That the LPG cylinder contains a liquid can be ascertained by shaking the cylinder. On opening the top valve, however, one gets gas. A cylinder of about 35 litres (which you can compute based on the dimensions measured) contains about 15 kg of LPG (Fig. 2.1). Typically, the pressure inside the cylinder is about 0.6 MPa (note that the atmospheric pressure at sea level is approximately 0.1 MPa; 0.101325 MPa to be precise), which is about 6 times the ambient pressure. This pressure depends on ambient temperature. If the ambient temperature falls below −10°C, which is common in winter in some northern parts of India close to the Himalayas, one may get very little gas on opening the valve. (This effect is evinced after the cylinder has experienced the temperature for about a day or two, for it takes quite some

Table 2.1 *Fuels, oxidisers and their uses (LH_2 =liquid hydrogen, LO_2 = liquid oxygen, RFNA = red fuming nitric acid)*

Fuels	Oxidisers	Uses
I. Gaseous fuels		
1. Liquefied petroleum gas (LPG)	Air	Domestic purposes, furnaces
2. Biogas	Air	Domestic purposes, engines
3. Producer gas	Air	Engines (reciprocating), furnaces
4. Acetylene	Oxygen (O_2)	Gas welding/gas cutting applications
5. Basic fuel species, methane, propane, butane, carbon monoxide, hydrogen	Basic oxidising species, O_2 (N_2 is generally inert)	All combustion
II. Liquid fuels		
1. Gasoline	Air	Spark ignition engines, aircraft piston engines
2. High speed diesel (HSD)	Air	Compression ignition engines, furnaces
3. Light diesel oil, furnace oil	Air	Furnaces
4. Kerosene (wide cut)	Air	Aircraft gas turbines, ramjet, domestic applications (wide cut)
5. Alcohols	Air	Engines
Special fuels		
6. Hydrazine, unsymmetrical dimethyl hydrazine, triethyl amine, LH_2	Nitrogen tetroxide (N_2O_4), RFNA, LO_2	Liquid rocket engines,
7. LH_2, kerosene	Air	Scramjet
III. Solid fuels		
1. Biomass like firewood, sawdust, rice husk, groundnut shells, coffee husk, charcoal	Air	Domestic heat, furnaces, engines with gasifiers
2. Coal, coke	Air, O_2	Furnaces (blast furnace—to make steel) (boilers for power generation), domestic heat
3. Polymers like polybutadiene, with hydroxyl termination and aluminium powder	Ammonium perchlorate	Composite solid propellant
4. Nitrocellulose (NC) + others	Nitroglycerine (NG)	Double-base solid propellant
5. Aniline formaldehyde, rubber	N_2O_4, LO_2	Hybrid rockets

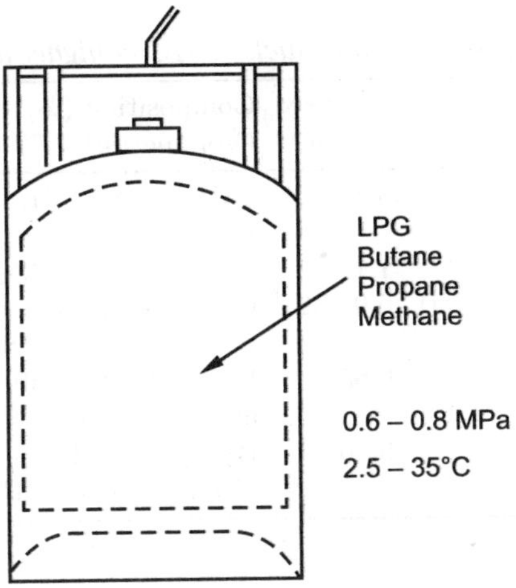

Figure 2.1 *An LPG cylinder*

time for the cold to penetrate the cylinder. A large part of the liquid then gets solidified due to the cold.) Thus, the pressure inside the gas cylinder depends on the ambient temperature, much like the boiling point of water being dependent on pressure (readers will recall the familiar example of elementary physics which tells you that lentil (*dal*) cooks well at sea level but poorly at high altitudes, this being related to lower boiling point at higher altitudes).

Liquid petroleum gas is composed of a few chemical species like propane and butane, which are composed of the chemical elements C and H. The primary component, butane, has a boiling point of –0.5°C at 0.1 MPa. Therefore, it is a gas at ambient temperature. If the pressure reaches 0.6 MPa, the boiling point is raised to 26°C. If the ambient temperature is 20°C but the pressure 0.6 MPa, you see that butane has to be in liquid form. If the ambient temperature reaches 35°C, the pressure inside the cylinder will become 0.8 MPa and both liquid and gas will exist in equilibrium. At typical draw rates of the gas in cooking stoves—0.03–0.05 g/s (108–180 g/h), the cylinder is able to maintain the flow rate without any loss of pressure because it will compensate for the heat of vaporisation of the liquid by drawing heat from the ambient.

However, if you draw much more gas at larger flow rates—something which can be done in a combustion laboratory and should be avoided at home—the cooling effect will dominate and the pressure in the cylinder will begin to fall. Consequently, water drops form on the outer surface of the cylinder due to condensation of atmospheric moisture, reducing the gas flow drastically.

The composition of LPG depends on the source of the crude used for

Table 2.2 *Composition of fuels (HHC = higher hydrocarbons)*

Substance	Density kg/m^3	Composition (%) (Volumetric)
LPG (liquid)	540–560	C_3H_8 = 18, C_4H_{10} = 80, HHC–rest
Biogas	1.1–1.2	CH_4 = 60–80, CO_2 = 40–20
Producer gas (wood)	0.9–1.2	CO = 16–20, H_2 = 16–18, CO_2 = 8–10, trace, HHC–, rest N_2–
Blue water gas	0.65	H_2 = 50, CO = 40, CO_2 = 6, N_2 and others–rest
Coke oven gas	0.40	H_2 = 54, CH_4 = 24, CO = 8, CO_2 = 6, rest (HHC + N_2)

refining and the effort put into refining it. Table 2.2 shows the typical composition and density of LPG. Notice that it is much lighter than water, in fact close to half of it.

Next we take up biogas. Biogas is produced by anaerobic digestion of biomass. Its use has gone up significantly in the last decade, and in several parts of India, large rural households now have biogas plants based on cow dung. The cow dung (which has several microbes in it) is mixed with water and allowed to settle in a sealed container with sufficient space left above the liquid level for the gas to collect. The microbes attack the biomass and generate a gas composed largely of methane and carbon dioxide. A typical composition of biogas is given in Table 2.2. The gas stoves that run on biogas are similar to the LPG stoves used for cooking purposes. Biogas can also be used to run gasoline (spark ignition) engines as well as diesel (compression ignition) engines in a dual-fuel mode, i.e., both gasoline diesel and biogas can be used as fuels but it is largely run on biogas.

Producer gas is a product of oxidation–reduction reactions of air with biomass. Oxidation results in products of combustion like carbon dioxide and water. This is because biomass is chemically composed of elements C, H, O and some N. The molecules of O_2 in air, augmented by bound oxygen, oxidises C and H to produce these products. The gases that are at high temperature due to partial oxidation pass through a bed of charcoal (which is produced because of oxidation reaction itself) and the reduction reaction of these gases with carbon leads to carbon monoxide and hydrogen. Nitrogen gas can be treated as inert in all these situations except for the generation of pollutants like oxides of nitrogen.

There are other variants of combustible gases called blue water gas, coke oven gas, coke producer gas and blast furnace gas, all produced as a result of oxidation–reduction reactions of coal or coke with air (and steam sometimes).

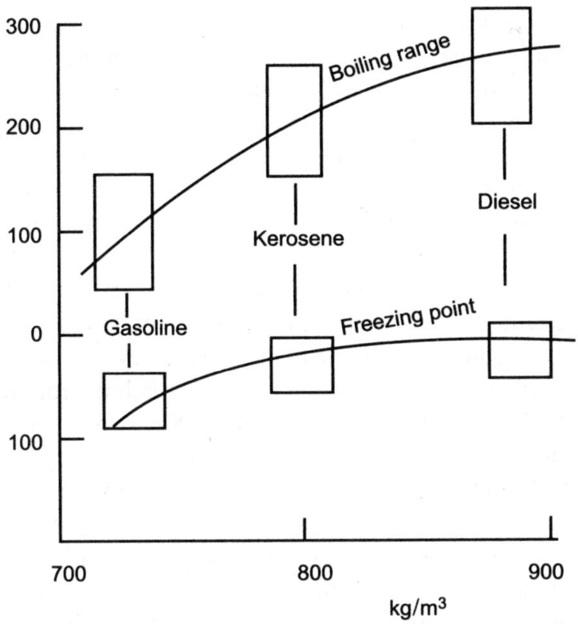

Figure 2.2 *Boiling and freezing range vs density of petroleum-based liquid fuels*

2.2 Liquid fuels

In the second group of fuels listed in Table 2.1 comes the liquid fuels. The first five liquids, namely gasoline, HSD, LDO, furnace oil and kerosene, are products of petroleum distillation. They are composed of C and H in various proportions. They are not pure compounds. They contain a mixture of what are known as straight chain compounds (like the family of methane, ethane, propane, etc.) and aromatics (like benzene, toluene etc.). Figure 2.2 shows the boiling ranges and densities of these fuels. One can see clearly that gasoline vaporises better than kerosene, a fact which is easily surmised because one can smell gasoline more than kerosene under ambient conditions. You may wonder what smelling has to do with boiling point. If something does not vaporise easily, its molecules are not found in the atmosphere and therefore cannot be smelt. The fact that you cannot smell diesel as easily as gasoline implies that gasoline vaporises better than diesel.

Kerosene comes in a variety of compositions. It includes the variety used in homes as well as those meant for gas turbines of aircraft, called aviation turbine fuel (ATF). The ATF is a refined kerosene obtained by particularly eliminating sulphur so that the life of turbine blades (which experience the combusted hot gases of the fuel–air mixture) is extended.

Gasoline is most extensively used in reciprocating spark ignition (SI) engines. They vaporise easily and are mixed with air in the right proportions before their entry into the combustion chamber.

Diesel fuels are used in compression ignition (CI) engines where no spark is required to initiate the combustion process. These engines work at much higher compression ratio than gasoline engines. The fuel is injected in the form of spray into hot compressed air. The fuel ignites and combustion follows.

The liquids mentioned under special fuels and oxidisers in Table 2.1 are used in rocket engines. Rocket engines are basically designed to work independently of the surrounding atmosphere so that they can go out of earth's atmosphere and still function. They are non-air breathing engines for which one can consider several fuels and oxidisers. Since one has to carry the oxidiser also, the choice of air is avoided because 77% (by volume) of air is nitrogen, which is inert, and its density is too low (about a thousandth of that of a liquid). One can, for instance, use liquefied oxygen. Alternatively, there are several liquids which have excess oxygen, like nitric acid (HNO_3), red fuming nitric acid (RFNA), which has about 12–14% dissolved nitrogen tetroxide in it), and nitrogen tetroxide (N_2O_4), which is liquid at near ambient conditions (nitrogen tetroxide should be kept below 21°C for it to retain its liquid form). Liquid oxygen (O_2) has a boiling point of −183°C and is called a cryogenic oxidiser since its storage requires a special design. Very good, low temperature cryogenic fluid insulation should be used, which should itself be chilled before liquid oxygen is stored in the container.

Several liquid fuels have been listed under the category of special fuels. Hydrazine (N_2H_4) is an interesting liquid—it can decompose by itself exothermally at high temperatures and release heat. If, for instance, an insulated tube is initially heated to 600°C and hydrazine is sprayed into it continuously, then the hydrazine decomposes into ammonia, nitrogen and hydrogen and releases enough heat to maintain the temperature inside the tube for continuous decomposition. But this is not the way hydrazine is actually used since what is required is that the liquid must decompose even at ambient temperatures. For this purpose, exotic catalysts made of iridium and molybdenum in the form of small pellets packed into a cylindrical chamber are used. Hydrazine is then sprayed on the catalyst bed. The catalysts decompose the liquid into gases almost instantaneously. Liquids which exhibit such a property are called monopropellants. They are used in rockets attached to satellites for producing small force (or thrust as it is called) required for correcting the attitude and position of the satellite.

An important feature of liquid fuels is what is known as hypergolic ignition. To appreciate its meaning, let us take two containers—one containing a fuel like unsymmetrical dimethyl hydrazine, $N_2H_2(CH_3)_2$ (not usually available in chemistry laboratories but available in rocket laboratories) and the other containing an oxidiser like red fuming nitric acid. A pipette and a glass dish are the other accessories needed. A small amount of fuel is first placed in the glass dish. Then a small amount of fuming nitric acid is pipetted (not by sucking, but by just dipping the pipette into the liquid, closing the top of pippette and lifting the pipette off) and dropped into the fuel. A bright flame erupts instantly. Such reactions between liquids in liquid phase, releasing gaseous components which are so exothermically reactive that the entire combustion process occurs in less than ten to fifteen milliseconds (0.01–0.015 s), are called hypergolic. Combinations of liquid fuel and oxidiser with this property are called hypergolic combinations. An important advantage of such combinations is that one can dispense with the igniter. Opening the valves in the fluid path in a rocket engine would automatically ensure ignition even in near-vacuum ambient conditions. It is for ensuring very high reliability of ignition that the Apollo mission (which landed crew on the moon and got them back) used a hypergolic combination of aerozine (50% hydrazine + 50% unsymmetrical dimethyl hydrazine) as the fuel and nitrogen tetroxide as the oxidiser in the lunar module engine that lifted off from the lunar soil.

Among liquids, most amines (substances with chemical formula ending in group NH_2) are hypergolic with nitric acid and nitrogen tetroxide. Liquid oxygen is not hypergolic with most substances, even with kerosene. One of the most powerful oxidisers, namely liquid fluorine, reacts with almost everything including glassware, and is hypergolic with all fuels. It is also very toxic and consequently not used much in rocket applications.

The last liquid without which this description is incomplete is liquid hydrogen. It boils at −253°C (20 K) and, hence, is a cryogenic fluid that must be stored with care, even more so than liquid oxygen since its boiling point is much lower than that of liquid oxygen. Liquid hydrogen is an excellent fuel with low molecular weight (2) and high energy. It is used with liquid oxygen in many rockets.

2.3 Solid fuels

The first of these listed in Table 2.1 is biomass. The term biomass is used for the natural product of plants that have the ability to generate carbon by photosynthesis. Biomass used for fuel includes firewood, leaves, bark, tiny branches, agricultural residues like rice husk, rice straw, wheat husk, wheat straw, groundnut shells and a host of other plant materials. The use of biomass for combustion dates back to millions of years. Yet, it is less investigated than liquid petroleum fuels whose use began just a little more than a hundred years ago. The composition of all biomass is about the same on a moisture-free and ash-free basis. The ash content of most biomass is about 0.5–5%. But straw, hulls of wheat and rice may have ash content

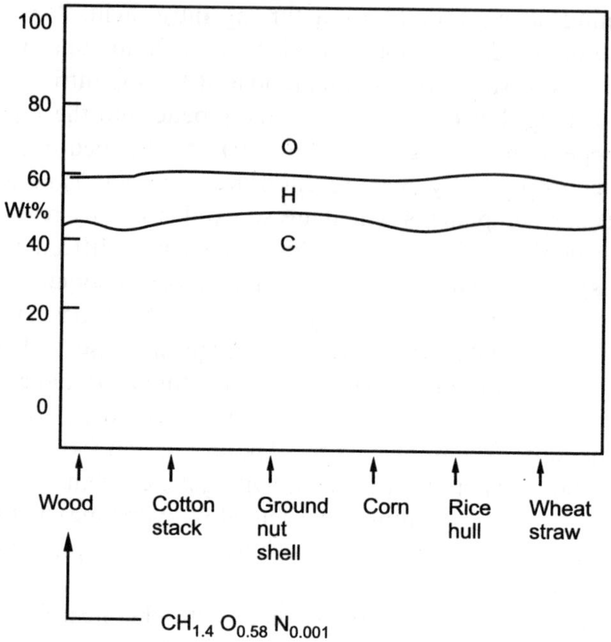

Figure 2.3 *Composition of biomass on an moisture-free, ash-free basis*

as high as 22%. Figure 2.3 shows the compositions of different types of biomass.

Though the composition of all biomass is about the same, their structure and form of availability vary widely, with their moisture content-ranging from the normal 8–10% in the case of water lilies or hyacinth to 90% in the case of coir pith. Hence their use for combustion calls for a consideration of these factors. There are, of course, technologies developed in the last century for using biomass for generating power as well as meeting combustion requirements. These were ignored soon after petroleum fuels became naturally available. The developing world has to grapple with the lack of both petroleum fuels as well as biomass to meet its energy needs. The need to understand the combustion behaviour of biomass is apparent. Biomass in the form of firewood is used for combustion on the grate. Its use for the generation of electrical power has been mentioned earlier while describing producer gas. Most biomass is lighter than water, with densities typically in the range of 40–90% of water.

Coal is the largest and most widespread fossil fuel resource available, providing 70% of India's energy and 23% of the world's energy needs. It will remain a fuel of relevance for a long time even though widespread concerns about environmental emissions have begun to limit the growth of its use. Coal is produced by natural processes over a span of geological times when biomass gets crushed under a load created by volcanoes and other natural phenomenon. Such processes, however, reduce the volatile content of the biomass and what is left in the coal is much lower than its original constituents as can be noted from Table 2.3. Coal is classified by a term known as rank, which is a measure of the alteration the coal has undergone during its formation. The consecutive stages in the evolution of the coal from biomass are: peat, lignite (brown coal), sub-bituminous coal, bituminous coal, and anthracite, in the order of increasing rank or the extent of carbonisation. Sub-bituminous coal, bituminous coal and anthracite are together called black coal or hard coal. Lignite (or brown coal) is relatively soft with a heating value of only about a quarter of that of black coal. Coal is very dense, as much as twice to thrice that of biomass because it is formed under highly stressed conditions. Interlayered with other inorganic matter, coal beds extend up to many metres in thickness and are known as seams. It is mined from open mines or from deep the underground.

Coal varies widely in its composition. It is composed chiefly of rings of six carbon atoms joined together in an extremely complex structure of layered arrangements which have not only hydrogen but significant amounts of oxygen and nitrogen. The composition also includes varying amounts of sulphur, which on combustion leads to sulphur dioxide, and other inorganic matter that would end up as ash when coal is burnt. The analysis of coal for moisture fraction, ash fraction, volatile matter and fixed carbon are set out in Table 2.3. When coal is burnt in boilers, the content of sulphur and nitrogen in it (sulphur is about 0.3 to 0.8 % of the coal) becomes important from the point of view of emissions of sulphur dioxide and oxides of nitrogen (see Chapter 16 on emissions from combustion systems). The exhaust gases have to be treated to ensure compliance with emission norms of a state or a country. Coals are burnt in furnaces fixed to boilers to generate high pressure steam that runs turbines used for running electric generators. Indian coals are characterised by their high ash content compared to coals available in rest of the world, as can be seen from Table 2.3. This can lead to ash fusion and clinkering on grate, tackling of which calls for carefully thought-out strategies. Sometimes the coal is finely powdered (called pulverised coal) and burnt directly in furnaces.

There have been attempts to produce liquid fuels from coal by distillation process. Though these have met with some success, the process is not yet widely accepted. There are also methods by which the coal is gasified. The gases so obtained are cleaned and subjected to a process known as Fischer–Tropsch synthesis to get a diesel-like liquid fuel.

Special fuels and oxidisers are largely used by the aerospace industry, although some of the special fuels like polymers have been extensively used in other areas as well. Polymers are essentially long-chain molecules of a basic chemical unit called monomer. All plastic materials are polymers. In

Table 2.3 *Composition of solid fuels: volatile fraction and fixed carbon in moisture free (mf) fuel*

Item	Moisture fraction, %	Ash in mf fuel,%	Volatiles in mf fuel, %	Fixed carbon in mf fuel, %
Wood	¡ 55	¡ 1	75 – 80	20 – 25
Bark	¡ 55	2 – 4	70 – 75	20 – 25
Rice husk	¡ 10	16 – 20	60 – 65	20 – 25
Peat	∼ 60	¡ 3	55 – 65	30 – 35
Lignite	∼ 40	¡ 4	50 – 55	40– 45
Bituminous coal	∼ 10	¡ 5	30 – 40	45 – 45
Anthracite coal	∼ 5	¡ 15	15 – 20	60 – 65
Indian coal (E)	∼ 5	∼ 25	30 – 35	35 –40
Indian coal (F)	∼ 5	∼ 35	30 – 35	25 – 30
Indian coal (G)	∼ 5	∼ 45	30 – 35	15 – 20

fact, many natural products are also polymers. Typical molecular weights of polymers vary from 10^3 to 10^6. At molecular weights of the order of 10^3, one has a very viscous liquid. At 10^6, what one gets is a hard solid. The monomers or liquid polymers, called prepolymers, become large molecular chain polymers on the addition of appropriate catalyst and/or suitable thermal curing. Polymers were conceived for solid propellant use because of (a) the need to mix a crystalline oxidiser like ammonium perchlorate powder at high solid loading, (i.e., when the amount of solids in the mix is 75%–87%) with a liquid binder, and (b) the fact that after curing it would lead to a solid with good mechanical integrity. Since low temperature properties are required to be good, terminated polymers like CTPB, HTPB were developed and currently, several such polymers with excellent properties are available. Most of these fuels are based on C and H, but O and N elements are present to a certain extent. The oxidisers are composed of C, H, N, O and Cl elements. Table 2.4 shows the molecular composition of some of the oxidisers and fuels.

Propellants are of two categories: composite and double base. In composite propellants there is only physical continuity; there is no molecular mixing of the fuel and the oxidiser. In double-base propellants on the other hand, the oxidiser (NG) and the fuel (NC) cannot be distinguished once the propellant is made. Composite propellants are more recent and can be tailor-made to meet stringent performance specifications. In the case of a composite propellant, the fuel, which is essentially a polymer, is first taken in the form of what is known as liquid prepolymer and mixed with the oxidiser particles (∼ 20–600 μ m; 1 μ m = 10^{-6} m) in appropriate proportion; a curing agent is then added to make the prepolymer a polymer and the entire

Table 2.4 *Molecular composition of rocket fuels (HTPB = hydroxy terminated polybutadiesne, CTPB = carboxy terminated polybutadiene, AP = ammonium perchlorate, HMX = cyclo tetramethylene tetranitramine, NC = Nitrocellulose, NG = nitroglycerene)*

Species	Fuel/Oxidiser	Elemental composition
HTPB	F	$OH—(C_4H_6)—OH$
CTPB	F	$COOH—(C_4\ H_6)—COOH$
AP	Ox	$NH_4\ ClO_4$
HMX	F	$(H_2CNNO_2)_4$
NC	F	$C_6H_7O_{11}N_3$ (14% N_2)
NG	Ox	$C_3H_5O_9N_3$

mixed material is cast into specific geometry in a mould. This material is then cured at an elevated temperature (~ 150°C) to obtain a hard solid. In the case of double-base propellants, nitrocellulose (NC) in the form of fine strips or pieces is mixed with liquid nitroglycerine and other ingredients and the entire material is made into a dough which is then extruded. Alternatively, nitrocellulose nodules (small spherical particles) are immersed in nitroglycerine liquid in a container, called a mould, and allowed to gel at temperature of 60°C or so. The extruded propellants are mechanically stronger than the propellants made by the second process called the casting procedure.

The propellants are cast in combustion chambers, of sizes small to large. A space shuttle engine booster uses several hundred tonnes of propellant. The Indian Polar Satellite Launch Vehicle (PSLV) has hundred and twenty-five tonnes of composite propellant cast into its first stage alone. Since solid propellants have their own oxidiser and fuel, they can be ignited accidentally, posing a serious fire hazard. Therefore, great care is to be taken while handling propellants in rocket applications. More about the way propellants burn and the way to control them will be taken up in a later chapter.

2.4 Overview

There are natural fuels and synthetic fuels and natural oxidisers and synthetic oxidisers. The most abundant fuels are biomass or biomass-related. Synthetic fuels are used for special applications like rocket propulsion. Most fuels are based on carbon and hydrogen and contain some oxygen and nitrogen. They are available in gaseous, liquid and solid forms.

The most natural oxidiser is the oxygen present in air. Examples of synthetic oxidisers are liquid oxygen or specially prepared inorganic liquid or solid compounds.

There are many properties of the fuels/oxidisers which matter in their selection for a specific purpose. The most important property is the energy content of the substance, which decides how high the combustion temperature will be. It is also important to know the quantity of oxidiser required to be mixed with a given amount of fuel in order to obtain the peak combustion temperature. This is called stoichiometry and is discussed next.

3 Chemistry and Stoichiometry

Stoichiometry implies the proportions of reacting elements in a chemical reaction. Conventionally, it is used to refer to the ratio of oxidiser to fuel which just leads to complete products of combustion. The important elements for consideration in a combustion reaction are C and H for fuel and O for oxidiser. The complete products are CO_2 and H_2O. In the case of a hydrocarbon's combustion with air, if there is no excess of oxygen left with the products being CO_2, H_2O and N_2 (inert), the proportion of air-to-fuel is termed stoichiometric. More air than this leads to lean mixtures, less air than this to rich mixtures. The stoichiometric reactions are represented typically as

$$H_2 + (1/2)O_2 \rightarrow H_2O \tag{3.1}$$

$$H_2 + (1/2)O_2 + [79/(21 \times 2)N_2] \rightarrow H_2O + [79/(21 \times 2)N_2] \tag{3.2}$$

$$CH_4 + (3/2)O_2 \rightarrow CO_2 + H_2O \tag{3.3}$$

$$CH_2+(3/2)O_2+(79/21)\times(3/2)N_2 \rightarrow CO_2+H_2O+(79/21)\times(3/2)N_2 \tag{3.4}$$

In equation (3.1), one molecule of hydrogen reacts with half a molecule (!) of oxygen to lead to one molecule of H_2O. The half molecule does not mean much except for stoichiometric purposes. Since there are millions of molecules randomly moving around in any gas, the statement is taken to mean that every 2 molecules of H_2 react with one molecule of O_2 and the product consists of 2 molecules of water. One thing that must be understood is that the reaction never proceeds from reactants to products the way shown in equations (3.1) to (3.4), but by much more complex paths (see Chapter 5).

Another way of describing reaction (3.1) is that one mole of H_2 reacts with half a mole of O_2 to give one mole of H_2O. The word mole is taken to imply a molecular weight equivalent of mass. That is, one mole of hydrogen implies approximately 2 grams of H_2. Similarly, half a mole of oxygen implies (1/2)×32 = 16 grams (g) of oxygen. Thus one can state the reaction 3.1 as: 2 g of hydrogen reacts with 16 g of oxygen to give 18 g of water. Notice that there is mass conservation here. It is one of the underlying principles of chemical reactions that no mass is created or destroyed in a chemical reaction. Only the form of the species changes. It is also to be noticed that there is no mole conservation. In fact, in reaction (3.1) the total number of moles has gone down from one and a half to unity.

The mass conservation can be stated by writing an equation like

$$(\Sigma n_i \mathcal{M}_i)_{\mathbf{reactants}} = (\Sigma n_i \mathcal{M}_i)_{\mathbf{products}},$$

where n_i are the number of moles and $\mathcal{M}_i$ the molecular weight of species, i. The stoichiometric ratio in case (3.1) is 16/2 = 8. Thus every gram of H_2 requires 8 grams of oxygen for complete combustion. If more than 8 grams of oxygen is used, then one gets a fuel-lean system and if less than 8 grams of O_2 is used, one gets a fuel-rich system.

We now move on to reaction (3.2). If one looks for stoichiometry with respect to air, then it will be [16+ (79/21) ×2×28]/2 = 34.4. In this reaction nitrogen is treated as inert. Nitrogen is a very stable molecule with a very high energy binding the nitrogen atoms. If nitrogen were to enter into any reaction, then this strong bond must be broken. It requires very high temperatures, ~2800–3000 K for a fair fraction of the molecules of N_2 to be dissociated into element nitrogen (N). The temperature attained in reaction (3.2) would be of the order of 2300 K. Hence one finds that nitrogen is virtually inert. In reaction (3.4), the species considered is CH_2. There is no specific species like CH_2, excepting as a radical, which is an intermediate in reactions. Rather, it represents an extreme case of straight chain hydrocarbons described by $C_n\ H_{2n+2}$. The value $n = 1$ gives CH_4, methane, a gas at ambient conditions; $n = 3$ gives C_3H_8, propane, a gas. $n = 4$ gives C_4H_{10} butane, a gas at ambient conditions. It is the primary constituent of liquefied petroleum gas (LPG). C_5H_{12} is pentane, a liquid. The series goes on like this till at $C_{12}H_{26}$ when one gets solids like waxes. Thus all the straight-chain compounds can be described by $CH_{2+2/n}$. CH_2 is an approximate representative of the series. The stoichiometric ratio in the case (3.3) is 3.4 and in the case (3.4) is 3.4/0.232=14.7. The last number is very familiar. For many hydrocarbons like kerosene, diesel and gasoline, the air-to-fuel ratio at stoichiometry is about 15. It decreases slightly from methane (17.2) to about 15 for larger size fuel molecules like hexadecane ($C_{16}H_{34}$).

One should be careful about the use of stoichiometry in actual situations. At flame temperatures of the order of 2300 K or so, dissociation of the molecules of CO_2 and H_2O occurs to a reasonable extent. Consequently, one obtains some CO, OH, HO_2 and others. These are incomplete products of combustion. One, therefore, needs additional oxygen to oxidise these. This is one of the reasons why in many IC engines, 15–20% excess air is used (to make sure combustion is complete).

As far as stoichiometry is concerned, for hydrocarbons the products are CO_2 and H_2O. What will happen with other elements like Cl, Al etc? In the case of chlorine, HCl is taken as the stable product; for Al it is Al_2O_3. Similarly, one can determine the stable product for other species as well.

One of the useful qualities related to stoichiometry is the equivalence ratio (e.r). It is the ratio of fuel to oxidiser by weight in a given case to that at stoichiometry. Stated in the form of an equation,

$$\text{e.r} = \frac{(\text{fuel}/\text{air})}{(\text{fuel}/\text{air})_{\text{stoichiometry, wt-basis}}}$$

Thus, all stoichiometric mixtures have equivalence ratio of unity. Rich mixtures have e.r greater than unity. Lean mixtures have e.r less than unity. By rich and lean, one generally refers to the extent of fuel.

Till now the discussion has been about fuels which have no oxidising element in them and vice versa. In rocket propellants, fuels and oxidisers have both the elements and need to be treated for fuel richness or otherwise.

For instance, one could ask about stoichiometry or equivalence ratio of ammonium perchlorate (AP), nitroglycerine (NG) or nitrocellulose (NC). Take $NH_4\ ClO_4$ (ammonium perchlorate).

$$NH_4ClO_4 \rightarrow (1/2)N_2 + HCl + (3/2)H_2O + (5/4)O_2$$

Ammonium perchlorate is oxidiser rich to the extent of two and a half atoms of oxygen. This amounts in weight basis to 40/117 = 34%. Thus, one describes ammonium perchlorate as being oxidiser rich to the extent of 34% by itself and is called an oxidiser.

It can be similarly shown that nitrocellulose is slightly fuel rich and nitroglycerine is slightly oxidiser rich. If one wishes to stoichiometrically balance the combination to make a high-performance propellant, one needs NG about six times as much as nitrocellulose. This mixture gives a liquid-like material and a fuel rich mixture close to 1:1 (NC : NG).

For all propellants based on HMX, the solid crystals of HMX are set into a fuel binder matrix. HMX is slightly fuel rich. Hence all solid propellants turn out to be fuel rich to varying extents.

In the case of liquid propellants, monopropellants like hydrogen peroxide (H_2O_2) or (N_2H_4) can be used in single propellant mode; there is no oxidiser in such cases. H_2O_2 is oxidiser rich to the extent of (1/2)O_2, implying 47% oxidiser richness. In the case of N_2H_4, exothermic decomposition takes place because of relatively unstable molecular configuration and not quite due to 'oxidiser' or 'fuel' molecules both being present. In

Table 3.1 *Valencies of various elements*

Element	H F Cl	O S N	P Al B
Valency	1	2	3

Table 3.2 *Stoichiometric ratio for several fuels*

Fuel	Formula	Molecular Weight	$(O/F)_{stoi}$ with Oxygen	Air
Hydrogen	H_2	2.0	8.00	34.50
Magnesium	Mg	24.0	1.66	7.10
Aluminium	Al	27.0	3.80	16.40
Methane	CH_4	16.0	4.00	17.20
Butane	C_4H_{10}	58.0	3.58	15.40
Carbon monoxide	CO	28.0	0.57	2.46
Kerosene	$CH_{1.8}$	13.8	3.36	14.50
Ethyl Alcohol	C_2H_5OH	46.0	2.09	9.00
Methyl Alcohol	CH_3OH	32.0	1.50	6.46
Hydrazine	N_2H_4	32.0	1.00	4.30
Wood	$CH_{1.4}O_{0.6}$	23.0	1.46	6.29
Peat	$CH_{1.3}O_{0.5}$	21.3	1.61	6.94
	$CH_{1.0}O_{0.3}$	17.8	1.98	8.53
Bituminous coal	$CH_{0.9}O_{0.1}$	14.5	2.59	11.16
Anthracite coal	$CH_{0.4}O_{0.05}$	13.2	2.66	11.46

fact, at the temperatures considered (~1000–1400 K) nitrogen is inert and hydrogen is of course a fuel.

In all cases where a single molecule has both fuel and oxidiser elements or elements in an unstable configuration, there is a way of defining fuel or oxidiser richness. This is done by using the concept of equivalence ratio defined as

$$e.r = (\Sigma N_i V_i)_f / (\Sigma N_i V_i)_{ox}.$$

where N_i is the number of atoms of elements, fuel or oxidiser and V_i, the valencies of the specific elements. Table 3.1 contains a list of valencies of various elements normally encountered in combustion phenomena

For H_2O_2 the formula gives $e.r = (2 \times 1)/(2 \times 2) = 0.5$, from which one can see it is fuel lean. Similarly

$$(e.r)_{NC} = (6 \times 4 + 7 \times 1)/(11 \times 2) = 1.41; \quad (e.r)_{NC} = 0.94.$$

$$(e.r)_{NH_4ClO_4} = (4 \times 1)/(1 \times 1 + 4 \times 2) = 0.44.$$

As can be noticed, the values of equivalence ratio confirm the expected feature regarding fuel richness or otherwise.

Table 3.3 *Volumetric and mass O/F_{stoi} for biomass-based producer gas*

			Mol Wt	(Air/Fuel) Volume	(Air/Fuel) Weight
Producer gas	0.2	CO			
	0.2	H_2	24.4	0.95	1.12
	0.1	CO_2			
	0.5	N_2			

Tables 3.2 and 3.3 give the stoichiometric ratio for a range of fuels with oxygen or air as the oxidiser. A few features are interesting to note. Those fuels which have oxygen as an element in their structure will need a smaller amount (weight) of oxygen or air for combustion as compared to those with greater amount of hydrogen in them. The stoichiometric ratios vary from about 2.5 to as much as 35.

Another feature emerges from the observation of data on solid fuels. The data shows that the composition of the fuels changes from wood to anthracite coal by successive carbonisation. The actual amount of oxygen and hydrogen stripped from the starting material depends on the process that occurs at high pressure and temperature inside the earth. The net result is that the oxygen-to-fuel ratio continues to rise from wood to coal as shown in Table 3.2. The implication of stoichiometric ratio on combustion is very significant. If one were to observe a flame from a burner which issues fuel gas into an otherwise undisturbed atmosphere, one would find that a hydrogen flame at the same mass flow rate is thirteen to fourteen times as long as that for carbon monoxide in the laminar range of flow rates. (See Chapter 10 for further details). If in a confined atmosphere leakage takes place in the presence of a very hot spot, smaller amount of hydrogen will consume all the air available in comparison to hydrocarbons.

3.1 Fuel? Oxidiser?

Till now we have been talking of fuels and oxidisers as though we know what they are. Indeed how can we say what is oxidiser? Is oxygen always an oxidiser? Chemically, an oxidiser is defined as one which acquires electrons and fuel as the one which can donate electrons. The various elements are categorised in terms of either their richness in donating electrons or their hunger in accepting electrons. Such a table is called electronegativity table. Table 3.4 shows the Pauling's electronegativity values in decreasing order.

As can be seen, fluorine has the largest capability of receiving electrons, oxygen comes next, chlorine, bromine and iodine follow. In the fuel range we have carbon, hydrogen, aluminium, magnesium, lithium, iodine, and

Table 3.4 *Electronegativity of various elements*

F	4.0	C, S, I	2.5	Mg	1.2
O	3.5	H, P	2.1	Li, Ca	1.0
N, Cl	3.0	B	2.0	Na, Ba	0.9
Br	2.8	Be, Al	1.5	K	0.8

potassium. Thus in a compound like F_2O_3, fluorine has the oxidising capability and oxygen acts as a fuel. Since fluorine is a very powerful oxidiser, it would react quickly and form stable products. Nature, therefore, is bestowed with relatively small amounts of fluorine. Oxygen, then, remains the next most abundant and powerful oxidiser. The power is reduced only by dilution with inert substance namely, nitrogen. On the fuel side, the more reactive of the fuels are sodium and potassium. Given a certain amount of oxygen, in an environment of mixture of fuel elements like C, H, Al, or Na, it is the metal elements which get oxidised largely, followed by hydrogen and carbon elements. The most common fuels are based on hydrocarbons. But metals are used as well to meet the requirements in special cases like rocket engines.

3.2 Overview

In this chapter we have seen some elementary, but important aspects of combustion, namely stoichiometry. We have also seen what fuels and oxidisers are and why they are so. Fuels are donors of electrons and oxidisers are acceptors of electrons. The most powerful oxidiser is fluorine; metals are very reactive fuels (though this quality alone does not make them most eminent at all times). Stoichiometric ratio refers to the amount of oxidiser required to completely oxidise the fuel to stable products of combustion at ambient (or more correctly, standard) conditions.

We shall now see what happens when reactions like the above take place. You may have already concluded that heat is evolved during the reaction—how much heat and what happens to this heat and how high the gas temperature rises are some of the questions we will try to answer as we go along.

4 How Much Heat? How High a Temperature?

Heat is an intrinsically self-evident quantity experienced when say, a warm object is touched or when a person lights a fire in an open field on a cold day for warmth. To develop from this qualitative understanding of heat a scheme by which quantities are measured, interrelated and predictions made requires the science of thermodynamics. We need the major results of thermodynamics for finding the temperature and composition of combustion products when fuels and oxidisers burn. This subject is called chemical thermodynamics, to emphasise the presence of many species and their chemical interactions.

Thermodynamics deals with quantities of state at equilibrium–temperature, internal energy, enthalpy, entropy, availability and so on. In the true sense of its description, it is only thermostatics that attempts to answer certain questions concerning transformations, not the rate. The question of how fast heat is transferred from one point to another or how fast a reaction takes place is outside the purview of classical equilibrium thermodynamics (as it is called). One needs to study non-equilibrium thermodynamics for this purpose. We shall presently review the elements of thermodynamics for understanding the way flame temperature or other equilibrium properties are calculated.

Firstly, what does the concept of equilibrium mean? It simply means that the characterisable properties do not change over space or time. For this definition to be useful, it is modified to state that the properties do not change over appropriate scales of space and time. To appreciate what this means, let us consider an example.

It is quite often stated that the temperature in the northern hemisphere is a few degrees higher than the southern hemisphere, or that the peak temperature in Bangalore or some other city is 25°C. Surely, the temperature over as large an area as say, Bangalore, is never the same. Even in a small area the temperature can vary by as much as several degrees. So all that the above statement implies is that in all regions which are shaded from sun, the measured temperature is about the same as that measured at the meteorological station. However, the temperature quoted at the airport, for instance, will be a few degrees different from that recorded at the meteorological station. Thus, one can say that the 'temperature' of Bangalore is at equilibrium over distances of possibly several kilometres around the meteorological station, but not over larger scales—for instance at places as far as the airport—because the temperature is not the same over this distance. All that this implies is that equilibrium is said to exist over certain smaller scales in a system; by itself the temperature in totality is at non-equilibrium.

Consider a candle flame. The temperature measured through different parts of the flame is significantly different. Yet we talk of temperature at a point. This means that the total non-equilibrium system is split into a number of states which can be described by equilibrium properties—pressure, temperature, etc.

Thermodynamics, as distinct from mechanics, introduces an additional quantity of state (equilibrium) needed for specifying a system—the temperature. Zeroth law gives it a shape by indicating that several bodies in contact with each other are said to be in thermodynamic equilibrium provided they have the same temperature. Stated differently, a quantity called temperature has to be the same if systems in physical contact are to be at equilibrium.

The first law summarises the experience of life that energy can neither be created nor destroyed but only transformed; that one cannot continue to extract heat continuously without any other change in the system. Conceiving that all descriptions require a system, its surroundings and interactions between them, thermodynamics distinguishes between those in which there is no transfer of mass, momentum and heat (called isolated systems, its those in which there is no mass transfer but momentum and heat transfer can occur (called closed systems) and those in which nothing is forbidden (called open systems).

In the closed system, one can conceive of a constant volume or constant pressure system to state the limits. No work will be done in the case of a constant volume system. Any heat transferred to this system (dq) will result in a raise in internal energy (de) of the system, which in perfect gas is $c_v dT$.

$$(dq)_{v=\text{constant}} = de = c_v dT, \tag{4.1}$$

where c_v is called the constant volume specific heat $= de/dT$. In the systems where pressure–volume work can be done—like a cylinder fitted with a piston at the top and on which one can set weights to change the pressure—the transfer of heat into the system causes a rise in internal energy along with the work required to move the piston.

$$(dq)_{p=\text{constant}} = de + pdv. \tag{4.2}$$

To treat such cases, a quantity called enthalpy (h) is defined as

$$h = e + pv \tag{4.3}$$

so that at constant pressure one gets

$$dh = de + pdv = (dq)_{p=\text{constant}} \tag{4.4}$$

and thus, the enthalpy change of the system represents the heat transfer to the system at constant pressure. The difference between changes in enthalpy and internal energy represents the work done by the system. Like internal energy, enthalpy is also uniquely related to temperature in a perfect gas. To see this, we need to make use of the equation of state, an equation relating pressure, density (or volume) and temperature resulting from Boyle's and Charle's laws.

$$p = \rho \mathcal{R} T = \rho RT/\mathcal{M} \tag{4.5}$$

or $pv = m\mathcal{R}T$, where R is the universal gas constant and $\mathcal{M}$, the molecular weight of the gas. This gives,

$$dh/dt = c_v + \mathcal{R} = c_p, \tag{4.6}$$

where c_p = constant pressure specific heat.

It is now the right time to discuss the properties of mixtures because we need to deal with situations of a number of species being together. The fundamental principle that applies here is the one given by Dalton, who stated that in a container containing a mixture of gases, the total pressure exerted by the mixture equals the sum of the pressures of the gases which can be taken to exert pressure as though each alone were present. Such individual pressures are called partial pressures, By the statement of this definition, one can write

$$p_i v = m_i \mathcal{R}_i T = m_i RT/\mathcal{M}_i, \tag{4.7}$$

where p_i is the partial pressure of species i and m_i is the mass of the species i.

If we express the total pressure by $pv = m\mathcal{R}T = mRT/\mathcal{M}$, we can state Dalton's law as,

$$p = \Sigma p_i. \tag{4.8}$$

In combustion literature, one uses molar units, one mole implying mass equivalent to molecular weight. Thus, we have

$$n_i = m_i/\mathcal{M}_i \tag{4.9}$$

and $p_i v = n_i RT$, $pv = nRT$. The ratio n_i/n equals X_i, called the mole fraction.

$$X_i = n_i/n = p_i/p. \tag{4.10}$$

In addition, one defines mass fraction as

$$Y_i = m_i/m, \tag{4.11}$$

the ratio of the mass of the species i to the total mass.

Equations (4.10) and (4.11) concerning X_i and Y_i can be used to write $Y_i = m_i/m = (n_i\mathcal{M}_i)/(n\mathcal{M})$ and we get

$$Y_i = X_i\mathcal{M}_i/\mathcal{M} \tag{4.12}$$

or

$$Y_i/\mathcal{M}_i = X_i/\mathcal{M}. \tag{4.13}$$

Summing (4.12) over all i, one gets

$$\mathcal{M}_i = \Sigma X_i\mathcal{M}_i, \tag{4.14}$$

the average molecular weight.

Summing (4.13) over all i gives an alternate but equivalent expression for $\mathcal{M}$,

$$\mathcal{M} = [\Sigma(Y_i/\mathcal{M}_i)]^{-1}. \tag{4.15}$$

The properties e and h defined earlier can be obtained for a mixture, given that for individual species $e = \Sigma e_i Y_i$ or $\Sigma e_i X_i$.

$$h = \Sigma h_i Y_i \quad \text{or} \quad \Sigma h_i X_i, \tag{4.16}$$

depending on whether e_i and h_i are given in mass or molar units, i.e., one can give e_i and h_i in kJ/kg or kJ/mole. The expression with weighting of mass fraction is to be used if kJ/kg units for e_i or h_i are used. The above relations (4.16) are valid for specific heats, entropies and Gibbs free energies (to be treated later). The enthalpy of any species is composed of two parts. One of this is the sensible enthalpy. This is a function of temperature alone and is the integral of specific heat with temperature,

$$h_{si}(T) = \int c_{pi} dT. \tag{4.17}$$

The values of specific heat are obtained from measurements and used in the above expression to obtain the enthalpies. If the temperature includes a phase transition like vaporisation, the enthalpy of vaporisation is to be introduced as follows.

$$h_{si}(T) = \int_{T_{\text{ref}}}^{T_{\text{boiling}}} c_{pi} dT + L + \int_{T_{\text{boiling}}}^{T} c_{pi} dT, \tag{4.18}$$

where L is the latent heat of vaporisation.

The second part of enthalpy due to the chemical and physical state of the substance, called the heat of formation, is due to differences in enthalpy between different species at the same temperature. If there were no such differences one would not have exothermic reactions (and therefore, flames). The heat of formation is essentially the heat of a reaction (which is a general form of the term heat of combustion) but, in a special reaction. It is the heat of reaction in a reaction in which the species alone is the product and the component elements of the species are the only reactants at standard state (standard state is 298.16 K, 0.1 MPa). The heat of formation of the reactants at standard state is set to zero while compiling tables of the complete data on heats of formation (denoted by h_{fi}).

Consider the following reactions.

$$CH_4 + 2O_2 \rightarrow CO_2 + 2H_2O \tag{A}$$

$$CO + (1/2)O_2 \rightarrow CO_2 \tag{B}$$

$$H_2 + (1/2)O_2 \rightarrow H_2O \tag{C}$$

$$C(s) + (1/2)O_2 \rightarrow CO_2 \tag{D}$$

In which of the above reactions can we talk of heat of formation? Since the heat of formation refers to a species, the first reaction (A) cannot qualify for consideration at all. In (B), the component elements are CO and O_2 and these are not the reactants. Hence (B) does not qualify either. Reactions (C) and (D) do qualify for consideration of heats of formation. The heats of reaction here give the heat of formation of H_2O and CO_2. For others, a table is formed from the measurements of heat of combustion/reaction in various reactions. For example, H_2, O_2, N_2, F_2, Cl_2, Br_2, C(s), Mg, Al, B, are all taken to have zero heat of formation. The heats of formation of H, O, OH, H_2O, N, F_2O_3, HCl, HBr, etc., are obtained from experimental data and by imposing conditions of self-consistency.

In a sense, the idea of heat of formation is no different from that of heat of combustion, which an engineer is most familiar with. Heat of combustion refers to a reaction while heat of formation refers to a species. The latter can be seen to be a great advantage since the same species can be involved in several kinds of reactions and one needs to keep track only of heat of formation of each of the species and not heats of reaction of several hundreds of combinations. Table 4.1 shows the values of heats of formation (h_{fi}) of some important species, while Tables 4.2, 4.3, and 4.4 show the specific heats, sensible enthalpies and other properties of relevance to combustion. How do we use it to get the heat of combustion?

For any reaction $\Sigma a_i A_i \rightarrow \Sigma a' A_i$, where a, and a'_i are stoichiometric coefficients and A_i refers to species,

$$\text{heat of combustion} = \Sigma(a_i - a'_i)[h_{fi} + h_{si}(T) - h_{si}(298.16)]. \quad (4.19)$$

As an example, we can calculate the heat of combustion for reaction (A) at 298.16 K. For this reaction, we identify various coefficients as $A_1 = CH_4$, $A_2 = O_2$, $A_3 = CO_2$, $A_4 = H_2O$ and $a_1 = 1$, $a_2 = 2$, $a_3 = 0$, $a_4 = 0$, $a'_1 = 0$, $a'_2 = 0$, $a'_3 = 1$, $a'_4 = 2$.

$$H_c = -74.5 + 394.0 + 2 \times 242 = 803.5 \text{ kJ}$$

The heat of combustion per kg of fuel will be (803.5/16) MJ = 50.2 MJ/kg. For reaction (C) the value of H_c at 298.16 K is 242 − 0 − 0 = 242 kJ and for H_2 it will be 242/2 MJ = 121 MJ/kg. If, in reaction (C) or any of the other reactions for that matter, one adds an inert substance like nitrogen, the heat of combustion is not affected. It is true that this heat is now absorbed by a mass augmented by inerts and hence one can expect the final temperature to be lower. The heat released however, will remain the same. Table 4.5 lists the heats of combustion for some reactions.

4.1 The second law

The second law of thermodynamics states a principle indicating directions of processes. For instance, heat flows from a higher temperature to a lower temperature. The reverse does not happen unaided. This part of the observation is not indicated in the first law. The first law states that either of the processes can take place provided energy is conserved.

The second law is variously understood and discussed. The useful viewpoint here concerns the feature indicated above. Is there a quantity which is related to state variables ($T, h, e \ldots$) such that on evaluation one can state which direction a process proceeds?

The answer lies in the statement that there is a quantity called entropy defined by the ratio of the reversible heat change $(dq)_{rev}$ to temperature, T:

$$ds = (dq)_{\text{rev}}/T \quad (4.20)$$

so that if ds is positive (for isolated systems), the process is natural and proceeds along $ds > 0$. If $ds < 0$, as in an isolated system, the system is not

Table 4.1 *Heats of formation (h_{fi}, kJ/mole), l= liquid, s = solid*
*b=0.75–1.2 (depends on nitrogen content)

Species	Formula	h_{fi}, kJ/mole
Oxygen	O_2	247.4
Hydrogen	H_2	0.0
Element hydrogen	H	218.1
Hydroxyl	OH	42.3
Water	H_2O	−242.0
Water (l)	H_2O	−286.0
Hydrogen peroxide	H_2O_2	−133.2
Hydrogen peroxide (l)	H_2O_2	−187.5
C (graphite, s)	C	0.0
Carbon monoxide	CO	−110.5
Carbon dioxide	CO_2	−394.0
Methane	CH_4	−74.5
Ethane	C_2H_6	−86.2
Propane	C_3H_8	−103.8
Butane	C_4H_{10}	−131.8
Octane (l)	C_8H_{18}	−208.4
Kerosene (l)	$CH_{1.842}$	−51.6
Acetylene	C_2H_2	226.9
Benzene	C_6H_6	82.9
Methyl alcohol	CH_3OH	−201.0
Methyl alcohol (l)	CH_3OH	−238.6
Ethyl alcohol	C_2H_5OH	−239.0
Ethyl alcohol (l)	C_2H_5OH	−277.4
Nitrogen	N_2	0.0
Elemental nitrogen	N	471.0
Ammonia	NH_3	−46.2
Hydrazine (l)	N_2H_4	50.4
Nitric acid (l)	HNO_3	−171.8
Chlorine	Cl_2	0.0
Chlorine atom	Cl	121.4
Hydrogen chloride	HCl	−92.1
Ammonium nitrate (s)	NH_4NO_3	−365.3
Ammonium perchlorate (s)	NH_4ClO_4	−290.5
UDMH (l)	$(CH_3)_2N_2H_2$	88.4
Ethyl amine (l)	C_2H_5N	91.0
Nitrogen Tetroxide	N_2O_4	9.63
Nitrogen dioxide	NO_2	33.9
Nitric oxide	NO	90.4
Nitromethane (l)	CH_3NO_2	−113.1
Aluminium (s)	Al	0.0
Alumina (s)	Al_2O_3	−167.0
Magnesium (s)	Mg	0.0
Magnesium oxide (s)	MgO	−601.5
HMX (s)	$(H_2CNNO_2)_4$	+75.0
NC (s) (b=1.0)*	$C_{1.2}\ H_{2-b}O_{1+2b}\ N_b$	−292.5
NG (l)	$C_3\ H_5(ONO_2)_3$	−370.0

Table 4.2 *Specific heat*

T	Species								
K	H_2	H	O_2	O	OH	H_2O	CO	CO_2	N_2
	kJ/mol K								
300	28.5	20.7	30.0	21.7	22.6	32.8	29.0	39.3	29.0
1000	30.7	20.7	34.0	21.0	30.7	41.0	33.0	52.6	32.7
2000	33.9	20.7	38.1	20.7	34.6	50.9	36.3	60.6	36.0
3000	36.7	20.7	40.0	21.0	36.7	56.1	37.3	62.4	37.1
4000	38.5	20.7	41.1	21.2	37.9	58.6	37.5	62.1	37.4

Table 4.3 *Sensible enthalpy*

T	H_2	H	O_2	O	OH	H_2O	CO	CO_2	N_2
K	kJ/mol K								
300	8.4	6.2	8.8	6.7	10.2	9.8	8.6	10.0	8.5
1000	29.1	20.8	31.4	21.6	29.7	36.0	35.2	42.8	30.1
2000	61.5	41.6	67.7	42.4	62.5	82.8	64.8	103.5	64.6
3000	96.8	62.4	106.8	63.2	98.3	136.5	102.1	162.5	101.3
4000	134.5	85.2	147.4	84.4	135.6	194.1	139.6	224.8	138.5

Table 4.4 *Entropy*

T	H_2	H	O_2	O	OH	H_2O	CO	CO_2	N_2
K	kJ/mol K								
300	130.6	114.7	205.2	161.0	187.1	188.7	197.9	214.5	195.6
1000	166.2	139.8	243.6	186.7	219.7	232.8	234.8	269.3	228.1
2000	188.4	154.0	268.7	202.2	242.3	264.8	258.9	308.9	252.0
3000	202.6	162.6	284.6	209.7	256.8	286.6	273.7	334.0	266.6
4000	213.6	168.6	296.1	215.7	267.5	303.0	284.6	351.9	277.5

Table 4.5 *Heats of combustion H_c, fuel or propellant (v = by volume, w = by weight)*

System	H_c, MJ/kg
LPG [80 butane, 20 propane (v)] + air	44.0
Biogas + Air	32.0–36.0
Prod. gas 20 CO + 20 H_2 + 2 CH_4 + 58 N_2 (v) + air	4.6
kerosene + air	42.0
Wood (sun dry) + air	16
Bituminous coal + air	26
Indian coal (45 % ash) + air	14
Solid propellant	
50 NC + 50 NG (w)	5.4
70 AP+20 Al+10 CTPB (w)	6.0
Liquid propellant	
50 N_2O_4 + 50 N_2H_4 (v)	6.0
0.50 UDMH+0.50 N_2O_4 (v)	7.5

natural and will not drive by itself along the path. If $ds = 0$, then the system is at equilibrium and no further change takes place.

Thus the second law introduces a quantity called entropy whose change will give the direction of the process. The second law does not define the absolute value of entropy. It is defined by the third law which states that entropy of a crystalline substance is zero at absolute zero temperature. Using the data on specific heats and enthalpies, entropy is calculated for various species and presented in Table 4.4 for the same species.

For closed systems operating at constant pressure and temperature, the quantity that indicates direction of processes is called Gibbs free energy. It is defined as $g = h - Ts$ so that

$$dg = dh - Tds - sdT = dh - Tds. \tag{4.21}$$

Since $dT = 0$, $dg < 0$ for natural processes, $dg = 0$ for equilibrium, and $dg > 0$ for processes which do not take place by themselves.

It can be seen that when $dh = 0$, the principles noted above with respect to g are equivalent to those of entropy. The fact that $dg = 0$ at equilibrium is used in the calculation of chemical composition at constant pressure and temperature. Armed with the basic information we now have, we begin answering two questions:

- Will the reaction proceed along a direction indicated?
- What is the composition for a given set of reactants at a given pressure and temperature?

Let us take an example. Is N_2O (g)$\rightarrow$ N_2 (g) + (1/2)O_2 (g), at 300 K and 0.1 MPa a natural reaction?

To do this we compute $g_{\text{rhs}} - g_{\text{lhs}}$ and see if it is positive or negative. Depending on this value we declare the reaction to be not natural or natural at equilibrium.

$$h_{\text{lhs}} = h + h_{s,\text{N}_2\text{O}}(300) - h_{s,\text{N}_2\text{O}}(298.16) = 81.6\,\text{kJ}$$

$$h_{\text{rhs}} = h_{f,\text{N}_2} + (1/2)h_{f,\text{O}_2} + h_{\text{N}_2}(300) - h_{s,\text{N}_2}(298.16)$$
$$+(1/2)h_{s,\text{O}_2}(300) - h_{s,\text{O}_2}(298.16) = 0$$

$$\Delta S = [S_{\text{N}_2} + (1/2)S_{\text{O}_2} - S_{\text{N}_2\text{O}}](298.16)$$
$$= (0.191 + 0.102 - 0.2198) = 0.074\,\text{kJ/K}$$

$$g_{\text{rhs}} - g_{\text{lhs}} = -81.6 - 0.074 \times 298.16 = -103\,\text{kJ} = \Delta g.$$

Δg is negative and hence the reaction must be a natural one.

In making these calculations the data on heats of formation, sensible enthalpies and entropies taken from Tables 4.1 to 4.3 have been used. Let us take another example. Consider H_2O (l, 0.1 MPa) $\rightarrow$ H_2O (g, 0.1 MPa).

The question is at what temperature is this transformation (called vaporisation) a natural one.

$$(g_{H_2O(g)} - g_{H_2O(l)}) < 0$$

$$(h_{H_2O(g)} - h_{H_2O(l)}) + T(S_{H_2O(g)} - S_{H_2O(l)}) < 0$$

$$T > (h_{H_2O(g)} - h_{H_2O(l)})/(S_{H_2O(g)} - S_{H_2O(l)})$$

$$> (40.1\ \text{kJ/mol})/(0.1075\ \text{kJ/molK}) = 373.0\ \text{K}$$

Thus, at $T > 100°\text{C}$, vaporisation of water is a natural process, a fact we are all familiar with.

Whether the reaction is natural or not depends on enthalpy changes as well as entropy changes. Table 4.6 indicates the qualitative behaviour of reactions under various conditions.

An example of Type 1 is the one already illustrated. All association reactions ($H + OH \rightarrow H_2O$, for example) are most probable at low temperatures but not so at high temperatures (Type 2). Type 3 is the opposite of association reactions, i.e., dissociation reactions of the type $CO_2 \rightarrow CO + (1/2)\ O_2$ which are more probable at high temperatures and not so at low temperatures. Type 4 is the opposite of Type 1.

We now proceed to answer the second question. To do this we need a basic relationship concerning the dependence of Gibbs free energy on pressure, very simply obtained from the integration of differential relationship like $g_i = g_i^\circ + RT \ln p_i$ (per unit mole).

Table 4.6 *The effects of changes in sign of Δh and Δs*

Type	Δh	Δs	Δg	Conclusion
1	Negative (exothermic)	Positive	Negative	A probable reaction at all temperatures
2	Negative	Negative	Negative at low T	Probable reaction at low T but improbable at high T
3	Positive (endothermic)	Positive	Negative at high T	A probable reaction at high T but not probable at low T
4	Positive	Negative	Positive	Improbable reaction at all T. The reverse reaction is most probable

Applied to a species in a mixture, this amounts to

$$g_i = g_i^\circ + RT \ln p \quad \text{(per unit mole)}.$$

g_i° = free energy at $p_i = 1$ atm. It is a function of temperature.

We now consider reactions at equilibrium. At equilibrium the rates of forward reactions must equal those of reverse reactions so that there is no net production or destruction of any species. During the transition from initial state to equilibrium, the Gibbs free energy (at constant total pressure and temperature) will decrease till a minimum is attained. At this stage the Gibbs free energy of the reactants will equal those of the products.

$$g_{\text{reactants}} = g_{\text{products}}$$

Thus, for reaction

$$\Sigma a_i A_i \to \Sigma a_i' A_i$$

at equilibrium,

$$\Sigma a_i g_i = \Sigma a_i' g_i.$$

Using the relationship for g_i noted earlier, we get

$$\Sigma(a_i - a_i')g_i^\circ = \Sigma(a_i' - a_i)RT \ln p_i.$$

This can be recast as

$$\Pi p_i^{(a_i' - a_i)} = \exp(-\Delta g^\circ/RT), \quad \Delta g^\circ = \Sigma(a_i' - a_i)g_i^\circ.$$

The notation Π implies the product of all the subscripted variables.

The right-hand side is a function of temperature alone because Δg° is a function of temperature alone. This quantity is called equilibrium constant (K_p). Thus,

$$K_p(T) = \Pi p_i^{a_i' - a_i} \tag{4.22}$$

represents the relationship used for calculating equilibrium composition, given the temperature T and the pressure p.

4.2 How do we compute the composition?

Given:

Reactants: moles of various species; pressure p; temperature T (example H_2, 1/2 O_2, N_2, etc.).

The process of reaction causes change of species without loss of elements. For instance, while the final products may be HO, H_2O, H_2, H, O_2 and O

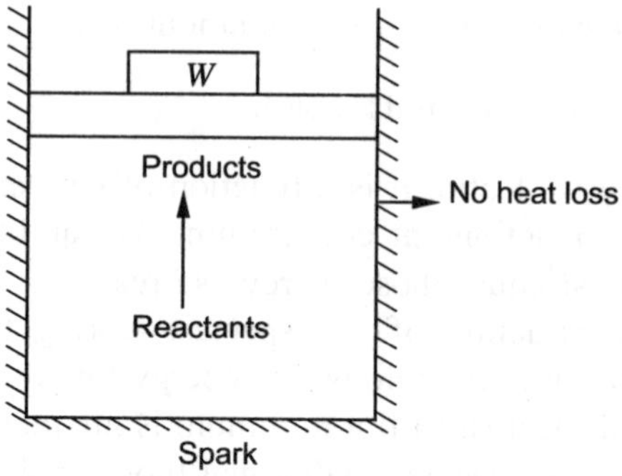

Figure 4.1 *Isolated cylinder with piston*

in different proportions, the total amount of H atoms has to be the same as initially introduced. This represents mass conservation relation of element H. In addition, the various species keep reacting with each other so that the net rate of production/destruction is zero, which gives rise to equilibrium relations. To calculate the composition, one must enunciate the possible products. In the case of H_2–O_2–N_2 reaction at high temperatures, one may have H_2, H, H_2, O, HO, H_2O, N_2, N, NO, N_2O and HNO (11 species) as the possible products. The number of elements is three. The difference, 11 – 3 (No. of species – No. of elements) = 8, is the number of equilibrium relations needed to complete the set of equations. After finding that some of the species have very small concentration at certain temperatures, one might simplify the problem by dropping the species altogether. This reduces the number of equations to be solved.

The equilibrium relations and element conservation equations are solved together to obtain the composition. These equations constitute a set of non-linear algebraic equations whose size is large even for 2 or 3 elements. From the early sixties to the seventies, several attempts were made to solve such equations by various means, and a very powerful computer technique was developed at NASA in the early seventies. This is a workhorse programme used all over the world for obtaining the equilibrium composition (and adiabatic flame temperature as well). This programme minimises the Gibbs free energy (at p = constant, T = constant) to obtain the equilibrium composition.

4.3 How do we obtain the flame temperature?

We have laid the foundations for calculating the flame temperature. We now make an important and reasonably good approximation: the flame temperature is attained as in an adiabatic situation. This implies that no heat is lost to the surroundings from the system. This situation is typified in Fig. 4.1.

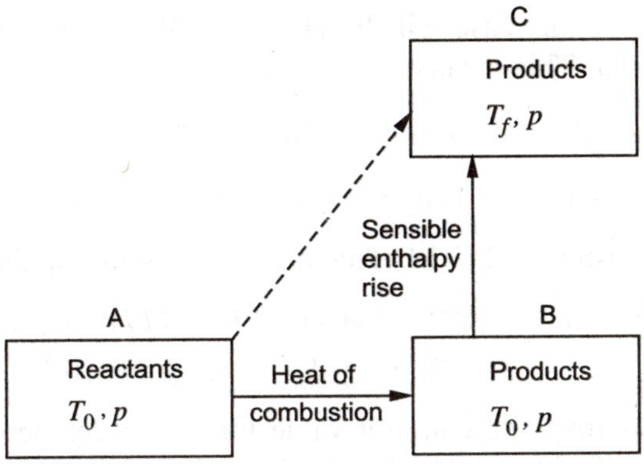

Figure 4.2 *Adiabatic flame temperature determination*

The reactants are kept in an isolated cylinder with a piston to simulate pressure. Then they are sparked to initiate ignition. After this the reactions proceed to completion. The temperature rises to adiabatic flame temperature. The calculations are made using of the idea described in Fig. 4.2.

A first estimate of the adiabatic flame temperature is made. Then the composition is calculated using the scheme enunciated earlier. This composition is set in box (B). The change in chemical enthalpy between (A) and (B) is obtained in the manner in which the heat of combustion is calculated. The heat of combustion is used to raise the temperature of products from T_0 to T_f. This part of the rise in temperature is in the form of sensible enthalpy rise. If all the heat of combustion is used up to raise the temperature to T_f, then one has obtained the adiabatic flame temperature. If some heat is left as balance or the heat absorbed is larger than what is available for an assumed temperature T_f, keep computing the composition and checking the balance till heat balance is satisfied to the required degree of accuracy. If the reaction is

$$\Sigma a_i A_i \rightarrow \Sigma a'_i A_i,$$

then $\Sigma(a'_i - a_i)[h_{f,i} + h_{s,i}(T_0) - h_{s,i}(298.16)]$ is the heat of combustion and $\Sigma a'_i(h_{s,i}(T_f) - h_{s,i}(T_0))$ is the sensible enthalpy absorbed.

The process of computation needs iteration because a'_i depends on the temperature T_f. In case the composition is known, then T_f can be obtained in one step. We shall take a few examples to clarify the procedure.

Reactants: H_2, O_2, (79/21)N_2; initial temperature: 298.16 K; pressure: 0.1 MPa. The initial composition has an air-to-fuel ratio (A/F) = 68.6. The A/F for stoichiometry is 34.3, and so this implies that the initial equivalence ratio is 0.5.

The products in this case will be H_2O and N_2 with excess oxygen remaining unutilised. This means

$$\mathrm{H_2 + O_2 + 3.76N_2 \rightarrow H_2O + (1/2)O_2 + 3.76N_2},$$

and therefore, $a_1 = 1$, $a_2 = 1$, $a_3 = 3.76$, a_1'=0, $a_2' = 1/2$, a_3'=3.76, $a_4' = 1$.

Heat of combustion = 242 kJ. This heat is absorbed by the products as

$$[h_{s,\mathrm{H_2O}}(T_f) - h_{s,\mathrm{H_2O}}(298.16)] + (1/2)[h_{s,\mathrm{O_2}}(T_f) - h_{s,\mathrm{O_2}}(298.16)] \\ +3.76[h_{s,\mathrm{N_2}}(T_f) - h_{s,\mathrm{N_2}}(298.16)] = 242.0\ \mathrm{kJ}.$$

If we take an approximate constant value for c_p in a temperature range of 1000–2000 K as 45, 32 and 34 kJ/mole K for H_2O, O_2 and H_2 respectively, we can write the above equation as

$$(45 + (1/2) \times 32 + 3.76 \times 34)(T_f - 298.16) = 242.0\ \mathrm{kJ}.$$
$$T_f - 298.16 = (242.0 \times 10^3)/189.0 = 1250\ \mathrm{K}.$$

Therefore, T_f = 1548 K. This value is about as accurate as can be obtained from detailed calculations. If there were no nitrogen in the initial mixture, one would get

$$(40 + 1/2 \times 40)(T_f - 298.16) = 242.0\ \mathrm{kJ}.$$
$$T_f - 298.16 = 242000/60 = 4330\ K,\ T_f \simeq 4630\ \mathrm{K}.$$

At this temperature the product H_2O will not remain undissociated. Therefore, a fair amount of enthalpy will be absorbed in dissociation. The products contain H_2O, O_2, OH, O, H, etc., and the process of creating the elements and radicals makes lesser amount of enthalpy available for raising the temperature. This makes the temperature to be about 2600 K or so.

One can make detailed calculations (given the initial data) using the NASA programme referred to earlier. This programme is so powerful that in most cases one can obtain a result in less than a few seconds of computational time on any modern personal computer.

Till now the discussions were centred on reactions at constant pressure because in several practical situations like in rocket engines or diesel combustion, combustion occurs at constant pressure. There may be situations where combustion occurs at constant volume. In such cases the quantity to be used for minimisation is Helmholtz free energy function, which is equal to $e - Ts$. Using the procedure already illustrated but replacing Gibbs free energy function by Helmholtz free energy function, one obtains the composition and the flame temperature at constant volume conditions. Generally, these values will be larger than those corresponding to constant pressure by 100–200 K because there is no work output in a constant volume reaction. We shall take a look at some results.

Table 4.7 *Flame temperature, equilibrium composition and other properties of kerosene–air system*

Kerosene: $CH_{1.942}$; $h_f(\text{l}) = -52.6$ kJ/mol
Air: $O_{0.149}N_{1.56}C_{0.0003}$; $h_f(\text{g}) = -0.118$ kJ/mol
Pressure: =0.1 MPa

A/F	10.0	12.0	15.0	20.0	30.0
e.r	1.47	1.22	0.98	0.735	0.5
T, K	2007	2198	2266	1949	1493
X_i					
H_2O	0.117*	0.129	0.121	0.095	0.065
CO_2	0.058	0.088	0.117	0.098	0.067
CO	0.114	0.065	0.012	0.0004	–
N_2	0.650	0.69	0.724	0.741	0.755
H_2	0.0500	0.018	0.002	–	–
H	0.0004	0.0007	0.0004	–	–
OH	0.00009	0.0007	0.00316	0.001	–
O_2	–	–	0.0085	0.051	0.102
$\mathcal{M}$	26.5	27.7	28.7	28.9	28.9
c_p, (J/ mole K)	9.6	10.6	15.2	10.2	9.0
γ	1.26	1.24	1.17	1.24	1.28

*Mole fractions

Table 4.7 shows the results of flame temperature and product composition for kerosene–air system for various air-to-fuel ratios. The stoichiometric ratio is about 15. The flame temperature peaks around this value and drops on either side. The products at this condition contain about 1.2% (vol) of carbon monoxide. If we use about 30% excess air, then carbon monoxide becomes negligible. At A/F of 30 or beyond, the only products are H_2O, CO_2, N_2 and excess O_2. It is under these conditions that the approximations made earlier for the calculation of flame temperature in the example are valid.

One can notice that the molecular weight of gases is lower for fuel-rich conditions and achieves the value of air at oxidiser-rich conditions.

The typical values of temperature for several common fuel and oxidiser combinations are shown in Table 4.8. The flame temperature does not depend significantly on the nature of hydrocarbon fuel as long as the oxidiser is air. It is about 2300±50 K. Replacing air by oxygen raises the temperature by 600–800 K. Increase in initial temperature does not raise the flame temperature by the same increment. It is particularly true for flame temperatures beyond 3000 K because most of the energy goes into the dissociation of the stable molecules so that the temperature does not change much. Increase in pressure is helpful in reducing dissociation, thereby causing a rise in flame temperature. The change in flame temperature, again, beyond some pressure is very limited because the change in composition beyond pressures of 5.0–8.0 MPa is not much. Acetylene, with its high heat of formation,

Table 4.8 *Flame temperature of some typical fuels*

Fuel	Oxidiser	Pressure MPa	Initial temp K	Peak temp K
Methane	Air	0.1	300	2210
Methane	Air	2.0	300	2270
Methane	Air	2.0	600	2500
Methane	Oxygen	0.1	300	3030
Methane	Oxygen	2.0	300	3460
Hydrogen	Air	0.1	300	2400
Hydrogen	Oxygen	0.1	300	3080
Acetylene	Air	0.1	300	2600
Acetylene	Oxygen	0.1	300	3400
Carbon monoxide	Air	0.1	300	2400
Butane	Air	0.1	300	2250
Kerosene	Air	0.1	300	2270
Producer gas	Air	0.1	300	1500
Wood (dry)	Air	0.1	300	1900

has a flame temperature with air distinctly higher than other straight chain hydrocarbons.

Producer gas and wood are low-energy fuels compared to hydrocarbons. Producer gas has about one-tenth the heat of combustion of kerosene on weight basis. Since it needs little air to burn stoichiometrically, it still can raise the temperature to a significant value ($\sim$ 1500 K). Wood (dry) has a calorific value of about 16–20 MJ/kg, being a little more than one-third that of kerosene; it also has oxygen in it. It needs about six and a half times its weight of air to combust stoichiometrically and ideally attains a temperature of 1900 K.

Combustion properties of three typical examples of rocket engine systems are shown in Fig. 4.3(a) and 4.3(b). The figures show the plots of T_f, $\mathcal{M}$, γ and a quantity called c^* with oxidiser/fuel for a solid propellant as well as two liquid propellant combinations. c^* is called the characteristic velocity. It is given by

$$c^* = \sqrt{RT_f/(\mathcal{M}\Gamma(\gamma))}, \tag{4.23}$$

where $\Gamma(\gamma)$ is a function of the ratio of specific heats ($\sim$1.2) and is about 0.62.

Higher c^* means better performance of a rocket's propellant combination. It has an interestingly curious dependence on $(T_f/\mathcal{M})$. This increase in performance does not necessarily have to take place by an increase in T_f. It can also be accomplished with a decrease in $\mathcal{M}$. Whereas in the case of a solid propellant (not shown here) as well as UDMH–N_2O_4 liquid propellant,

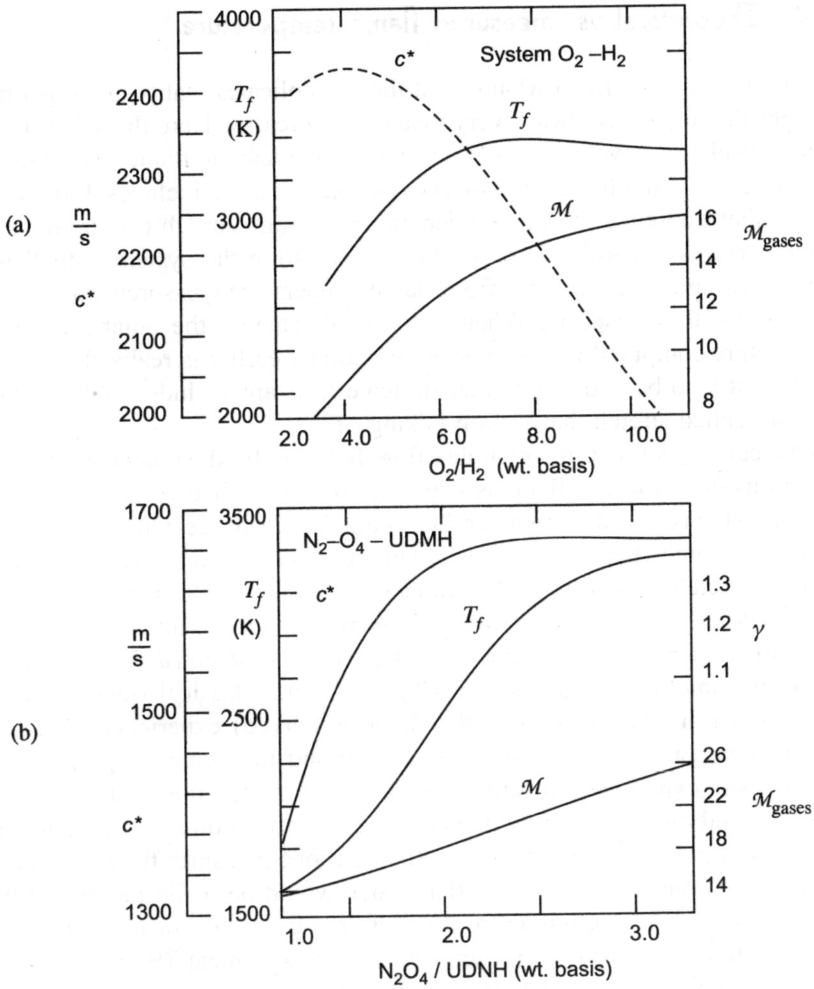

Figure 4.3 *Equilibrium combustion properties*

the peak in T_f corresponds roughly to peak in c^*, implying that molecular weight variation does not play a major role, in the case of liquid hydrogen–liquid oxygen (LH_2– LOX) system, variation in $\mathcal{M}$ plays a significant role. As can be noticed, $\mathcal{M}_{H_2} = 2$ and $\mathcal{M}_{H_2O} = 18$; the average molecular weight varies between 8 and 18 in the figure. Since this variation is large, making the mixture H_2–LOX fuel-rich causes an increase in $T_f/\mathcal{M}$ even though T_f decreases because $\mathcal{M}$ decreases even more when the mixture becomes more fuel-rich. This fact is made use of in LOX–LH_2 engine, where the operating oxidiser to fuel ratio is only 4.5 to 5 even though the stoichiometric ratio is 8. The flame temperature is reduced, which reduces the thermal problem on the engine.

4.4 Theoretical vs. measured flame temperature

It is useful to examine to what extent theory replicates reality, for it is often thought that theory is always very distant from reality. Here the word 'theoretical' itself has several levels. The first is the adiabatic flame temperature. This does not involve flow aspects. The next aspect includes fluid flow effects that influence the flame temperature through stretch (or straining of flame surfaces). Thirdly, there are heat losses from the system with flame to the surroundings. Inference from flame temperature measurements should account for these aspects. When it is asked whether the adiabatic flame temperature computed by the procedure outlined earlier is realised in actual practice, it is to be understood that stretch effects are excluded. What is this quantity called stretch that we are talking of?

One can expect that in a complex flow field the fluid elements will move in various directions. A flame is expected to be stretched if there is change in fluid velocity in a direction parallel to the flame surface. One also talks of strain rates somewhat synonymously. This stretch can be positive or negative. Positive stretch makes the flame thinner. Negative stretch makes the flame thicker. When a flame is flat and the *premixed fluid* flows through the flame in a direction normal to it, one would have an *unstrained* flame. This is the ideal flame, to be discussed in Chapter 6. In a classical Bunsen flame, the region near the top (where the flame is curved) experiences negative stretch (also called compressive strain rate) and the conical region below this segment experiences positive stretch. In a complex flow field the flame surface could move unsteadily and curve up in various directions, leading to various strains being imposed on the flame. If one measures the temperature in the burnt zone just after a flat flame, one would be really measuring the adiabatic flame temperature corresponding to the *mixture ratio of premixed mixture*. If one measures the temperatures in a conical (Bunsen) flame, one will find that to stretch is to reduce the 'flame speed' or the local consumption rate, and at extreme stretch there could be flame extinction as well. If the flame is turbulent, one could have flame extinguishment at several locations at different instants leading to temperature fluctuations from the ambient value to high temperature largely because of these effects.

The effect of heat losses will be severe in small systems and lesser in larger systems—the governing factor to control this would be a geometry which minimises the surface area contributing to heat loss while having the necessary volume to release the heat. Such a geometry is essentially a sphere. Increasing the combustion throughput or power in such a spherical combustor will reduce the role of heat loss in determining the peak temperature achieved in a combustor. The heat losses can contribute to the observed reduction in temperature by a few hundreds of Kelvin.

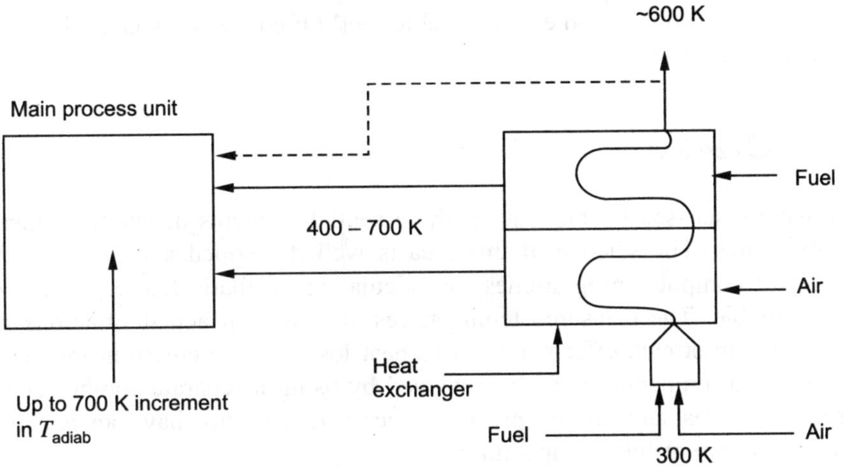

Figure 4.4 *Schematic of an arrangement to raise the peak temperature of a fuel–oxidiser combination*

Thus, both the above factors can reduce the observed temperatures in actual systems by several hundreds of Kelvin.

4.5 Can we raise the peak temperature from a given reactant set?

This question becomes relevant in industries which use low quality fuels to perform thermal operations requiring high temperatures like glazing ceramic material or melting iron. In the former case at least 1350 K is required while in the latter, at least 1600 K is required. If we are using a fuel–oxidant mixture that generates 1100 K, how can we achieve the objectives noted above? Figure 4.4 is a schematic of how this can be achieved. The fuel–oxidant mixture is burnt in two locations, with the hot gas from the first location being used in a heat exchanger to preheat the oxidant alone or the fuel as well before being used in the second combustion system. Since the entry conditions for the second combustion system have reactants at sufficiently high temperature (even up to 800 K, depending on the quality of the heat exchanger), it is possible to raise the temperature even up to 1700 K. In many practical situations the waste heat from the process itself can be used for preheating the reactants, either in part or completely. This is true for many metal melting industries designed and built at a time when fuel was considered cheap and the burnt gases were simply sent up into the atmosphere. By putting up a heat exchanger to heat the air for combustion, such industries would have derived enormous financial benefit and would have saved the planet some considerable fuel! Of course, they can effect the changes even now.

4.6 Overview

We have discussed in this chapter the essential elements of chemical thermodynamics. The science of this area is well developed and understood. Powerful computer programmes for calculating adiabatic flame properties are available. The measured temperatures of flames in actual situations is lower due to stretch effects as well as heat losses. An increase in the peak combustion temperature can be achieved by using a separate combustor to preheat the reactants if the process concerned does not have an exhaust (waste) stream at high temperature.

Equilibrium adiabatic flame temperature sets the upper limit for the observed flame temperature for most systems — gaseous oxidiser, fuel; solid propellant, liquid bipropellants. There is one important exception in some liquid monopropellants, hydrazine being one example, where the measured decomposition temperature exceeds the adiabatic flame temperature. The reason lies in the fact that ammonia, one of the products, decomposes endothermically very slowly to N_2 and H_2. Thus, in an actual system the decomposition is partial and not complete. This leads to a slightly better performance in terms of T_f and c^* in the actual system compared to equilibrium conditions.

5 How Does a Reaction Proceed? At What Rate?

We saw till now what reaction products are and how to compute their mass or mole fractions in the mixture. The question we ask now is how fast is an equilibrium state attained from a given initial state. In order to compute this we should describe the rate of generation or destruction of a given species in a reaction system. It may be recalled that a hydrogen–oxygen reaction was set out as

$$H_2 + (1/2)O_2 + pN_2 \rightarrow H_2O + pN_2.$$

Does the reaction proceed this way? If the products contain many species like we found in equilibrium products, will the reaction proceed differently?

The reaction does not proceed in the way indicated by simple stoichiometry. This is not due to the fact that equilibrium products contain many other species, for one can consider cases of low flame temperature with larger inert fractions and make sure that no species other than the stable products shown above are present in any significant measure. Yet the reaction does not proceed along the path shown. Why is this so?

To answer this we must understand how a reaction takes place. In a gaseous medium it is known that molecules are moving randomly with a range of velocities with a mean related to the temperature of the gas. Collisions occur during the random movements of molecules. These collisions are usually unproductive, i.e., the molecules after collision move away in different directions without any change in the molecular structure. Amongst these collisions, some occur at higher velocities. At these velocities the molecules act like bullets and when they collide, they end up breaking the molecules or forming bonds with other molecules. For instance, consider the following reactions:

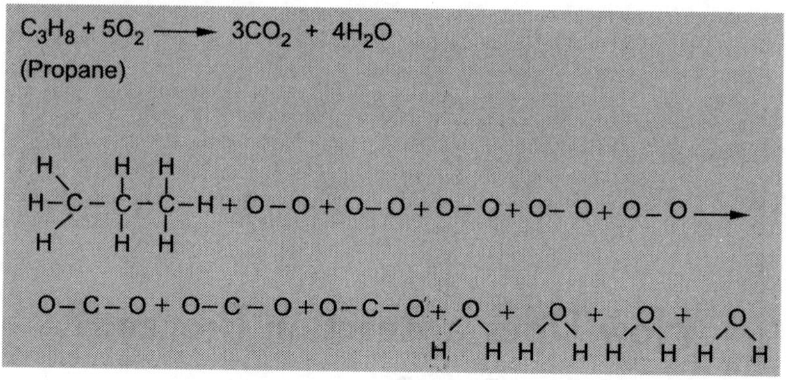

Figure 5.1 *Bonds in propane*

$$H_2 + H_2 \rightarrow H{+}H{+}H_2 \qquad (1)$$

$$H_2 + O_2 \rightarrow H{+}H{+}O_2 \qquad (2)$$

$$H_2 + M \rightarrow H{+}H{+}M \qquad (3)$$

$$HO{+}O \rightarrow O_2 + H \qquad (4)$$

$$H{+}O{+}M \rightarrow OH{+}M \qquad (5)$$

In the first reaction, H_2 collides with another H_2 and breaks up to form hydrogen atoms. Here only one bond is broken. In reaction (2), the collision of H_2 occurs with O_2 and dissociation of H_2 takes place. This feature is generalised in the third reaction. Here H_2 reacts with M giving hydrogen atoms and M. Here M represents any molecule in the field. In reaction (4), HO reacts with O to give O_2 and H. Here one bond is broken and another made. This process is a little more difficult than a simple event of breaking or making of a bond. In reaction (5) three species meet at a single location leading to products. These reactions, called three-body reactions, are not usual at low or reasonable pressures. The density of the gas has to be very high in order for the molecules to be, on an average, close to each other so that three species can meet at a point at the same time. Now we can see why a reaction like

$$C_3H_8 + 5O_2 \rightarrow 3CO_2 + 4H_2O \quad \text{(propane oxidation)}$$

cannot take place in one step. Notice that propane molecule is very large with eight hydrogen atoms attached at various points (Fig. 5.1). For the reaction to take place, five oxygen molecules have to meet one propane molecule at the same time, break it up such that all the eight molecules are pulled out and the carbon atoms separated from each other to form three molecules of CO_2 and four molecules of H_2O. In effect, 15 bonds are to be broken and 14 bonds are to be made. An obviously impossible task considering the fact that in a normal situation, one or two bonds are broken or made. What actually happens is that C_3H_8, reacts with some energetic atom like H or O, which will first break a bond to form C_3H_7 and H_2 or OH. Such a process will continue till very small molecules are formed (CH for instance). Most of these species like C_3H_7 and C_3H_6 are all short-lived unstable configurations and end up quickly as small molecules which will get oxidised to products. What is clear from this discussion is that a chemical reaction proceeds along molecular events. The making or breaking of a bond is the simplest event. The next complex event is the making of two bonds, breaking of two bonds or making of a bond and breaking of another. This is followed by the event in which three bonds are being made/ broken (or some combination of these happenings).

The reaction paths for a simple reaction system like H_2, O_2, are many. Typically, they are as follows:

$H_2 + M \rightarrow H + H + M$	Chain initiation
$O_2 + M \rightarrow O + O + M$	
$H_2 + O \rightarrow OH + H$	Chain branching
$O_2 + H \rightarrow OH + O$	Chain branching
$H + O_2 + M \rightarrow HO_2 + M$	
$HO + O_2 \rightarrow HO_2 + O$	Chain branching
$HO + O + M \rightarrow HO_2 + M$	Chain carrying
$HO + H + M \rightarrow H_2O + M$	Chain termination
$H + O + M \rightarrow H_2O + M$	Chain termination

Thus, one can see nine reversible reactions in the simplest case. The reaction system is called a chain reaction. One can notice a species like HO_2, called hydroperoxyl, being present. It is a species present at relatively low temperatures; nevertheless it is important. One can notice that the other active species and radicals are H, O and OH. The various steps in the chain reaction are characterised differently. The two initial steps when active species are generated from initial reactants are called chain initiation steps. Then we have chain branching reactions where more radicals and active intermediates are generated. The chain termination step is the step where the final products are produced and the radicals get used up.

5.1 How fast does a reaction take place?

The reaction rate is now understood to be due to collisions—largely between two molecules (called bimolecular). This means the rate of reaction is proportional to concentration of molecules of each of the participants, with higher pressure implying higher concentrations, linearly. Thus,

$$\text{Reaction rate (RR)} = AX_iX_2p^2, \tag{5.1}$$

where X_i, X_2 are the mole fractions of colliding species.

Next we examine the dependence of the reaction rate on temperature. It is to be recalled that energetic collisions are responsible for a reaction. It is not the molecules with mean energy that matter, but those with much larger energy levels. It implies that one can set a threshold value of energy E which must be exceeded for a reaction to take place. One can now ask what fraction of molecules have energy greater than or equal to E. The Boltzmann energy distribution law states that the probability of a molecule possessing energy E is proportional to $\exp(-E/RT)$. A more elaborate study obtains the expression for probability of molecules possessing energy equal to and larger than E to be approximately $\exp(-E/RT)$. Thus, the reactants (in a true situation, the single step molecular event in a large number of s) have to have energy larger than E for the reaction to be successful and the fraction of such molecules is $\exp -E/RT$. This dependence is also termed Arrhenius law. Thus, the reaction rate can be taken to be

$$\text{R}R = A_f X_1 X_2 p^2 e^{-E/RT}. \tag{5.2}$$

The quantity A_f is called the frequency factor and is a constant. It is proportional to collision frequency or the number of collisions per unit time. The study of chemical reactions this way is not special to combustion alone. Chemical engineers do deal with reaction rates but mostly isothermal. Biochemical reactions take place at temperatures near ambient temperature. In fact, most microorganisms die beyond 80–90°C. It is only in combustion that a temperature range of 300–3600 K is experienced in a single system like flame. A_f is estimated from kinetic theory based on collisions; it is molecular density and the relative orientation of the participating species which is given by what is known as steric factor. Consider the example of an h atom colliding with a propane molecule. One can notice in Fig. 5.2 that there are several paths of approach that the H atom can take when it attacks a large molecule like propane. Since the bond strength between

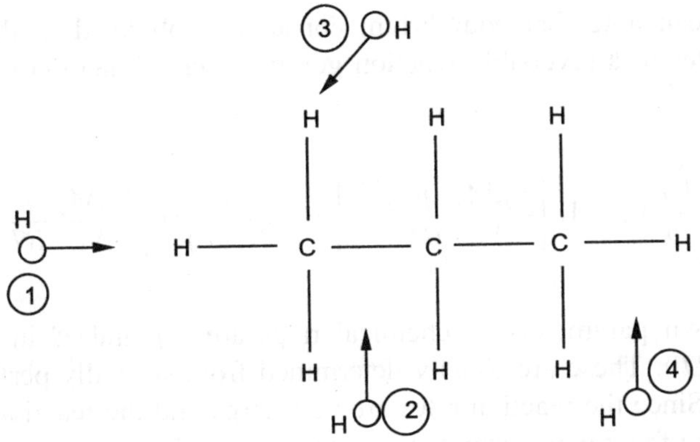

Figure 5.2 *Propane molecule*

various atoms is different, the ability of H atom to break up the propane molecule is different along the different orientations shown. Hence the reaction rate will get affected by the orientation of the molecule in the reaction. In a complex situation, the Steric factor could be as small as 10^{-3}. For a general reaction,

$$\Sigma a_i A_i \quad \xrightarrow{k_f} \quad \Sigma a_i' A_i, \tag{5.3}$$

one can write

$$dc_i/dt = (a_i' - a_i)\dot{w}''',$$

where $\quad \dot{w}''' = k_f \Pi c_j^{a_j}.$

k_f is the constant $= A_f T^\beta \exp(-E/RT)$ and the symbol Π refers to the product of the subscripted quantity over all the species. c_i = species concentration (moles/volume). This relationship is called the law of mass action. It describes the rate of reaction as a function of species concentrations and a constant dependent on temperature. If the reverse reaction, $\Sigma a_i A_i \rightleftharpoons \Sigma a_i' A_i$, is involved and if one uses the equation of state and relationships between molar and mass fractions, one gets

$$\frac{dY_i}{dt} = \frac{\mathcal{M}}{\mathcal{M}_i}\frac{RT}{p}\left\{k_f \times \Pi\left[\frac{Y_j\mathcal{M}_j}{\mathcal{M}}\frac{p}{RT}\right]^{a_j} - k_b\Pi\left[\frac{Y_j\mathcal{M}_j}{\mathcal{M}}\frac{p}{RT}\right]^{a_j'}\right\}, \tag{5.4}$$

where the first and second terms within the parenthesis are the rates of forward and backward reactions.

Now, if steady state or equilibrium is attained, one gets $dY_i/dt = 0$ and so,

$$\frac{k_f}{k_b} = \Pi\left(\frac{Y_j\mathcal{M}_j}{\mathcal{M}}\frac{p}{RT}\right)^{(a_j'-a_j)} = K_p = K_p(T). \tag{5.5}$$

Thus one can note that equilibrium constant is obtained in the limit of reaction rates in a reversible reaction going to zero. Equation (5.4) can be written as

$$\frac{dY_i}{dt} = \frac{\mathcal{M}}{\mathcal{M}_i}\frac{RT}{p}k_f \times \Pi\left[\frac{Y_j\mathcal{M}_j}{\mathcal{M}}\frac{p}{RT}\right]^{a_j}\left\{1 - \frac{1}{K_p(T)}\Pi\left[\frac{Y_j\mathcal{M}_j}{\mathcal{M}}\frac{p}{RT}\right]^{(a'_j - a_j)}\right\}.$$

The unknown parameters of chemical rates are A_f and E in $k_f = A_f \exp(-E_i/RT)$. These are usually determined from specially performed experiments. Since the reaction rates are very large and the reaction times are very small (a few micro seconds to a tenth of a millisecond or so), transient instrumentation techniques are used to obtain the data. Once k_{f_i} is known, the backward rate k_{b_i} is obtained from equilibrium constant, which is known from thermodynamics, the data being specific heats and entropies.

Some features of the reaction rate expression are interesting. Typical values of the activation energy E are of the order of 100–150 kJ/mol for most hydrocarbon-oxygen reactions. If we examine the dependence of reaction rate on temperature, we can write

$$RR_{T_1}/RR_{T_2} = e^{-E/RT_1}/e^{-E/RT_2}. \tag{5.6}$$

For E/R = 5000 K (note R = 8.346 J/mol K),

$$RR_{500\text{K}}/RR_{550\text{K}} = e^{10-9.09} = 2.46. \tag{5.7}$$

Thus, a 10% change in temperature more than doubles the reaction rate. This steep dependence of reaction rate on temperature makes the study of combustion very intriguing and interesting.

The reaction rate increases at a fast rate with temperature (Fig. 5.3). But in a premixed gas, as the temperature increases the reactants are consumed and the rate has to decrease beyond some temperature and go to zero eventually when the reactants are totally consumed. Thus, the plot of the reaction rate with temperature will show a peak, the temperature at which peak occurs being related to activation energy (overall).

Till now we have discussed the essentials of reaction paths and reaction rates of elementary steps or molecular events. It has been brought out that the single overall step written down is good enough for stoichiometric calculations although the reaction do not indeed take place that way. This implies that one cannot write down strictly an overall expression for the reaction rate. While this is indeed valid, engineering science does not get limited by such 'pure' thoughts. An engineering mathematician models reactions by a single step, assigns a rate equation with some parameters and conducts analysis and obtains general results. It is done so because the treatment of

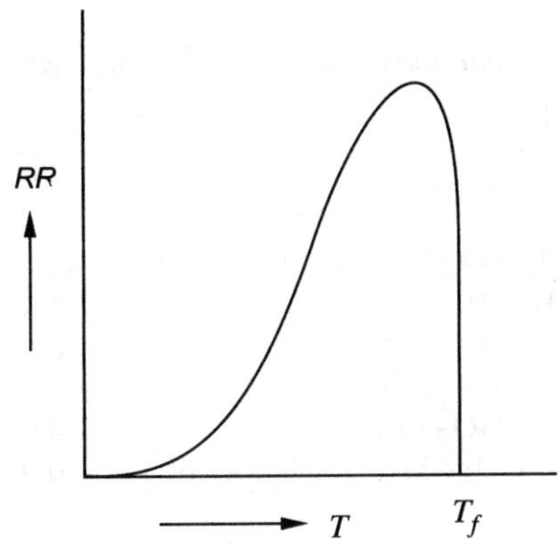

Figure 5.3 *Reaction rates*

complex kinetics is indeed very formidable. A typical way of expressing the overall reaction is

$$\dot{w}_f''' = A_f Y_f^{n_1} Y_o^{n_2} p^n e^{-E/RT},$$

where n_1, n_2 and E are constants estimated from experiments. Typically, n is 1.8 to 2.2 in most cases. Till the seventies, ninety per cent of the flame problems were treated based on single-step reaction assumption. It is only in the last two decades that complex kinetics has been treated using better numerical techniques and faster computers. A further feature is related to values of activation energy and pre-exponential factor like (like A_f in Table 5.1)—it was a common joke that these numbers were at best known to an accuracy of a factor of 10 and the activation energy to an accuracy of 20–30%. See Table 5.1 for data on several reactions and their rate data. So, it was argued that there was not much point in making accurate calculations because the data were so uncertain. In the last fifteen years chemical kineticists have improved the accuracy of data of many elementary steps and it has become worthwhile making detailed calculations. Some of the spectacular advances will be discussed in later chapters (see for instance, premixed flames, Chapter 6). Even so, efforts to obtain an equivalent single-step reaction rate expression based on initial reactant concentrations continue. Wherever a single-step reaction is inadequate, successively increasing number of steps is used to describe the chemical system so that some overall predictions on ignition, flame propagation, etc., can be accurately obtained. A great advantage now, in comparison to earlier times, is that a lot more experimental data of a discriminatory nature are available. Further, comparisons of simplified models can be made with the results of complex chemistry and the limitations of the simplified model obtained. Much of these are in the frontier areas of research.

Table 5.1 *Some reactions and reaction rate data* ($\dot{w}_f''' = A_f Y_o Y_f e^{-E/RT} p^2 T^m$)

Reaction	A_f mol/cm^3 s atm^2	m	E kJ/mol
$H+O+M \rightarrow HO+M$	3.6×10^{18}	-1.0	0.0
$OH+H_2 \rightarrow H_2+H$	1.14×10^{9}	1.3	15.1
$H+O_2 \rightarrow OH+O$	1.45×10^{14}	0.0	69.1
$NH_3+OH \rightarrow NH_2+H_2O$	3.0×10^{12}	0.0	9.2
$CH_3+O_2 \rightarrow CH_2O+OH$	5.2×10^{13}	0.0	144.5±4
$CO+O+M \rightarrow CO_2+M$	3.2×10^{13}	0.0	−17.6

5.2 Overview

Chemical reactions of importance to combustion are characterised by a strong dependence on temperature. Active radicals are a central part of the description of flames. These are generated by molecular events involving energetic collisions. Phenomena dependent on or affected by reaction dominance like premixed gas ignition and/or steady propagation calls for a more detailed description of reactions to be taken into account. For obtaining qualitative dependencies even in such cases, the idea of a single-step overall reaction is very useful. In overall reactions, a single-step equivalent reaction rate can be written as

$$d(Y_i/\mathcal{M}_i)/dt = A_f Y_f^{n_1} Y_o^{n_2} p^n e^{-E/RT},$$

where the exponents n_1, n_2 and n can all be different (generally $n_1 = n_2 = 1$, $n = 2$).

6 Premixed Flames

Premixed flames are those generated when the fuel and the oxidiser are mixed before letting them into the combustion zone. They are not common in nature because if they were, they would have posed serious fire hazards.

6.1 Propagating flames

Consider Fig. 6.1(a). A glass tube is initially filled with premixed gaseous mixture of a fuel and an oxidiser, say air, and sparked by using a high voltage source. When the mixture is sparked, a flame will propagate through the mixture. The flame will be planar in the early stages but becomes curved as it propagates further. The flame becomes curved because of the viscous effect of the glass tube. The speed at which the flame would propagate into the mixture if it were one-dimensional is called the flame speed (S_u).

In Fig. 6.1(b) the apparatus shows rotameters to measure the flow rate and a mixer to mix the fuel and air and pass the mixture so that it attains uniform velocity at the exit end. If the mixture is sparked, a flame issues, which is plane and thin and would remain nearly stationary. The velocity of the unburnt fuel–air mixture entering the flame when it is stationary is the flame speed, denoted normally by S_u, the subscript u referring to the unburnt condition. This situation is similar to the one described earlier excepting that in (a) the gases are quiescent and flame propagates and in (b) flame is stationary and gases are moving in. In apparatus (b), the fuel and air flow rates can be varied so that the air-to-fuel ratio can be varied and the flame speed measured (one can also vary the air-to-fuel ratio in Fig. 6.1(a); it is not shown here). At mixture ratios far from stoichiometry, the flame speed reduces to very small values and eventually, at very lean and very rich mixtures, the flame does not propagate at all. These lean and rich mixture ratios are called flammability limits. Figure 6.1(c) shows the flame over a Bunsen burner. As the flow rate increases, the flame becomes more deeply conical. The velocity of the incoming gases along a direction normal to the flame is the flame speed. If the flow rate is increased, the flame adjusts itself such that the speed of the incoming gases normal to the flame will still be the flame speed.

Typical flame speeds are about 0.30–0.5 m/s for hydrocarbon-air fuels, about 2.0 m/s for H_2–air and 10 m/s for H_2–O_2 flames near stoichiometry. The peak flame speed occurs near stoichiometry in most cases on the fuel-rich side (for e.r.$\sim$ 1.1 or so). In the case of H_2–air and CO–air, the peak flame speed occurs at tremendously fuel-rich mixture (e.r.$\sim$ 1.7). The flame thickness varies from 0.2 mm to as much as 10 mm, faster flames being thinner. Figure 6.2 shows the plot of flame speeds vs. mixture ratios for a few gaseous mixtures. The flame speeds depend only to a little extent on pressure. If the flame speed S_u varies with pressure p as $S_u \simeq p^m$, m varies from −0.3 to +0.3, depending on the chemical system and the equivalence ratio of the mixture. But the flame speed depends strongly on the initial temperature.

6.2 Why are we interested so much in flame speed?

Before we answer this question, we shall examine the dependence of the flame speed on various parameters through a simple analysis.

If $\dot{w}_f'''$ is the reaction rate (kg/m^{3}s) of the fuel and H the heat of combustion, then $H\dot{w}_f'''d_f$ represents the heat flux (W/m^2) caused by chemical reaction. (If it is multiplied by unit cross-section, then one gets the heat generated in kW.) The heat flux so obtained causes the gradient between T_f, the adiabatic flame temperature, and T_0, the initial temperature over the flame thickness d_f. Thus,

$$H\dot{w}_f'''d_f = k\frac{(T_f - T_0)}{d_f} \tag{6.1}$$

(k = thermal conductivity of the gas). An overall heat balance leads to $H \simeq c_p(T_f - T_0)$. If we use this we get

$$\dot{w}_f'''d_f^2 = \frac{k}{c_p}. \tag{6.2}$$

Another relationship is obtained if we recognise $\rho_u S_u = \dot{w}_f'''d_f$ (=mass flux of mixture). Hence,

$$d_f = (k/c_p) \times (1/\rho_u S_u) \tag{6.3}$$

and

$$\rho_u S_u = \sqrt{(k/c_p)\dot{w}_f'''}. \tag{6.4}$$

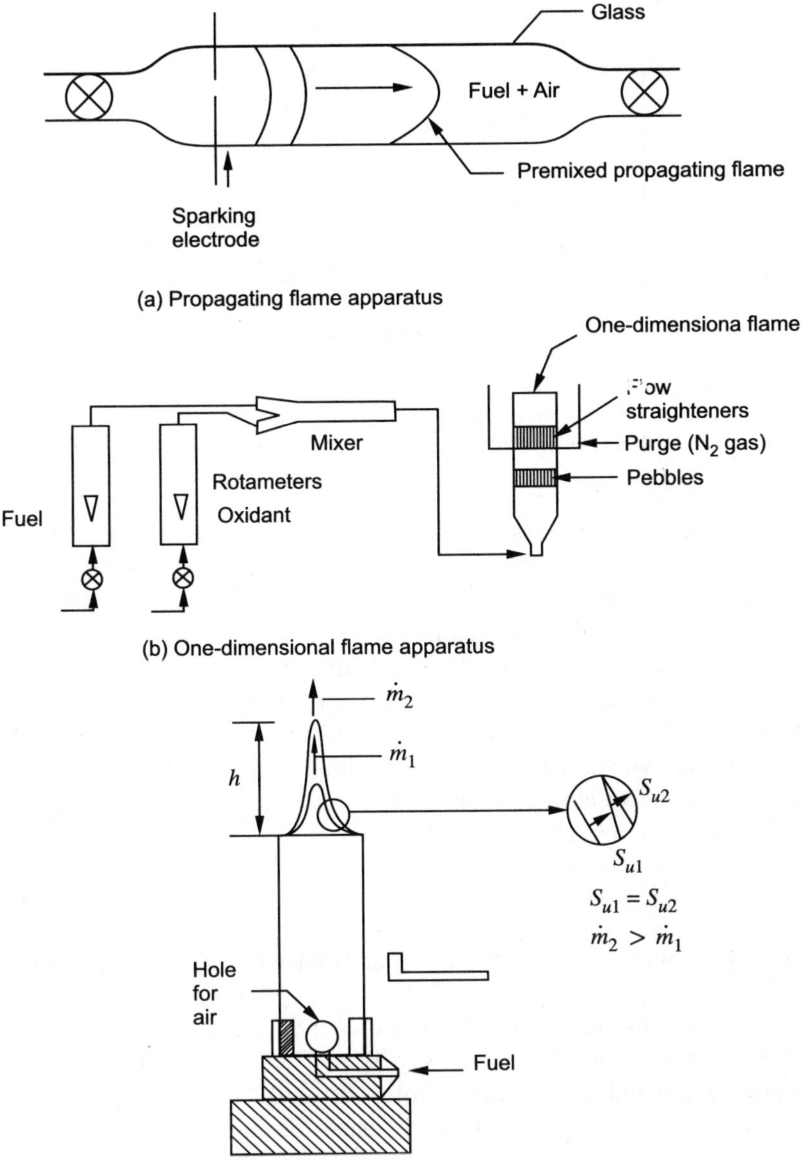

Figure 6.1 *Premixed flame apparatus*

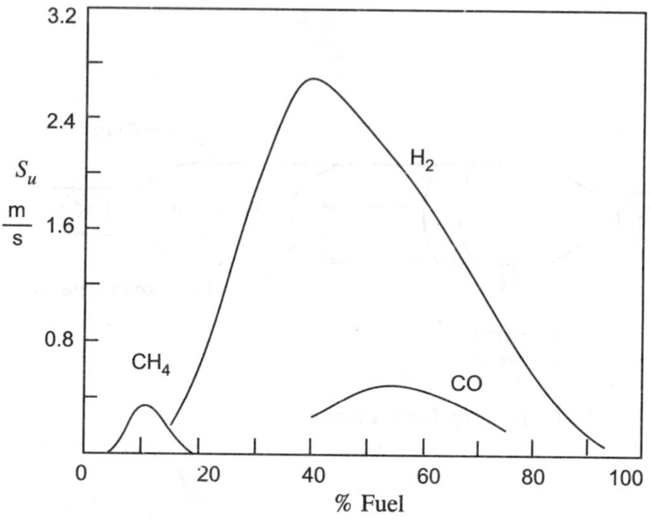

Figure 6.2 *Flame speed of fuel–air mixtures*

These are the two major results. The flame thickness is inversely proportional to the flame speed (Fig. 6.3). Experimental results confirm this, as already indicated. The flame speed varies as the square root of reaction rate. The reaction rate in the above expression should be treated as an average value. The expression indicates that the flame speed is representative of the reaction rate of the premixed mixture. If we now recall the results of flame speed indicated earlier, we conclude that H_2–O_2 stoichiometric mixture is lot a more reactive compared to H_2–air, which itself is more reactive compared to LPG–air system. If we introduce the structure of $\dot{w}_f'''$, averaged in some sense, we write

$$S_u \simeq \sqrt{(k/c_p)A_f \frac{RT_{in}}{p} p^{n/2} e^{-E/2RT_f}} \simeq p^{(n/2)-1} e^{-E/RT_f}, \tag{6.5}$$

where n is the overall order of reaction and T_f the adiabatic flame temperature.

If most reactions are taken as bimolecular, $n \simeq 2$, then $S_u \sim p^0$, i.e., S_u is independent of pressure. If $n \simeq 2.4$, say, $S_u \sim p^{0.2}$ and if $n \simeq 1.8$, $S_u \sim p^{0.1}$. Thus the pressure index of S_u varies from -0.1 to 0.2 for this range of overall orders of reaction (1.8 to 2.4), which is usual for most systems. This result is in complete conformity with experimental observations. The dependence on initial temperature is caused through a change in flame temperature.

Let us consider the question of the importance of the flame speeds in combustion processes. Several phenomena like ignition, quenching, lifting and blow-off of diffusion flames, blow-off of high-speed premixed mixtures, are all related to chemical reactivity of a gaseous mixture. These can

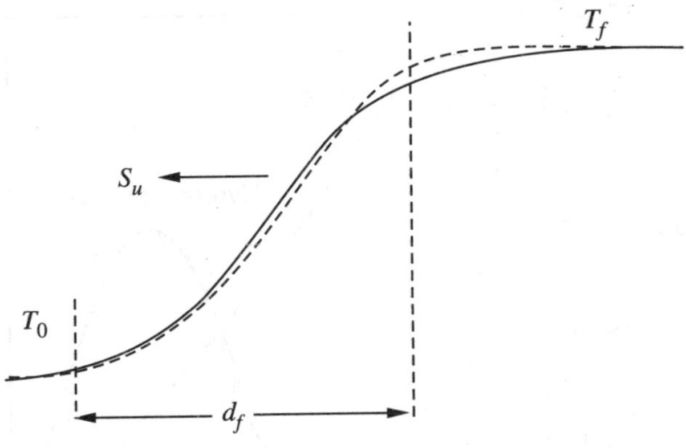

Figure 6.3 *Flame front*

therefore be directly related to the burning velocity of a mixture. In situations where chemical reactivity is to be treated, one can use the flame speed as the representative quantity. If a solid propellant is burning in one-dimensional geometry, then the configuration is similar to the flame in gaseous media excepting that a solid interface is accepting the heat transfer from the flame and burning. The quantity $S_u = \rho_p \dot{r}$, where ρ_p = density of the solid and $\dot{r}$ the linear burn rate, can be treated by a similar approach. If a porous bed of pieces of solid fuel (like bio-fuel or coal) is burning with the flow of air through the bed, the flame front propagates through the bed against the air flow. This process is similar to the propagation behaviour in gaseous fuel–oxidiser mixtures.

While the simple analysis described above is adequate to understand the overall features of flame speed, more effort is needed to elucidate the dependence of flame speed on pressure. This is because what is being done is to relate the pressure index of the flame speed to reaction rate pressure index, something which is unknown because the reaction proceeds in several steps and it is not clear *a-priori* which of the steps is/are important.

In order to take complex kinetics into account, one needs to solve conservation equations involving mass, momentum and energy in general. In respect of deflagration (subsonic flame propagation), it is adequate to solve species (mass) and energy conservation equations. The conservation equations of many species being formed or destroyed via various steps are solved on a computer, resulting in flame speed, temperature and mass fraction profiles. Computation performed for several pressures will reveal the pressure index. The resulting profile can also be used to obtain the overall heat release rates as a function of local temperature. One can then determine the reactivity of the gaseous mixture. Figure 6.4 shows the plots for H_2–O_2 and hydrocarbon–air systems. It can be seen that peak heat release rates are as high as 10^6–10^7 MW/m^3. Referring back to Fig. 6.1, wherein various

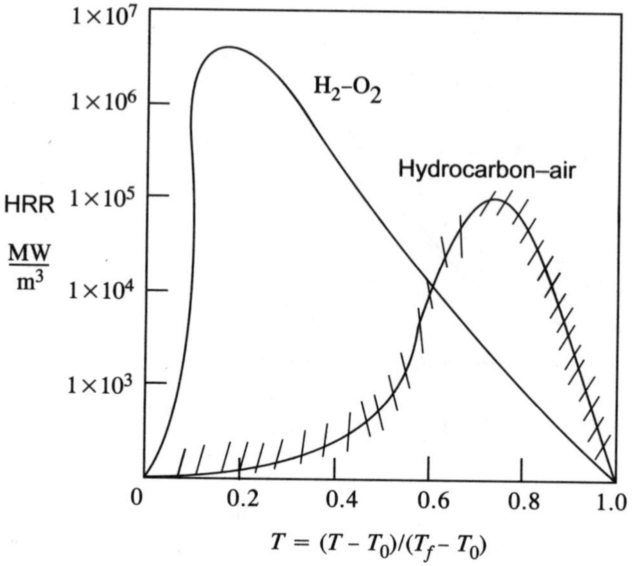

Figure 6.4 *Heat release rate vs. non-dimensional temperature*

geometries of premixed flame are shown, it is possible that the flames could be produced with large ducts and at reasonably high velocities as well. In such cases the flames no longer remain laminar. High speed pictures will show combustion zones randomly moving around; the flame will be noisy as well. Such flames are said to be affected by turbulence. Turbulence begins to play a significant role in ducts for Reynolds numbers larger than 2300 or so. The Reynolds numbers are calculated based on mass flux through the duct, ρu (where ρ is the density and u is the velocity of the gas mixture), the duct diameter, d and the viscosity of gases issuing out of the duct, μ ($Re = \rho u d/\mu$). Turbulence is characterised by intensity and scale. Intensity is essentially the ratio of root mean square of the fluctuating velocity to the mean local velocity ($\sqrt{\bar{u}'^2}/\bar{u}$). Scale refers to the length scale or distance of influence of fluctuations at any point. It is usually defined using correlations between fluctuations of velocity at different points and the extent of influence of the fluctuations at one point in its neighbourhood. At any level of intensity, if the scale of turbulence is large, it is taken that the flame is simply contorted (or more generally called wrinkled), and this increases the consumption rate by increasing the surface area for combustion. Following this suggestion, the ratio of turbulent to laminar flame speed is written as S_T/S_u = area of wrinkled surface/area of cross-section The area ratio is calculated from geometrical considerations using some model descriptions and one obtains, area ratio $= 1 + (\sqrt{\bar{u}'^2}/S_u)$. Thus,

$$S_T = S_u + \sqrt{\bar{u}'^2} \tag{6.6}$$

as a result for one extreme condition. In another extreme of small scale turbulence, the turbulence is expected to simply enhance the diffusivity of the fluid.

If we note

$$S_u = \sqrt{k\dot{w}_i'''/c_p},$$

it is taken that

$$S_T/S_u = \sqrt{(k/c_p)_{\text{Turbulent}}/(k/c_p)_{\text{Laminar}}}.$$

It also implies that the ratio of flame thicknesses of turbulent to laminar is the same, namely

$$d_T/d_l = \sqrt{(k/c_p)_{\text{Turbulent}}/(k/c_p)_{\text{Laminar}}}. \tag{6.7}$$

An approximate expression for the ratio of diffusivities is quoted as 0.01 Re and so

$$S_T/S_u = d_t/d_l = \sqrt{(0.01Re)} = 0.1Re^{1/2}. \tag{6.8}$$

Thus, at high Reynolds number ($\simeq 10^4$), the turbulent flame can be ten times as thick and propagate ten times as fast as a laminar flame. While these overall results are quite in agreement with experimental observations, the foundations are by no means sound. For instance, it is not clear why the reaction rates in turbulent range should be the same as that for laminar range. This is an area of current research where theoretical description is refined to predict details of flame structure in addition to overall results.

It is often understood that laminar flames are only of theoretical importance and it is the turbulent flames that are of practical relevance. This is not true. Laminar flames are also of practical importance. Solid propellant combustion processes occur at length scales of a ten to hundred microns with gas efflux velocities of a few m/s. With viscosity being high due to high temperatures (of 1000 to 2000 K), the effective Reynolds number of the flow is 10 to 100. The flows coming out of the propellant surface would be unsteady, but laminar. Flame quenching (see the next chapter) is a process that occurs at dimensions and velocities that are in the laminar flow regime. A new subject called micro-combustion process, being evolved now, occurs in the laminar flow regime.

6.3 Overview

This chapter has dealt with laminar flames. Flames propagating at constant speed can be treated as stationary by reversing the inflow at the speed required to maintain the steady behaviour. The speed at which the unburnt mixture approaches the steady flame is termed the burning velocity and it characterises the chemical reactivity of the mixture. The propagation speeds are weakly dependent on pressure, but strongly on initial temperature of the mixture. Reducing the amount of dilution increases the propagation speed. Premixed combustion process behaviour dominates the combustion of double-base propellants at all pressures and composite propellants at low pressure. The specific qualification in terms of pressure arises from the consideration that the propellant ingredients are in a molecularly-mixed state in double-base propellants and the length scales of combustion at low pressure are large compared to the particle sizes in a composite propellant. Turbulent flames existing in some regimes can be treated as wrinkled laminar flames. In fine scale highly-turbulent combustion, turbulence interacts deeply with the reaction process.

7 Inflammability, Quenching

Suppose you had to light an LPG gas stove manually. You would possibly use a mechanical spark igniter. You would open the valve on the front and cause the spark a few seconds later. Unless you time the spark properly, the gas would not ignite. You do it a few times at various locations around the gas exit region. At one moment you may find that the entire gas mixture ignites. Also, if you open the valve and start the sparking operation too late near the gas exit region, you would not achieve any success. What is it that is happening? The gas will ignite and flame will stabilise provided the mixture is neither too rich nor too lean in the spark region. If you sparked too early (after you complete the operation of opening the valve), the gas would not have arrived at the spark region after mixing with air, and so the mixture will possibly be too lean to ignite. If you sparked too late, the mixture of fuel and air issuing out of the gas outlet would possibly be too fuel-rich and so it would not ignite at all.

To give another example, if the valve of a gas stove or gas cylinder is inadvertently left open (or is leaking), gas accumulation takes place in a confined area. Suppose that somewhere in the vicinity there is a naked flame. A short while after the leakage is noticed, and before any corrective action can be taken, the whole gas is up in flames. In this situation the leaked gas would be mixing with air and the mixture, which would be moving around possibly due to ambient wind, encounters an excellent ignition source and the gas (in the appropriate mixture ratio range) ignites.

In both these cases, the essential feature is that the gas mixture is inflammable only over a limited range of mixture ratios. Inflammability limits are the range of fuel–oxidant mixture ratios within which a flame can propagate, and beyond which the flame cannot propagate. It is experimentally measured by a rather simple apparatus. A long tube (of length 10–12 times the diameter), typically of 40–60 mm diameter (diameter cannot be too small) is filled with a mixture of chosen mixture ratio. It is sparked at the top, middle, or bottom. If the flame propagates, then the mixture ratio is moved further to the lean or rich side. That mixture ratio at which the flame hesitates to propagate (or does not just propagate) is the inflammability limit. There are slight differences between results of upward and downward flame propagation. But we will not consider this.

For instance, consider the results of methane–air mixture as shown in Fig. 6.2. If you notice the left-hand side region, the curve is approaching very low flame speed at fuel fraction of 5% (by volume). This is typically about 0.02 m/s. Similarly, on the rich side, the curve drops down to very small values at fuel fraction of 15%. The flammability limits may therefore be taken to lie between 5–15% for methane–air at ambient temperature. An important question concerning these values has been raised in literature. If we have an adiabatic flame propagation, would there be limits or would the propagation occur at any mixture strength?

It is indeed true that an adiabatic flame should be capable of propagation at any mixture ratio. This fact has been proved by systematic calculation of the propagational behaviour. In reality however, there are heat losses—the irreducible heat loss due to radiation from the flame. If one calculates the propagation speed as a function of mixture strength, one finds that the difference between the speeds without and with heat loss is very small at stoichiometry (about 2 %) which increases towards the lean and rich conditions. At low propagational speeds, the energy present in the flame is so small that relatively small heat loss is enough to quench the flame. One can impose natural heat loss behaviour and calculate the limits. These match with the observed limits. Some typical values of flammability limits are given in Table 7.1.

It may be noticed from Table 7.1 that: the limits get enlarged because of oxygen, essentially due to greater reactivity; that in the case of acetylene the upper limit is 100% because acetylene is exothermically decomposable by itself; hydrogen has very wide limits compared to hydrocarbons due to its higher reactivity; the upper limit (rich) is about 2–4 times the stoichiometry; the lower limit (lean limit) is about 30–60% of the stoichiometry.

The limits get enlarged at higher initial temperatures. The lean limit remains unaltered because of the increase of pressure. The upper limit is enhanced substantially at higher pressures. The data on Table and the discussion in the earlier paragraph imply that the behaviour is different for lean and rich operating conditions. These are due to chemical kinetic effects which should be taken into account along with heat losses if the predictions are to be realistic. While simple theories explain many observed features qualitatively, computational studies with realistic chemistry and multi-dimensional geometry have captured many observed features.

Table 7.1 *Flammability limits (0.1 MPa, 300 K)*

Fuel	Oxidiser	Lean limit %(Volume of fuel)	Rich limit %	O/F$_{stoi}$ %
Hydrogen	Air	4.0	75.0	29.5
Hydrogen	Oxygen	4.0	95.0	66.0
Methane	Air	4.5	14.0	9.5
Ethane	Air	3.0	12.4	5.6
Propane	Air	2.1	9.1	4.0
Butane	Air	1.8	8.4	3.1
Acetylene	Air	2.5	100.0	7.8
Methyl alcohol	Air	6.7	36.0	12.2
Carbon monoxide (Moist)	Air	12.0	76.0	29.5

7.1 Quenching

Quenching is an extension of flammability limits. Suppose one keeps conducting the experiment on flammability limits with cylindrical tubes of successively lower diameters. The flammability limits remain about the same till a certain value, typically about 20 mm or so. Below this diameter if the duct size is reduced, the limits begin approaching each other till the stage when the flame will not propagate at all at any mixture ratio. This diameter, at which flame will not propagate at all, is called the quenching diameter and half of it is called the quenching distance. Why does a quenching distance exist at all?

The answer lies in the fact that the heat production or the release rate of the flame is not adequate enough to overcome the heat losses for the flame to propagate. Another way of stating this result is that the flame speed keeps decreasing from its adiabatic value to lower values depending on the extent of heat loss till it becomes zero, when the heat loss rate is a significant fraction of the heat generation rate.

The heat generation rate is calculated by multiplying the following: the volumetric reaction rate, heat of combustion, volume of combustion zone given by the cross-sectional area of the duct and flame thickness. Therefore,

$$\text{Heat generation rate} = H\ \dot{w}_f'''\ (\pi d^2 d_f/4). \tag{7.1}$$

Heat loss can occur by conduction or radiation. For propagation through tubes, which is being considered at present, it is the loss by conduction to the walls that matters. This heat loss is estimated by stating

$$\text{Heat loss rate} = \text{Flux} \times \text{Area} = \frac{k(T_f - T_0)}{(d/2)}(\pi d\ d_f).$$

If heat generation rate is comparable to rate of heat loss, then quenching may be considered to occur ($d = d_q$, is the quench diameter).

$$H\dot{w}_f'''\frac{d_q^2\,d_f}{4} = C\,k\frac{(T_f - T_0)}{(d_q/2)}d_q\,d_f,$$

where C is a constant.

We note that $H = c_p(T_f - T_0)$ and obtain

$$d_q^2 = 8\,C\frac{k}{c_p}\frac{1}{\dot{w}_f'''}. \tag{7.2}$$

If we further note that $\dot{w}_f'''d_f^2 = (k/c_p)$, we get

$$d_q^2 = 8\,C\,d_f^2 \text{ or } d_q = \sqrt{8\,C}d_f. \tag{7.3}$$

Alternately, one can state

$$d_q = \frac{\text{Constant}}{\rho_u\,S_u}. \tag{7.4}$$

Experimental measurements seem to confirm the above relationship between **quench distance** and flame speed. The proportionality constant, C, varies **between** 10 and 30. The dependence of quench distance on pressure and initial temperature is essentially through the laminar flame thickness or flame speed. This implies

$$d_q \sim p^{-n/2} \text{ and } d_q \sim e^{-E/2RT_f}. \tag{7.5}$$

Typically, $n \sim 2$ and so $d_q \sim 1/p$. The dependence of d_q on initial temperature is felt through its effect on the flame temperature. Typical values of quench distance for some gases are shown in Table 7.2.

One can notice from Table 7.2 that the lowest quench distance is as low as 0.2 mm. Thus, it is difficult to prevent H_2–O_2 flame from moving across any barrier in ducts.

What do we use the information on inflammability limits and quenching distances for?

The information on inflammability limits is useful for causing ignition as well as preventing fires. If a fuel–oxidant mixture needs to be ignited, it must lie within the limits of flammability. Thus, one simple check to determine if a mixture is ignitable is to examine the limits of flammability. There are occasions when one does not want a mixture to ignite. One practical instance is as follows. Most submarines have a device for surfacing rapidly from the depths in case of an emergency. Typically, the time to surface from 200 m

Table 7.2 *Quench distance (d_q) of some gases*

Mixture	Stoichiometry mm	Minimum mm
Hydrogen–air	0.5	0.50
Hydrogen–oxygen	0.2	0.18
Methane–air	2.5	2.00
Ethane–air	2.3	1.80
Butane–air	3.4	1.80
Acetylene–air	0.8	0.70
Methyl alcohol–air	1.8	1.50
Carbon monoxide–air	2.8	2.50

depth may be about 20–30 s. For doing this, the water in its interior regions are expelled by a gas generator based on hydrazine, which produces gases at high pressures. These gases act on the surface of water in the chamber so that it is ejected. The products of decomposition of hydrazine are ammonia, hydrogen and nitrogen. This mixture, at a temperature of about 400–500°C, mixes with the air in the ballast tanks. Pressures are anywhere between 2.5–3.0 MPa (25–30 times the ambient pressure). It is not immediately clear if the mixture will ignite in the environment. If it ignites, the results would be disastrous. Examination of the data in the light of knowledge of flammability limits indicates that the possibility of ignition cannot be ruled out. Experimental evidence indicates a high incidence of ignition (and explosion) in several tests made at various conditions.

Similarly, quenching has several useful practical aspects. Several chemical industries deal with hydrogen and hydrogen–air or other mixtures. In industries, these gases are handled at fairly high flow rates. If there happens to be ignition anywhere, the flame will propagate (at as much as 1.5–2.5 m/s for hydrogen–air system) throughout the system and may enter the hold of gas and cause explosion. In all such cases, it is important to isolate various systems so that the possibility of flame in any one region does not affect the other units/systems. For designing flame isolators, one needs to use the information on quench distances. Two systems, if connected through a large number of parallel tubes, each of diameter less than quench distance (the large number is to provide for adequate total cross-sectional area) and preferably made of high conductivity material, would become decoupled because a flame cannot cross from one to the other.

A somewhat similar scheme is employed in the design of a flare used for burning combustible gases from a biomass gasification system. This system needs to be used certainly at start-up, in emergency shutdowns, and also at other times during the plant's operation. While in normal conditions the combustible gas without any oxidant is the only gas that passes through the system, it may turn out that some leakages develop during the system's

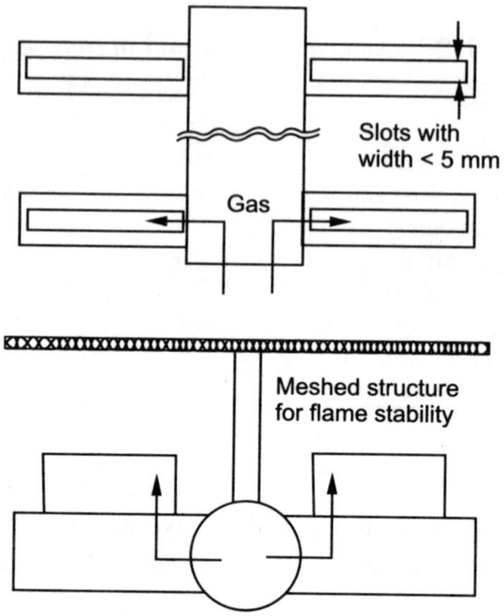

Figure 7.1 *A schematic for ensuring that the flame does not flash back even if the gas that flows out of the slots gets premixed subsequently*

lifetime which may generate a good combustible mixture passing through the system. If, at the time when the flare is operating an emergency shut-down occurs, the average speed through the system keeps falling and could go below the flame speed. When this happens the flame will propagate up-stream, which can cause undesired combustion in large volumes of gaseous mixtures, if present, leading to thermal explosion. Figure 7.1 shows the schematic of a design to prevent this happening. The gas from a duct is divided into two, four (or more, if needed) paths and the exit occurs from a rectangular section where the width is smaller than the quench distance. The total cross-sectional area is made comparable to the gaseous inlet area so as not to cause any additional pressure drop in the line. The gases coming out of the rectangular slots can be ignited and the flame maintained. If the exit velocities are large enough to blow the flame off, they can be countered by maintaining a meshed structure to enable the flame to be stabilised outside. If, now, the blower (or any other source) delivering the gases is turned down or turned off, the flame tends to move back (flash back). This movement is prevented by the small cross-section of the path where the flame extin-guishes because the heat generation rate here is inadequate to overcome the heat loss rate.

7.2 Overview

In this chapter we looked at flammable mixtures and quenchable regions of flames. The two are connected with flame speeds as is amply clear from the simple expressions for quench distance and other aspects discussed. Understanding these would help to bring a mixture to the ignition range or take it out of it, and to permit transmission of ignition from one region to another or prevent it.

We now move on to ignition and stability of flames.

8 Ignition

It is a matter of experience that a gas stove can be ignited more easily than a kerosene wick stove, which in turn is easier to light than a solid fuel stove. Since ignition implies a flame in gaseous phase, one has to generate fuel vapours from liquid/solid before ignition can take place. That is why it is easier to ignite a gaseous fuel. It is more difficult to vapourise a solid in comparison to a liquid, which explains the greater difficulty in igniting solid fuels.

Aircraft engines use kerosene as a fuel. Kerosene is usually injected as a fine spray into the combustion chamber. Ignition is performed by a spark source. It must be noted that the flow velocities in the combustor are by no means small, typically 20–50 m/s. Hence, it is quite difficult to re-ignite the fuel under these conditions. Let us assume that ignition has taken place and the aircraft is at a cruising altitude. Suppose the aircraft moves into a zone of heavy rain and water ingestion causes a 'flame-out', as it is called. It should be possible to re-ignite the system at this altitude and at reasonable flight speeds. This is however a tough task and if achieved, makes the aircraft engine qualify for acceptance as a propulsion system. To find how much must be the energy of the spark to cause ignition in such conditions and where to locate the spark in the flowing fluid requires an understanding of the processes of ignition.

We begin now to try and understand the processes during ignition. There are two methods of ignition—(i) high energy spark, (ii) a naked flame. The high energy spark is created between two electrodes kept at some distance away from each other. Generating a high voltage across the electrodes (typically of the order of 10 kV) causes a breakdown of the resistance in the gaseous atmosphere and the region between the electrodes is filled with ions and high energy species. The local temperatures are also high. These high energy species diffuse to the surroundings, recombine at a distance and generate heat. The chemical reactions begin in the entire region around the spark. Whether these reactions decay away or sustain into a propagating flame will depend on the relative levels of energy generated locally to that which is diffused away. The minimum energy required can be estimated by calculating the energy of a flame whose thickness (cross-section) equals the quench distance. The logic for this comes from the following observation. If the energy of the spark is restricted to the cross-section equal to or less than the quench distance corresponding to the gas–air mixture, the energy will simply be diffused away or lost by conduction through the surrounding medium. The energy of the flame is the product of the sensible enthalpy per unit mass of the gas taken from the ambient to the flame temperature and the mass of the gas confined within the quench diameter and flame thickness. As long as the ignition energy (IE) is larger than this value, ignition will take place.

$$\mathrm{IE} = c_p(T_f - T_0)((\pi d_q^2/4)d_f\rho_u). \tag{8.1}$$

This states that the ignition energy is equal to the product of the sensible enthalpy per unit mass multiplied by the mass of the gas. If we note that $d_q \sim 10d_f$ from (7.2), we get

$$\mathrm{IE} = 100\rho_u c_p(T_f - T_0)d_f^3. \tag{8.2}$$

This expression correctly describes the qualitative behaviour of ignition energy with pressure and initial temperature through ρ_u and d_f. Again, recalling the relationship between d_f and the flame speed (Eq. 6.3), we get an alternate expression for ignition energy as,

$$\mathrm{IE} = 100\frac{k^3(T_f - T_0)}{c_p^2\rho_u^2 S_u^3} = 100\alpha_u^2 k\frac{(T_f - T_0)}{S_u^3}, \tag{8.3}$$

where α_u = gas thermal diffusivity = $(k/\rho_u c_p)_g$.

If we set $S_u \sim p^{n/2-1}$, $\rho_u \sim p^1$ and k/c_p as independent of pressure for a perfect gas, IE $\sim p^{-2}$ if $n = 2$.

Thus as the pressure decreases, the ignition energy becomes larger by a factor p^{-2}. This is a steep dependence on pressure. Let us look at some typical values for vapours of kerosene or natural gas in air, viz. $k = 0.04\mathrm{W/mK}$, $T_f - T_0 = 2000$ K, $c_p = 1.3$kJ/kg K, $S_u = 0.4$ m/s, $\rho_u \sim 1.2$ kg/m^3. These values lead to an ignition energy of 0.11 mJ. This value is in the right range of values determined experimentally, observing that this is an upper estimate of the limit. Some of these values are shown in Table 8.1. Note that these values are for a quiescent atmosphere. If pressure is a third of the sea level pressure, as it happens for a flying aircraft, the ignition energy will be about thirty times this value, 1–2 mJ. If now we superpose the effect of flowing stream at velocities ~20–50 m/s, the energy goes up substantially. While the actual calculations can indeed be made, the typical ratio of ignition

Table 8.1 *Ignition energies (IE) at 0.1* MPa

Fuel	Oxidiser	*IE* mJ
Hydrogen	Air	0.01
Hydrogen	Oxygen	0.003
Methane	Air	0.003
Ethane	Air	0.4
Butane	Air	0.3
Acetylene	Air	0.03
Methyl alcohol	Air	0.2
Carbon monoxide	Air	0.05

energies with flow compared to that at quiescent conditions is about 100 or so. This brings the ignition energy in the range of 0.1 J or so. Typical values of ignition energies in spark igniters of aircraft engines are about 1–2 J, and this is consistent with the fact that in aircraft engines the ignition is of kerosene spray (fine droplets) and not gaseous fuel.

Ignition by a naked flame is always easier than ignition by a spark. This is because a flame has a copious amount of active radicals at reasonably high temperature—even a match stick flame carries with it energy of as much as 20–50 J. Thus the energy available for ignition is very large. Of course, one will not be able to use a simple flame in relatively high speed streams because the flame will get quenched. (Why? See Chapter 9 on extinction and stability of flames.) A spark is a very stable source of energy especially since it is tiny and can be arranged easier. This does not mean pilot flame ignition is not used in practice. It is indeed used even in rocket engines. The pilot flame is spark ignited and it becomes the ignition source for a much larger system.

8.1 Ignition of liquid pool and solid fuels

Under unforeseen contingencies it may so happen that a liquid pool gets formed. A typical instance could be the breaking up of a fuel tanker at sea. The entire liquid fuel spreads on the sea surface. During the breaking up, should there be an unwanted fire, the entire liquid pool could go up in flames or, be not in a position to be burnt-up—a condition less desired under such circumstances because of the environmental hazard it poses. So we ask a question: under what conditions does a pool of liquid ignite?

Suppose one were to take a burning matchstick near a pool of kerosene. You may find that the kerosene will not ignite at all. You may then take the burning stick near a small pool of gasoline and be surprised by the speed of ignition. You might further provoke the kerosene pool by simply inserting the cinder of burning stick into the pool to find a few whitish vapours or a gasoline pool escaping into the atmosphere. Then even a small flame brought near the pool would quickly ignite and burn away the vapours obtained a little earlier. What do all these mean? For ignition, one needs fuel vapours. In the case of kerosene the boiling point is high and so vapours are found in small quantities in the region above the pool. On the other hand, one finds more vapours on a gasoline pool even at temperatures of 20–25°C. Therefore, bringing any tiny source of ignition is adequate to cause ignition. These aspects are covered under the concepts of flash and fire points.

Flash point is the temperature of the liquid at which an ignition source is able to flash a flame and consume the vapours. If the ignition source is taken away, the flame also will disappear. Stated differently, the flame is not self-supporting at the flash point. At fire point, any ignition makes the flame over the pool become self-supporting. Following ignition, the heat transferred by the flame will generate enough volatiles to continue burning in the gas phase. Igniting solid fuels is even more difficult. Consequently, if a person wants to light a wood stove, she would douse the ends of the firewood with some kerosene and then light the piece. It is not always certain that the wood piece doused with kerosene will ignite, for the kerosene could burn away leaving the wood unignited. How ignition works with dousing of kerosene is as follows. Firstly, it must be understood that kerosene is the first to vapourise because its boiling point is about 150–200°C. Volatiles from wood would get generated only at 300–350°C. Hence it is kerosene which would burn away first. But during this process, transfer of heat by radiation and conduction close to the flame should begin to generate volatiles from the wood to combust it. If this process becomes self-sustaining before the kerosene burns away, the process of ignition is successful. For instance, if the wood pieces had been doused with gasoline instead of kerosene, there would be less chances of the wood igniting. This is because gasoline would burn away faster and the chances that wood would generate volatiles within this time are lower. In fact, many a criminal has been unsuccessful in burning incriminating documents by dousing them with gasoline for the want of understanding principles of combustion!

It is not that one needs to use kerosene for ignition. One can ignite wood by itself, of course not a log of large diameter. This is because the ignition source, expectedly small, is not able to persuade regions of wood to release volatiles in a sustained manner. The heat transferred is shared by the larger portions in conduction mode and the heat is simply dissipated. Therefore, one needs to use a large number of small-sized fibrous dry sticks and ignite them with a matchstick. The fibrous wood pieces, particularly the sharp-edged ones, will ignite immediately and the entire bunch will start burning. They can then be put on the grate of a stove, and by suitably adding additional wood pieces of slightly larger sizes, the fire can be maintained. The energy utilised here will be close to 20 to 40 J.

8.2 Matchstick composition and ignition

Matchstick is used in many kitchens around the world, even though it has gone out of vogue in many other countries in favour of lighters and quartz-crystal based sparking devices. The composition used in the matchstick ignites on being rubbed against a special surface (as it happens in safety matches), holds the flame for the brief time sufficient for lighting a kerosene wick stove or a cigarette or any other combustible substances. The wood used for the matchstick is so chosen as to be porous enough to absorb various chemicals and be rigid enough to withstand the bending forces encountered when the match is struck. The trees whose wood is used for this purpose are usually white pine and aspen. With an automated process the wood is veneered (generating thin slices of wood in the form of a sheet) and matchsticks are cut out of it. In many cases, these are soaked in ammonium phosphate to act as a fire retardant. This prevents the stick from smouldering after the match has gone out. The striking end of the matchstick is dipped in hot paraffin wax to provide a small amount of fuel to transfer the flame from the burning chemicals on the tip to the matchstick itself.

Matchsticks come in the form of either strike-anywhere matches and safety matches. Safety matches embed safety in two ways: (i) by having two components that need to be used to cause a flame, viz. a composition on its head, a surface that is separate from the stick and of a different composition from the stick and, (ii) replacing the very highly reactive white phosphorous that was used earlier with red phosphorous. The striking of the matchstick against the surface causes the generation of frictional heat sufficient to cause the ignition, which involves, as an initial step, the conversion of a trace of red phosphorous to white phosphorous.

The compositions of the match head and the striking surface are not unlike those used in igniter compositions of rocket engines. Only, they are less expensive and less reactive. The match head is typically composed of 45–55% potassium chlorate, with a little sulphur and starch, a neutraliser (ZnO or $CaCO_3$), 20–40% of siliceous filler or powdered glass, diatomaceous earth and animal glue. Some heads contain antimony (III) sulphide and burn more vigorously. The striking surface is composed of typically 25% powdered glass, 50% red phosphorus, 5% neutraliser, 4% carbon black and 16% binder. Powdered glass aids the friction to generate heat. Inert fillers are added to give sufficient mass to maintain the fire for the required time. The typical mass of the composition on the match head is about 5 to 10 mg and its calorific value is about 1.5 to 2.0 J/g. Thus, the energy of a matchstick head is about 6 to 20 J.

8.3 Ignition in reciprocating engines

Spark ignition engines

In engines that use gasoline fuel, the carburettor mixes the fuel spray with air and sends it to the engine combustion chamber. After the mixture is ingested into the chamber, at an appropriate moment in the cycle in relation to top dead centre, a spark is fired so that ignition occurs. The spark is created by a voltage source of 3–5 kV.

Compression ignition engines

In such engines which use diesel fuel, the pressure ratio used is high (~15–20) so that compression causes the temperature to rise to such an extent that when liquid injection takes place, it can ignite by itself under conditions of high pressure and temperature. One of the important requirements in such engines is that ignition must take place very fast. The typical time available for combustion in an engine running at say 1500 rpm, is about 2–4 ms. This requires the droplet to be very fine—which indeed it is. The other condition is for the environment to permit ignition in the time scale of the kind indicated.

8.4 Ignition in rocket engines

It has already been indicated that there exists a combination of liquid fuels and oxidisers which on mixing will react and burst into flame. These are the hypergolic combinations. When the liquids are mixed, the liquid phase reactions (between UDMH and N_2O_4, or N_2H_4 and RFNA, for example) at the interface between the liquids is such that very reactive species are produced which enter the gas phase and react exothermically, leading to high temperature flames. While this feature is true in most combustion reactions, the essential point concerns the rate of reactions. The rate of reactions here is so large that the time between mixing and occurrence of a gaseous flame is as small as 3–10 ms. This duration between the start of mixing to the bursting into flame is called the ignition delay. Thus, even at extremely low pressures, when the gas phase reactions can be expected to be slow, the reactions are completed in as small a time as 20–30 ms and ignition is indeed smooth. It is for this reason that most rocket engines that need high reliability, e.g., the lunar module engine, use only hypergolic combinations.

There are rocket engines based on liquid oxygen–liquid hydrogen (LOX–LH_2) mixtures. These engines use igniters which by themselves are small rockets ignited by spark. Figure 8.1 shows schematically the arrangement for such an engine. Similar arrangements need to be made for LOX–kerosene engine. Such engines can also be made restartable if needed.

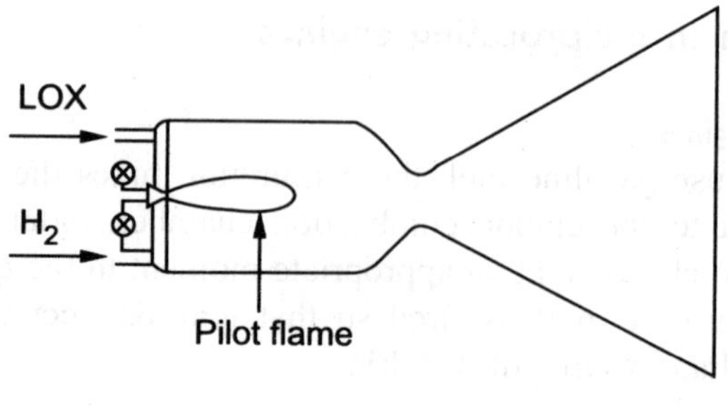

Figure 8.1 *Igniter for LOX–LH$_2$ engine (LOX–kerosene is similar)*

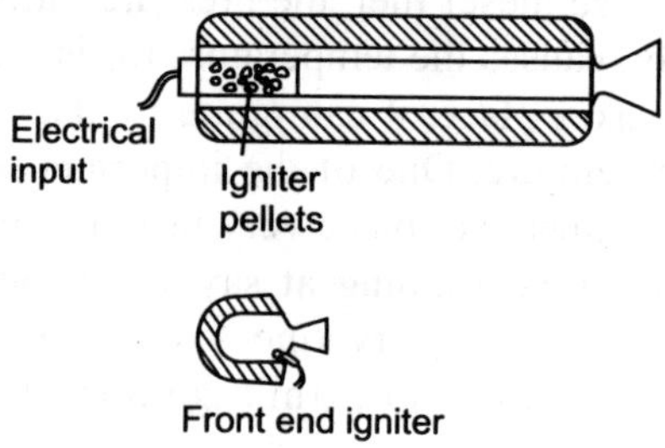

Figure 8.2 *Ignition system for solid rocket engines*

8.5 Ignition in solid rocket engines

In solid rocket engines, there is a solid propellant (configured geometrically) which needs to be ignited. Figure 8.2 shows two arrangements of the propellant and their ignition schemes.

In relatively small rockets, ignition is caused by an igniter charge consisting of pellets of appropriate composition—similar to the main propellant, but with more metal loading. A typical composition may be 50% ammonium perchlorate (AP), 35% boron or titanium and 15% polymer. The ignition is usually electrical—a fine wire coated with a heat sensitive explosive such as lead azide or mercuric fulminate causing ignition when an electrical current, typically 0.75–1 A, is passed through the wire. The heat sensitive material explodes and this causes the main charge to burn fast (in about 10–30 ms). The products are gases and hot metal and metal oxide particles. The rapid generation of gases causes a rise in pressure and the hot particles cause local ignition. The gases, when passing through the duct along the grain, cause convective heat transfer and thus enhance the possibility of local ignition. The flame then begins to spread across the entire surface of the propellant and steady operating conditions are achieved in about 0.3–2.5 s, depending on the size of the rocket being tested.

In large-sized rockets like India's PSLV stage rocket, the igniter constitutes a rocket by itself. Such igniters are called pyrogen igniters. In such cases a part of the igniter products, namely gas, is expected to raise the pressure in the chamber, and another to cause local ignition. This aspect needs to be addressed carefully in the design stage to make sure that there are no over pressures during ignition and that the transient blends smoothly into normal, steady operating conditions.

8.6 Overview

Ignition is the first part of any combustion process. It is affected by pressure and initial temperature of the system under consideration. Ignition delay, i.e., the time from start of the ignition process to achieving steady state, should be small in systems for the ignition process to be effective. The process of ignition is more difficult at low pressures and temperatures. In gas-phase fuel–oxidant mixtures, ignition energy is typically 0.1–0.2 mJ under quiescent conditions. In flowing mixtures the ignition energy increases a hundred-fold, depending on velocities, local mixture ratio, etc. Ignition in liquids is affected by the fire point of the liquid fuel, apart from the ambient pressure and initial temperature. Ignition in gasoline engines is spark-initiated and that in diesel engines compression-initiated. The combined action of high temperature and pressure towards the end of the compression stroke causes ignition of the tiny liquid droplets injected before the end of the compression stroke.

In rocket engines, hypergolic combinations for liquid engines eliminate the need for a separate ignition system. In other engines using non-self-igniting propellants, an ignition system is called for. These are usually based on the same propellant and ignition is caused in a smaller chamber with spark initiation. The hot gases then become pilot flame for the main engine ignition.

In solid rocket engines, the igniter serves the purpose of building pressure inside the combustion chamber and also produces hot particles of metal or metal oxides which impinge on the solid propellant and create many ignition sources for the entire propellant to ignite within a small time.

9 Stability, Extinction and Blow-off of Flames

Stability is a concept used in many scientific disciplines. Invariably, it means that the system in static or dynamic equilibrium gets restored to equilibrium on being displaced slightly from its original state. This interpretation is also appropriate for flames. There are many situations where the flame—premixed or diffusion—is subject to disturbances. If, in spite of these disturbances the flame gets restored to the original state when the disturbances are removed, then, the flame is said to be stable.

Let us first look at situations where the subject of stability is relevant. Figure 9.1 shows several such situations. The unstable flames may move to one of the more stable states—the no-flame state. In this case the flame is thought to be 'extinguished' or blown off.

In Fig. 9.1(a) is shown a classical Bunsen burner used in chemical laboratories and glass blowing units. It is mostly run on kerosene vapour and sometimes on LPG. When one runs out of either of these, acetylene is used. At comparable flow rates one may find that the flame flashes back in the case of acetylene–air mixture when it would not for LPG or perhaps kerosene-vapour–air mixture. If one had designed the system for acetylene–air, then allowing kerosene vapour–air to flow through causes the flame to blow off at the same flow rate. We should understand why.

In Fig. 9.1(b) the combustion chamber of a gas turbine engine is indicated. The combustion chamber of a gas turbine engine has to function over a wide range of fuel–air mixture ratios and pressures (sometimes even below sea level pressure). The speed of the high pressure air flow through the system does not vary during the operation. One would like to ensure that in the operating range of the parameters, the flame is stable.

In case (c) we have a candle flame or a matchstick flame. Candle flame represents an example of a diffusion flame. The initial flame from the matchstick on the other hand, represents the case close to premixed flame, as it

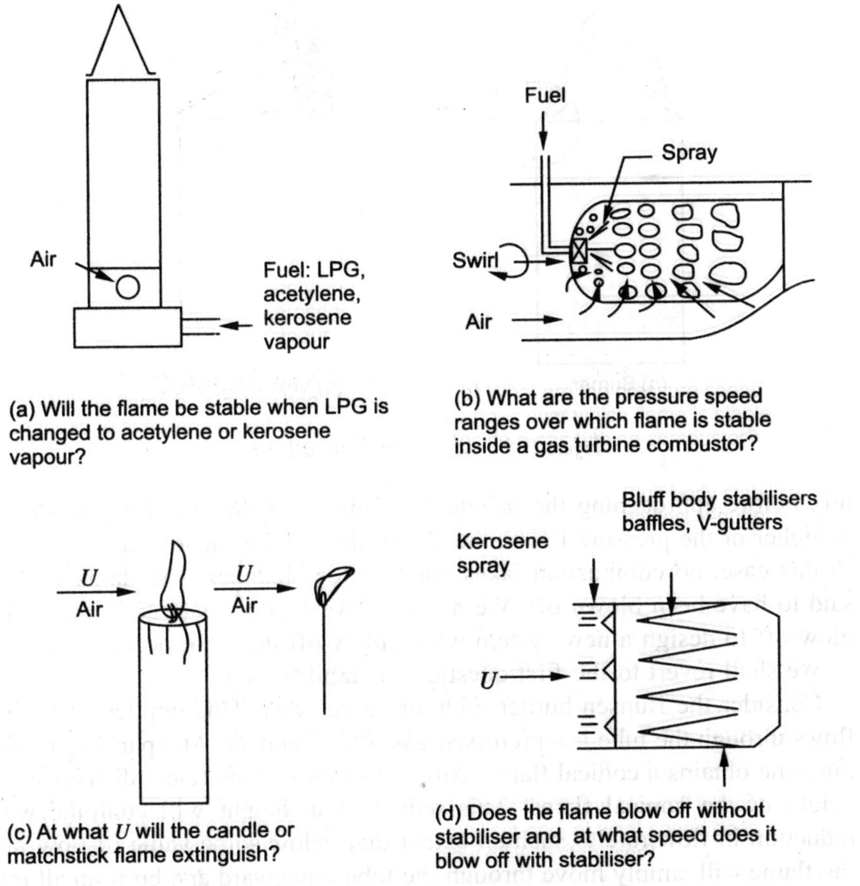

Figure 9.1 *Problems of stability, extinction and blow-off (U=air velocity)*

has oxidiser in the match composition. In both cases, a child can extinguish the flame by blowing air. The same fluid-air which supports combustion also can deactivate it. Why is it so?

In the fourth example drawn from what is known as the after-burner of an aircraft engine, one has a relatively high speed stream flowing through a straight duct. The gases flowing through the duct come from main combustion chamber and are quite oxidiser rich, with almost 70–80% of the capacity of air to oxidise (16–18% oxygen as compared to 23% oxygen in air) and are at temperatures ~600–700 K. Into this stream is supplied a fine spray of kerosene at various locations. The kerosene, in fact, may be sprayed upstream so that the mixing is good. At short distance downstream, the mixture becomes homogeneous with fine droplets in the hot stream. Baffles of cylindrical or other shapes are provided in the duct to help hold the flame in these locations. For this reason these are called flame holders. Downstream, the flame expands around each of these holders and the entire burnt gases

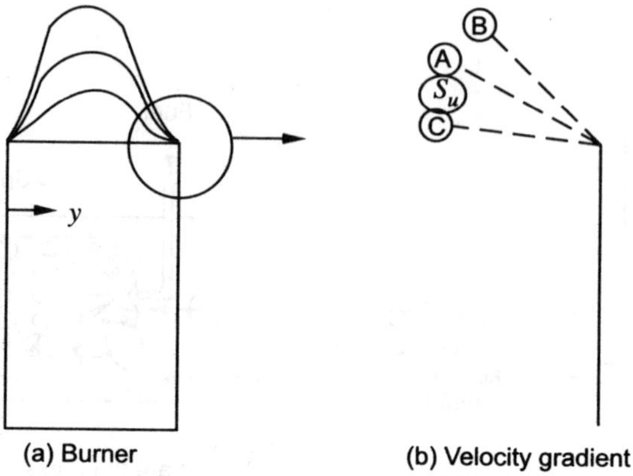

Figure 9.2 *Mechanics of stability*

mix before approaching the nozzle. Sometimes, if the speed of the stream is higher or the pressure lower, the flame may not be capable of being held. In this case, no combustion takes place in the chamber. The flame is then said to have been blown off. We need to investigate what conditions cause blow-off to design a new system where blow-off does not occur.

We shall revert to the first question of stability now.

Consider the Bunsen burner with air valve open. This implies that what flows through the tube is a premixed gas of fuel and air. At a particular flow rate, one obtains a conical flame. Any reduction in flow rate will reduce the height of the conical flame. This reduction in height will continue with reduction in flow rate to such an extent that below some value of flow rate the flame will simply move through the tube downward and burn up all that is in the tube. Then the flame will extinguish. If, on the other hand the flow through the tube is continuously increased, the flame will move beyond the edge of the burner, the difference in height being called the lift height. At one stage the flame will simply blow-off.

This implies that beyond some flow rates the flame blows off; below some flow rates it flashes back; and in a region in between, the flame is stable.

9.1 Stability of a Bunsen flame

The velocity profiles at the burner exit for different flow rates are shown in Fig. 9.2 (a). As can be seen, the profile is parabolic (for laminar flow conditions relevant here) and gets deeper as the flow rate increases. The region near the rim is shown in an enlarged manner in Fig. 9.2 (b). The flame speed is nearly constant in the middle portion of the tube and reduces to zero near the rim because of heat loss (and quenching). The lines A, B

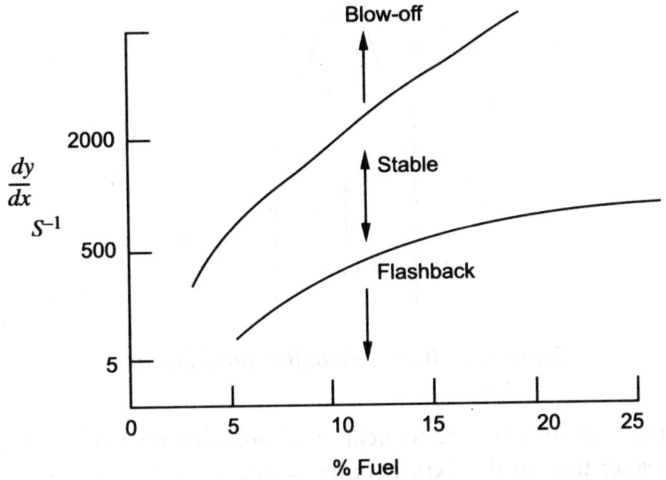

Figure 9.3 *Ranges of stability*

and C refer to velocity profiles at different flow rates. The coordinate y is along a radial line normal to the wall and u is the stream velocity at any y. At normal flow rates (A), the two curves (A) and (S_u) intersect. At large flow rate (B), the slope of the u vs. y curve is steeper than the S_u vs. y curve. At very low flow rates (C), the slope of u vs. y is smaller than S_u vs. y near the wall. It is only in case A that a flame over the tube is possible and in the other two cases the flame will either blow off or simply flash back. Thus, for (du/dy) such that

$$(du/dy)_{\text{low}} < (du/dy) < (du/dy)_{\text{high}},$$

the flame is stable. Experiments seem to confirm this behaviour as shown in Fig. 9.3. One can now understand why flames in burners flash back or blow off when the fuel is changed. If one changes LPG to acetylene, S_u goes up at the same flow rate and the flame will move towards flashback. On the other hand, if one moves from acetylene to LPG, the tendency of the flame is to blow off. One can change this behaviour by effecting a change in velocity profile near the rim. For instance, providing a reduced section near the exit as shown in Fig. 9.4 causes a reverse flow and the classical flow structure is destroyed. This enhances the flame stability.

9.2 Stability of flames in gas turbine combustors

We now move on to case (b) of Fig. 9.1. In this case we have to determine the range of velocities and pressures over which flame can exist inside the system. The flow rates are so large that the flow is turbulent. Air is injected partly axially and partly through the holes shown. The arrangement of holes

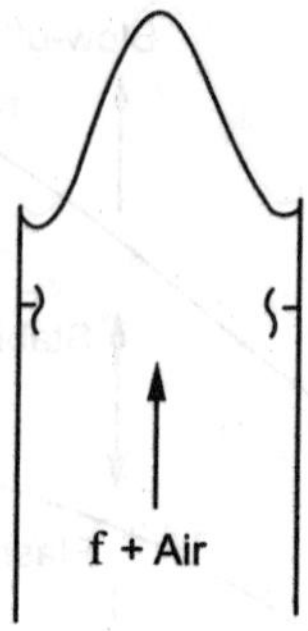

Figure 9.4 *Burner stability improvement*

regulates the fuel–air mixture to near stoichiometry near the fuel injection zone and leaner toward the exit. Mixing is intense in the first zone close to fuel injection. This region is called the primary zone. The combustion in this zone is likened to what is known as well-stirred reactor. A stirred reactor is one in which fuel–oxidiser elements are taken as completely mixed and the phenomenon is dominated by the reaction processes alone. At steady state, the reactants flow in at $\dot{m}$ (mass flow rate), react at a volumetric rate of $\dot{w}_f'''$ with heat of combustion H, and raise their temperatures from T_0 to T_f. The steady heat balance gives

$$\dot{m}c_p(T_f - T_0) = \dot{w}_f'''vH, \tag{9.1}$$

where v is the volume of the reactor, c_p = specific heat of the gases. One way of representing the overall reaction rate is as follows:

$$\dot{w}_f''' = A_f e^{-E/2RT_f}(T_{f0} - T_f)^m f(A/F)p^n. \tag{9.2}$$

Here A_f is the frequency factor, p^n represents pressure term, n being the reaction order ($\sim$ 1.8-2.4), the exponential term due to activation energy. $(T_{f0} - T_f)$ is representative of the mass fraction of fuel/oxidant and A/F is the air-to-fuel ratio. Since we are representing the reaction rate by an overall rate, the only way of accommodating the different air-to-fuel ratios of the gaseous mixtures is to treat it by an overall function as represented above. When the temperature reaches the adiabatic temperature T_{f0}, both the reactants are completely consumed and their mass fraction is zero. (Even if one reactant goes to zero as may happen when the mixture is fuel or oxidiser rich, the reaction rate goes to 0.) Effectively, $m = 1$ for uni-molecular and $m = 2$ for bimolecular class of reactions. Thus,

$$\dot{m}c_p(T_f - T_0) = A_f p^n e^{-E/2RT_f}(T_{f0} - T_f)^m f(A/F)vH. \tag{9.3}$$

T_f is a result of the heat balance noted above. We denote the left-hand side of the equation by LHS and the right-hand side, by RHS. We can plot both

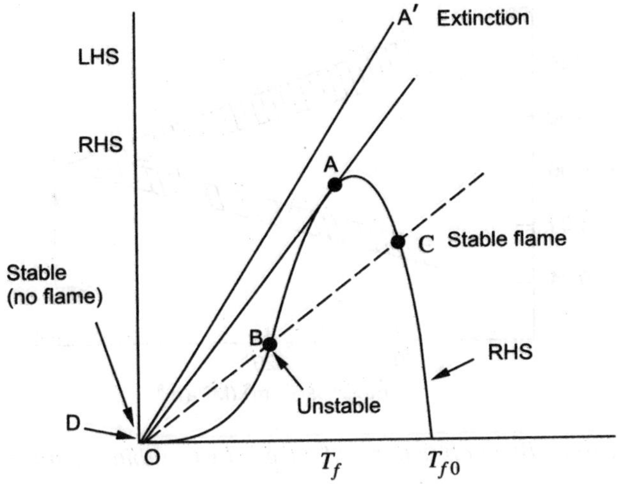

Figure 9.5 *Stirred reactor stability*

LHS and RHS as functions of T_f in a graph as in Fig. 9.5. The LHS plots as a straight line and can be taken to represent the rate of heat removal, with several straight lines corresponding to different values of $\dot{m}$. RHS is a curve which is close to the temperature axis at the left side and goes to zero at adiabatic temperature T_{f0}. RHS represents heat generation rate. The straight lines representing the heat removal rate intersect the heat release rate curve at points that can be identified as the points of solution of equation (9.3). The points of intersection can be one, two or three. If one takes line DA′, the solution occurs at D only. This represents cold flow. This is the case of extinction. It occurs because the heat generation rate is so small that the flame can be dissipated at near ambient temperature. The limiting line DA has two solutions—one at D and another at A. The solution at A has flame. If we decrease $\dot{m}$ we get a solution at points D, B, and C. The solution at B at an intermediate temperature can be argued to be unstable. Suppose, by some mechanism one disturbs the system by raising the temperature beyond B. Notice then that the heat generation rate is more than the heat carried away by the gases $[\dot{m}c_p(T_f - T_0)]$. This causes further increase in temperature and it goes on till point C is reached. If at C one raises the temperature, the heat taken away is more than the heat generated and the the temperature falls back to C. And if at B one disturbs the temperature toward the lower side, then the additional heat carried away becomes more than the heat generated and the temperature falls till point D is reached. Again, a similar argument shows that A is a stable operating point. If we reduce the flow rate further, the temperature of the flame reaches the adiabatic flame temperature. This is termed 'explosion', to signify that the rates of heat generation are so large that the balance occurs near the highest possible temperature.

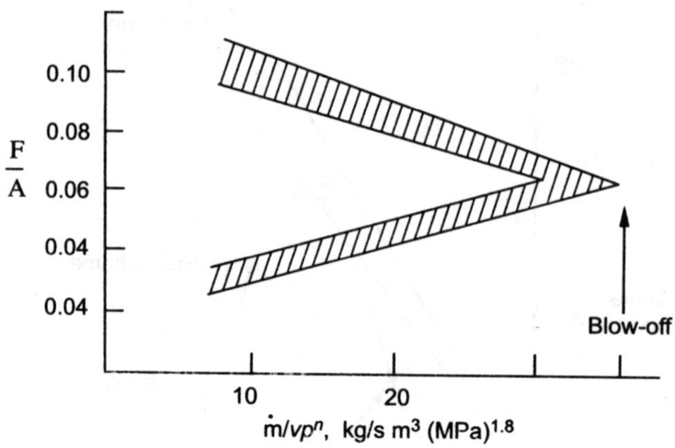

Figure 9.6 *Blow-off features of a typical gas turbine combustor*

Returning to the question of stability of flames in combustion chambers, the equation can be cast as

$$\frac{\dot{m}}{p^n v} = f(A/F, T_f). \tag{9.4}$$

Experiments of stability are conducted by first establishing a flame inside the combustor at specific equivalence ratio and increasing the flow rate till the flame is extinguished. It is useful to appreciate that the term 'stability' under circumstances implies essentially stable equilibrium. A typical stability plot for a gas turbine combustor is shown in Fig. 9.6. There are two branches to the curve—one fuel-lean and another fuel-rich. The two curves meet at a region and beyond a certain value of $\dot{m}/vp^n$, the flame blows off. The exponent n is about 1.8 for kerosene–air mixtures. One can notice that the operation of gas turbine combustor becomes critical at low pressures when the parameter $\dot{m}/vp^n$ indeed becomes large and so tends to blow off the flame. The volume of the chamber then has to be increased so that one has a reasonable stable operating range of fuel flows at worst conditions, namely highest altitude, lowest rpm of engine and flight velocity. Another interesting way of interpreting the above relationship, particularly in the light of blow-off, is as follows. The equation can be written as

$$\dot{m}/v \sim \dot{w}_f''' H/c_p(T_f - T_0). \tag{9.5}$$

$\dot{m} = \rho A V$, where ρ is the density, A the representative cross-section of the chamber and V the representative velocity. v can then be written as $v = Ad$, where d is a representative dimension of the chamber. If, in addition, we take $H = c_p(T_f - T_0)$, we get

$$V/d = \dot{w}_f'''/\rho \quad \text{or} \quad t_f^{-1} = t_{ch}^{-1}. \tag{9.6}$$

d/V can be taken as the travel time t_f of the fluid over the length d, and $(\dot{w}_f'''/\rho)^{-1}$ can be taken as time taken for completing reaction t_{ch}. Thus the previous result can be stated as $t_f = t_{ch}$. If t_f is very small, something which can be achieved by raising the velocities, there will be very little time for reaction and so the flame blows off. The ratio $t_f/t_{ch} = D_1$ is called first *Damköhler* number and is a very important parameter in combustion studies. $D_1 \to \infty$ represents the limit of fast chemical reactions and the attainment of equilibrium. $D_1 \to 0$ represents the limit of little time for reaction (or very slow reaction) and is called frozen limit, implying little change of composition during the passage of gases through the combustion chamber.

9.3 Stability of a candle flame

We now move on to the case (c) of Fig.9.1— candle and matchstick flames. The question here is: How is it that increased flow of oxidiser causes flame blow-off or extinction? And at what speed does it extinguish? The answer to this question has been discussed already. The only point of difference is that the system is not so simple as discussed above. As distinct from a stirred reactor model, the candle flame is a diffusion flame and mixing-controlled. The matchstick flame is somewhat premixed-flame-controlled, and yet affected by local distribution of flow rates.

Therefore, the changes to our earlier statements can be derived from the expression related to time scales. In candle flame the distribution of local velocities, mass fraction of species and temperature exist and hence the distribution of reaction rates over the region. One can examine if the peak temperature in the region will fall rapidly as a consequence of an air stream flowing around the flame. Detailed numerical calculations of this class for slightly simpler geometries like-opposed jet diffusion flame (flames stabilised between two opposite jets of fuel and oxidiser) or premixed flame (flames stabilised between two jets of premixed fuel-oxidiser mixture) yield plots as shown in Fig. 9.7 for various inlet stream temperatures. In this figure the peak temperature in the field ($T_{\max}$) is plotted against $D_1^{-1} = \tau_{ch}/\tau_f$ with $\tau_f = d/V$, where d is interpreted as the diameter of the jet and V is the jet speed. Assume that the system is at D at an ambient temperature of 300 K, under no flame conditions. At this condition or between D and C, ignition causes the point to shift to the upper branch—called the equilibrium branch, i.e., say from D to A. If now the speed of the stream is increased, point A moves to B. The temperature falls slightly (say, from 2300 to 2000 K or so). At condition B, any slight increase in speed causes the flame to suddenly extinguish and the system takes position C. This speed is the maximum that can be set with flame being present in the system. Beyond C (larger velocities), the system will not ignite at all. In this region the heat

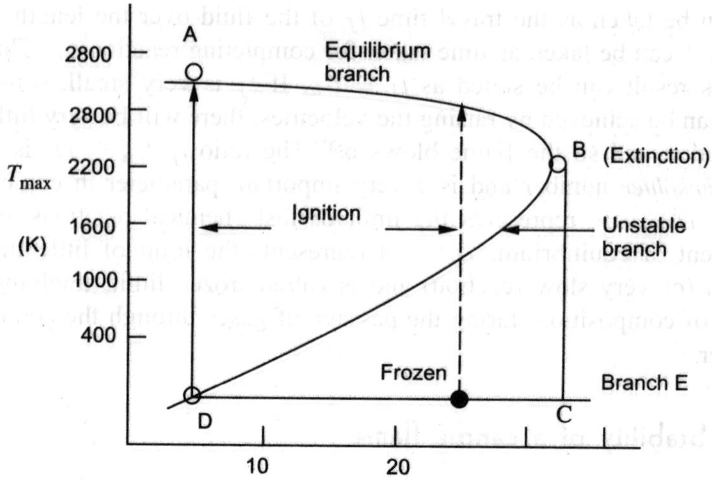

Figure 9.7 *Ignition – extinction features*

convected away from any region in the flow is much larger than the energy input rate and steady the state with no flame existing at all.

The curve joining B and D can be shown to be unstable; the branches AB and DE are stable. Such curves are called S curves (you can see an S curve for a plot of T_{max} vs. D_1 as is usually done). The curves are not special to combustion alone. They occur in many nonlinear problems of dynamics like vibration of nonlinear spring–mass systems. When the inlet stream temperature is large, say, 1200 K, the transition process does not have any discontinuities. There is 'flame' at all *Damköhler* numbers, with small, non-insignificant reactions at temperatures little above the stream temperature and reasonable reactivity at higher temperatures. The behaviour that is observed is similar both for premixed and diffusion flames. A typical experiment that illustrates this is the flame obtained near the stagnation region of opposed jet streams with identical premixed mixtures or air and oxidant components in the case of diffusion flame. If we interpret the fluid time scale (length scale/stream speed) as representative of stretch, i.e., increasing the speed by reducing the fluid stay time and hence increasing the strain rate on the flame, the above results can be used to explain the observed flame temperatures being lower than the adiabatic flame temperature in complex fluid flows. This was discussed in Chapter 4.

9.4 Bluff body flame stabilisation

We shall move on to case (d) of Fig. 9.1. Again, the case is typical of flame stability. The time taken for the fluid to traverse the after-burner is $t_f = L/V$, where L is the length of the after-burner and V is the mean speed. Typical

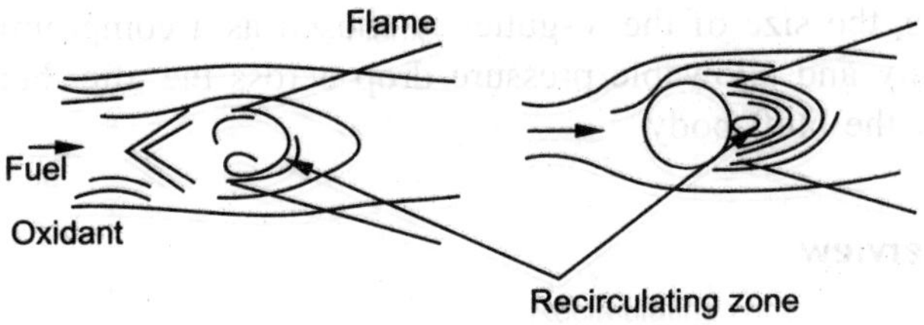

Figure 9.8 *Flame holders*

speeds are about 150 m/s and $L \sim 1.5$ m. This implies that t_f = 10 ms. The reaction time at the conditions of after burner inlet (800 K) is about 10–15 ms. Since these numbers are comparable, the reactions will not be complete. In order to complete the reaction, flame holders are introduced. The way flame holders work is shown in Fig. 9.8. The oncoming flow goes around the obstacle and causes a recirculation zone so much so that even if V is large, the zone behind the obstacles will have low velocities because the fluid will be recirculating in this zone. Because the velocities are low, the effective stay time of the fluids is enhanced significantly. Consequently, the flame will be stabilised in the recirculation zone. Again, even in the case with flame stabilisers, the flame would be blown off if the incoming velocity exceeds a critical value. The blow-off velocity can be estimated by the logic enunciated earlier. Taking the recirculation zone to be approximating a stirred reactor, we have

$$\dot{m}c_p(T_f - T_0) = \dot{w}_f'''vH.$$

Here v is the volume of the recirculation zone, scaling like d^3. The flow rate $\dot{m}$ can be calculated as ρAV, where A is the cross-sectional area of the fluid entrained in the recirculation zone, again scaling like d^2. Thus, we can can obtain a relationship for the velocity of blow-off, V_{bf}, as

$$\rho d^2 V_{bf} c_p(T_f - T_0) \simeq \dot{w}_f''' d^3 H \times \text{Const.}$$

$$V_{bf} \simeq \text{Const.}\ (\dot{w}_f'''/\rho) d\ \frac{H}{c_p(T_f - T_0).}$$

Since $\dot{w}_f''' \sim p^n$ and $\rho \sim p$, we get

$$V_{bf} \simeq \text{Const.}\ p^{n-1}\ d\ f(A/F) \simeq S_u^2 d/p. \tag{9.7}$$

This behaviour of the blow-off speed with pressure seen via pressure alone or through S_u is indeed found experimentally appropriate. The blow-off speed peaks around stoichiometry and falls off on either side like flame speed. It also scales like the characteristic dimension of the obstacle. In the after-burners, the size of the V-gutter is chosen as a compromise between flame stability and allowable pressure drop across the after-burner caused primarily by the bluff body.

9.5 Overview

In this chapter the elements of combustion theory relevant to flame stability and extinction/blow-off have been examined. The ideas of laminar flame speed representing reactivity of fuel–oxidant mixture along with quench distance are used in describing the stability of flames in the burner. The combustion stability and blow-off in gas turbine combustors and bluff body flame holders are described in terms of well-stirred reactors. An alternate but entirely equivalent view in terms of time scales invoking the first Damkohler number is shown to be very effective in extracting the dependence of speed at blow-off or stability limits in terms of pressure and geometric parameters. The extinction of diffusion/premixed flames in a complex situation calls for detailed calculations and plots of maximum temperature in the field with externally induced velocity (or its inverse). Reversed S curves (or S curve) result from such calculations, and one obtains branches involving flame or no flame and transition between them, depending on the fluid speed.

10

Diffusion Flames—Gaseous Burner Flames, Droplet Combustion, Boundary Layer Combustion

तव श्रमास आशुया पतन्त्यनु स्पृश धृषता शोशुचानः ।
तपूंष्य्म्ने जुह्वा पतङ्गानसंदितो वि स्रज विष्वगुल्काः ।।२।।

Swiftly rush thy wanderings; blazing up follow and touch with thy violence; O Fire, spread by thy tongue thy burning heats and thy winged sparks; unleashed, scatter on every side thy meteors.

Rig Veda

Diffusion flames, as different from premixed flames, are those in which the fuel and oxidiser are unmixed right up to the flame. The fuel and oxidiser diffuse and mix at the flame. Reaction rates are much larger in comparison with diffusion rates. Such flames are therefore diffusion limited. This is in direct contrast to what is observed with premixed flames in which the reaction rate is the most important factor in deciding their structure. There are other differences in the behaviour of diffusion and premixed flames which we shall examine later. It is also good to recognise that diffusion flames occur more often in nature and that when flames/ fires are caused, nature makes sure that the fuel and oxidiser elements are separate to increase the stability of life. When fire is caused, the oxidiser, usually air, gets to the fuel vapours at the flame, resulting in a diffusion flame.

Though we wish to talk of flames, one can include vaporisation as a natural subset of the investigation. We shall investigate three classes of flames—gaseous burner flames, droplet combustion and boundary layer combustion.

Gaseous burner flames occur in laboratories and in nature. The Bunsen burner flame with its air vent closed, flares in petrochemical complexes and unwanted gas duct explosions resulting in flames from underground gas jets in petroleum gas exploration sites are some instances of gas diffusion flames. A wood crib fire is another example of diffusion flame. The flow of oxidiser-rich gases past a burning fuel surface, e.g., a rocket engines (hybrid) is also an example of diffusion flame.

We shall first examine the case of laminar burner diffusion flame. When gaseous fuel issues out of a tube into ambient atmosphere of air and the gas is ignited, a flame, usually conical, is established (Fig. 6.1(c)) (notice that air entry hole is to be closed). The question being considered is—how high is the diffusion flame? While conservation equations can be written down under certain approximations and solved to obtain the flame height, one can make a simple set of arguments and obtain a relation for flame height which has all the elements in it.

Oxygen has to arrive at the flame by diffusion. The length scale for diffusion is $d/2$ because the flame tip is at the centre. The time taken for diffusion is $t_D = d^2/4D_{12}$, where D_{12} is the diffusion coefficient ($\simeq$ 2–6$\times 10^{-5}$m^2/s). One can ask the question: how did we write this expression?

In the phenomenology, one can see that there are two quantities: (a) a distance d over which diffusion should occur and (b) diffusion coefficient, D_{12}, unit of which is m^2/s. The only way of obtaining a time scale from these two quantities is to take d^2/D_{12}. That is how the expression is obtained. During the period t_D, the fluid has moved a distance Vt_D. And this distance must equal h because the flame ends at a point where all the fuel has got the necessary oxidiser (stoichiometric proportion). Thus,

$$h \sim \frac{Vd^2}{4D_{12}} \sim \frac{\dot{m}_f}{D_{12}\rho}. \tag{10.1}$$

The diffusion coefficient D_{12} is so subscripted because we must define the two species diffusing into each other. It is adequate for the present to take a mean diffusion coefficient between the fuel and the oxidiser, though systematic analysis uses what is known as the trace diffusion coefficient which treats the fact that one species diffuses into the gas mixture. Kinetic theory of gases allows the diffusion coefficients to be described by

$$D_{12} = 2.628 \times 10^{-3} \frac{T^{1.75}}{p} \frac{\sqrt{\frac{1}{2}(\frac{1}{\mathcal{M}_1} + \frac{1}{\mathcal{M}_2})}}{\sigma^2 \Omega_D},$$

where σ and Ω_D are molecular properties and $\mathcal{M}_1$, $\mathcal{M}_2$, the molecular weights of species. From the above equation the diffusion coefficient D_{12} is seen to vary as p^{-1} and $T^{1.75}$ (the dependence of σ and Ω_D on temperature is such that the overall dependence on temperature is of the form

$D_{12} \sim T^{1.75}$). Therefore, $D_{12}\rho$ varies as p^0 and $T^{0.75}$. Thus, $D_{12}\ \rho$ is independent of pressure. We then have from (10.1) that the height of the flame is independent of pressure at fixed mass flow rate of the fuel. Alternatively, as the mass flow rate (or velocity) is increased, the height varies linearly. The last fact was experimentally observed about thirty years ago, and can be represented in a dimensionless manner by stating

$$\frac{h}{d} = \frac{ReSc}{4}, \tag{10.2}$$

where $Sc = \mu/D_{12}\rho = \nu/D_{12}$, the Schmidt number, is a term of the order unity ($\sim$ 0.75–1.2). One would see that the expression shows no dependence on fuel properties. This is simply because we have not accounted for it yet. For the same flow rate and diameter of the duct, if the requirements of stoichiometry are higher (implying more air is required to burn a fixed amount of fuel), then the flame height has to be larger. Also, if the active oxidiser mass fraction in the surrounding air, $Y_{0\infty}$, is increased, one would expect the flame height to be lower. Thus, one would expect

$$h = \frac{ReSc}{4f_s Y_{0,\infty}^{m_2}}.$$

We will present a simple argument which includes these effects and obtain the expression for flame height.

Suppose the flame is enclosed in a cylinder of diameter d and height h. The fuel flow rate is $\dot{m}_f$. The flame will acquire just enough air for it to burn completely. This means that the air obtained by diffusion should be in stoichiometric proportion with fuel flow. This means $\dot{m}_{air}/\dot{m}_f = 1/f_s$. The flow rate of air is the product of mass flux and the area, πhd. The mass flux is given by Fick's law of diffusion as $D_{12}\rho(dY_0/dx)$. We can take $dY_0 = (Y_{0,\infty} - 0)$, $dx = d/2$ and write down the relationship for the stoichiometric air-to-fuel flow rate as

$$\pi hd \times 2D_{12}\rho \times \frac{Y_{0\infty}}{d} = \dot{m}_{air} = \frac{\dot{m}_f}{f_s}. \tag{10.3}$$

Thus,

$$h = \frac{\dot{m}_f}{2\pi f_s Y_{0\infty} D_{12}\rho}, \qquad \frac{h}{d} = \frac{ReSc}{8f_s Y_{0\infty}}. \tag{10.4}$$

We now have an expression that takes into account all the factors. It is also possible to set up the problem of jet diffusion by writing down the conservation equations and solving them to obtain $h/d = ReSc/(48 f_s Y_{0\infty})$. One can see that the relationship obtained from exact calculations confirms the results expected from simple approximations. One interesting and important

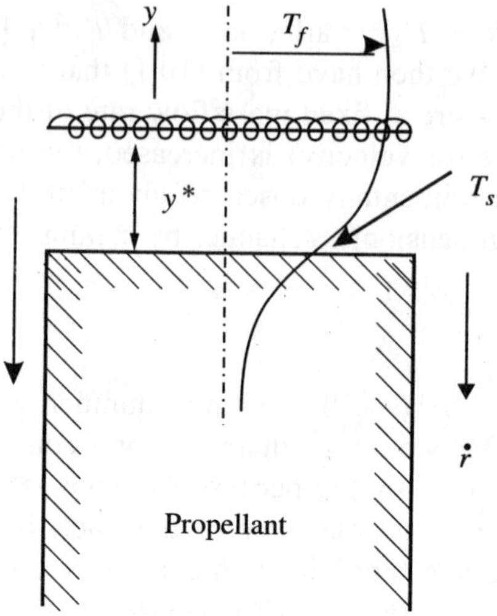

Figure 10.1 *One-dimensional propellant combustion*

conclusion is that diffusion-dominated phenomena have weak dependence on pressure; for instance, the mass burn rate of a solid dominated by diffusion is independent of pressure. The latter conclusion can be quickly drawn if we argue that the one-dimensional solid surface (Fig. 10.1) is diffusion dominated in regression (the term used for linear burn down of a surface); we can strike an energy balance (of fluxes) at the surface and write

$$k\left[\frac{dT}{dy}\right]_{y=0} = \dot{q}'' = \rho_p \dot{r} L,$$

where $\rho_p \dot{r}$ is the product of the density of the solid, the solid regression rate and L, the heat of phase change from solid to gas, $\dot{q}''$ is the heat flux expressed in terms of Fourier's law of conduction. Noting that dy can be replaced by a quantity proportional to h and dT replaced by the difference between an effective flame temperature and surface temperature, one can write $k(T_f - T_s)/h = \rho_p \dot{r} L$. So one gets

$$\rho_p \dot{r} = k(T_f - T_s)/hL.$$

Since h is independent of pressure, it follows that $\rho_p \dot{r}$, the mass burning rate (or mass flux) as it is called, is independent of pressure.

10.1 What will happen to the height in the turbulent range?

A turbulent flow through ducts begins when the Reynolds number is beyond 2300 or so. A velocity of air of 1 m/s through a tube of 20 mm diameter has a Reynolds number of about 2400. A larger diameter or higher velocity fluid passing through the duct leads to the flow being turbulent. The mechanics of diffusion in turbulent flows is different from that in laminar flows. In laminar flows, diffusion occurs because of the random motion of molecules. In turbulent flows, large scale motion caused by fluctuations (which themselves are triggered because of instability in the flow) makes diffusion occur over large length scales and with larger amount of effective diffusion. Turbulent diffusion is thus characterised by eddy diffusivity. There are various methods of describing this in conservation equations, most of which need improvement because of the lack of clear understanding of the phenomenon of turbulence.

It is adequate for an overall appreciation of the situation to treat the turbulent diffusion time scale t_D as $Cd/2V$, where $d/2$ is the characteristic distance of diffusion and V the velocity of the fluid. This expression appears more like a convective time scale. The justification for this is that eddies of various sizes flip over and transfer the fluid from the centre to the outer edge. Thus, effective length scale is $d/2$ and the velocity of the fluid stream flipping the gases from the centre is V.

With this expression we obtain

$$h = Vt_D = \frac{CVd}{2V} = \frac{Cd}{2}.$$

Thus in turbulent flow, the height of the flame is independent of the speed of the incoming fluid but depends on the diameter of the duct. If now, we add the effects of stoichiometry and oxidiser mass fraction, we get

$$h = Cd/f_sY_{0\infty}. \tag{10.5}$$

The constant C is related to the turbulent entrainment characteristics (or inverse of eddy diffusion constant) ($C \simeq 3$).

10.2 Droplet combustion

We now move on to droplet combustion. Droplet combustion is of relevance in many industrial applications as well as reciprocating, gas turbine and rocket engines. For instance, all furnaces in industries use light diesel oil or furnace oil which are less refined forms of crude petroleum. These liquids get injected in the form of a spray into the combustion chamber/furnace along with air; a bright flame results after ignition.

In reciprocating engines of the compression ignition kind, high-speed diesel is injected in the form of a fine spray into the combustion chamber at a time when the piston has compressed the air inside to a relatively high pressure. It is the droplet ignition and combustion process in the highly turbulent and highly varying environment in durations of the order of a few to a few tenths of milliseconds that keeps millions of Cl engines going.

All gas turbine engines, particularly aviation gas turbines, use ATF (aviation turbine fuel) consisting of refined kerosene. Kerosene is injected it the form of a fine spray into a complex fluid-mechanical environment, and the combustion takes place in this zone.

Liquid rocket engines invariably use injectors whose primary function is to atomise the liquids into a fine spray; the liquid droplets vaporise in the combustion chamber and then burn up before going through the nozzle.

In all these cases, it is of interest to determine the burn rate of a liquid droplet as a function of its diameter, and the thermodynamic and transport properties of the gaseous environment.

The burn rate is also affected by the flow of the oxidiser past the droplet, either forced or induced by gravitational environment. The effect of gravitational environment is called free convection and is due to velocities induced by differing densities in the $1g$ field that all of us experience. Because of this the flame will appear as in Fig. 10.2 (b). If the drop is burnt in a free fall condition, like in the case of a freely falling elevator which is one of the normal experimental methods adopted for such studies, one obtains a spherically symmetric flame as in Fig. 10.2 (a). If the drop is burning in a situation where the fluid (the oxidiser, say) is flowing past the droplet, the flame shape appears as in Fig. 10.2 (c).

The drop vaporisation and combustion rate in case Fig. 10.2 (a) will be in a sense the base burn rate. In the situation of Fig. 10.2 (b), free convection effects defined by a Grashoff number play an important role. The drop vaporisation/ combustion rate in case Fig. 10.2 (c) is dependent on the Reynolds number of the flow.

The problem of drop vaporisation at zero g can be obtained by solving energy conservation differential equation as follows.

$$\frac{d}{dr}4\pi kr^2\frac{dT}{dr} - \dot{m}\frac{d}{dr}c_pT = 0. \tag{10.6}$$

The first term represents the conduction heat transfer and the second the convection term. This differential equation states that at any radial location, r, the heat transferred by conduction per unit volume per unit time is balanced by that from convection. The differential equation is of the ordinary kind and of second order. Its solution has two constants. The constants are determined by using appropriate boundary conditions. The boundaries are the surface of the droplet, $r = r_s$ and $r \to \infty$, the infinite outer boundary. The droplet is at temperature T_s and the outer region is at T_0. For vaporisation to occur, T_0 must be larger than T_s. Let us for the moment assume that the surface temperature of the droplet, T_s, is constant all the time.

Thus for $T(r = r_s) = T_s$, and $T(r \to \infty) \to T_0$, the solution can be obtained. An additional condition is required to calculate the vaporisation rate: one needs to strike a heat balance at the liquid surface like

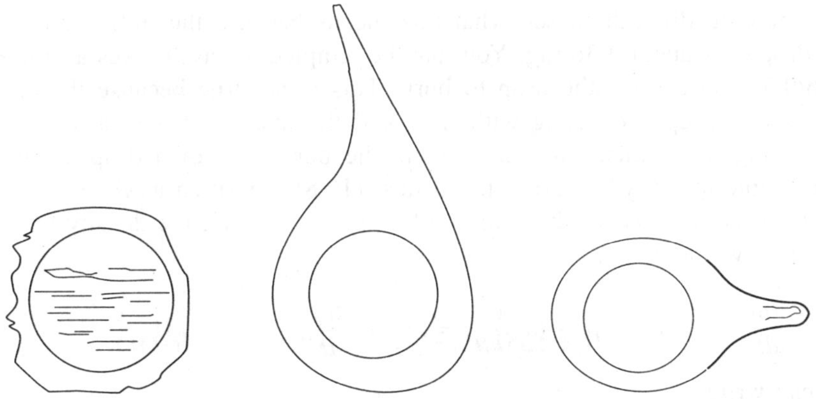

(a) Zero-g condition (b) Under natural gravity (1 g) (c) Forced convection

Figure 10.2 *Liquid droplet combustion modes*

$$\left[4\pi r^2 k \frac{dT}{dr}\right]_{r_s} = \dot{m}L, \tag{10.7}$$

where L = heat of phase change. This equation states that the heat transferred from the outer region to the surface is balanced by the heat taken away by the vaporising substance/liquid. Such an equation is indeed common in the solution process of combustion problems.

The solution of (10.6) subject to the boundary conditions noted above, along with the condition (10.7) gives,

$$\dot{m} = 4\pi r_s (k/c_p)_g \ln(1 + B_v). \tag{10.8}$$

The subscript g on k/c_p is to indicate that it is to be obtained for the gas phase. In the above equation, B_v is expressed as

$$B_v = c_p(T_0 - T_s)/L. \tag{10.9}$$

The quantity B_v is called transfer number and it indicates the thermodynamic potential to cause vaporisation. k is the thermal conductivity (transport property) and c_p is constant pressure specific heat of gas.

Equation (10.8) indicates that the mass vaporisation rate is proportional to the drop radius. The dependence on transfer number is weak since the logarithmic term changes little for large variations of B_v. Let us consider a numerical example. For $r_s = 1$ mm , $k_g = 0.02$ W/m K, $c_p = 1.0$ kJ/kg K, $\rho_l = 800$ kg /m^3, $T_0 = 800$ K, $T_s = 300$ K, $L = 300$ kJ/kg,

$$\dot{m} = 3.0 \times 10^{-4} r_s \text{ kg/s} = 3.0 \times 10^{-7} \text{ kg/s} = 0.30 \text{ mg/s}.$$

It may be difficult to see what this means because the initial mass of the droplet is about 3.36 mg. You may be tempted to say it takes a time of 3.36/0.3 = 11.2 s for the drop to burn. This is not true because the drop radius will keep decreasing with time and the mass burn rate also keeps decreasing. How then can we estimate the burn time of a drop, a more perceivable quantity? In order to do this, (10.8) is written as $\dot{m} = dm/dt$, where m is the mass of the drop $= (4/3)\pi r^3 \rho_l$, ρ_l being the density of the liquid. If we note

$$\frac{dm}{dt} = (4/3) \times \pi\rho_l \times 3r_s^2 \frac{dr_s}{dt} = 2\pi\rho_l r_s \frac{dr_s^2}{dt},$$

we can write

$$2\pi\rho_l r_s \frac{dr_s^2}{dt} = 4\pi r_s \frac{k}{c_p} \ln(1+B_v).$$

Hence,

$$\frac{dr_s^2}{dt} = 2\pi \frac{k}{c_p} \frac{\ln(1+B_v)}{\rho_l}$$

and

$$r_s^2 = r_{s0}^2 - K_v t. \qquad (10.10)$$

$$\boldsymbol{K_v} = 2\frac{k}{c_p} ln(1+B_v)/\rho_l, \quad r_{s0} = \text{initial drop radius.} \qquad (10.11)$$

Equation (10.11) is classically expressed in terms of diameter of droplet as

$$d_s^2 = d_{s0}^2 - \bar{K}_v t, \qquad (10.12)$$

where $\bar{K}_v = 4K_v$, d_{s0} = initial diameter. Equation (10.12) is called the d^2-law and $\bar{K}_v$ is the evaporation constant. We can obtain the drop evaporation time by setting $d_s = 0$ in (10.12) as

$$t_v = d_{s0}^2/\bar{K}_v = r_{s0}^2/K_v. \qquad (10.13)$$

This is an important relation showing the drop evaporation time varying as the square of the drop diameter. We can estimate the value of t_v for the example indicated earlier,

$$t_v = \frac{10^{-6}}{2 \times (\frac{0.020}{1000} \times \frac{1}{800} \times \ln(1+B_v))} = 16.6 \text{ s}.$$

One can note that this is larger than the linear estimate indicated earlier.

The treatment of the problem of droplet combustion (under zero g) is similar, but needs more work. A flame surrounds the droplet at a distance 10 to 15 times the drop radius from the centre and transfers heat to the droplet. In the treatment of this problem, one uses a well known (to combustion theoreticians) approximation called the thin flame approximation. It is good to understand the features of this approximation because most diffusion flame treatments invoke it.

In this approximation, which is based on the fact that diffusion is slower than reaction because the fuel and the oxidant are unmixed until the flame is reached, the reaction rates are taken to be infinitely fast compared to diffusion. Such an approximation makes the flame infinitesimally thin. Since the oxidiser and the fuel come from both sides of the flame towards it and the reaction is very fast, it implies that the fuel and oxidiser are completely consumed at the flame (their mass fraction is zero at the flame) and no leakage past the flame can take place (fuel mass fraction is zero on the oxidant side and vice versa). The temperature has a peak at this flame location.

The flame is located by assuming that the fuel and oxidiser fluxes approaching the flame are in stoichiometric proportions. This implies,

$$(D_{\mathrm{ox}}\rho dY_{\mathrm{ox}}/dr)/(D_{\mathrm{f}}\rho dY_{\mathrm{f}}/dr) = \text{stoichiometric ratio.} \tag{10.14}$$

Using this expression and other conditions, it is possible to solve the conservation equations in a straightforward manner. One interesting feature of these solution techniques is that one solves the enthalpy and element conservation relations first as these are unaffected by thin flame approximation. Subsequently, one obtains the complete solution after imposing the approximation. The solutions give

$$t_c = r_{s0}^2/K_c, \tag{10.15}$$

where

$$K_c = 2\frac{k}{c_p}\frac{\ln(1+B_c)}{\rho_l}. \tag{10.16}$$

It can be noted that the expression for the time of combustion (and for the mass burn rate) is similar to that of vaporisation, and the only difference is in the value of transfer number B_c.

$$B_c = \frac{HY_{0,\infty}/s + c_p(T_s - T_0)}{L}. \tag{10.17}$$

It can be noted that the temperature difference term in vaporisation is $(T_0 - T_s)$, whereas for combustion it is $(T_s - T_0)$. It is so arranged because vaporisation occurs only when the ambient temperature T_0 is larger than the surface temperature T_s, and for combustion, the surface temperature is usually larger than the ambient temperature. However, it is possible for combustion to occur with the surface temperature lower than the ambient temperature because the heat released from the flame will sustain the heat transfer to the liquid surface, enabling its vaporisation before reacting with the oxidant at the flame.

One can obtain from the solution procedure, $T_f = HY_{0,\infty}/sc_p + T_0$.

In the above expression, s is the stoichiometric ratio (same as $1/f_s$), and the other terms have the same meaning as in the previous case. If we now take similar numbers but include a few more needed for combustion, $T_0 = 800$ K, $T_s = 300$ K, $k_g = 0.03$ W /m K, $c_p = 1.2$ kJ/kg K, $\rho_l = 800$ kg/m^3, $H = 42$ MJ/kg, $s = 3.5$, $Y_{0\infty} = 0.232$, $L = 300$ kJ/kg (typical values for kerosene drop burning in air), $r_{s0} = 1$ mm, we get $t_c/t_v = 2.7$.

One can see that the time for combustion is much smaller than that for vaporisation and this is dominantly affected by the transfer number and mean transport property effects.

There is a minor point concerning the above results. In the case of combustion or vaporisation at high ambient temperatures, the liquid temperature will increase from the ambient to a value close to boiling point. This heat is to be included in the denominator of the expression for B_c by replacing L with $(L + mc_p(dT_s/dt)/\dot{m})$.

The second term approaches zero within a short time during droplet burning. One can now ask as to what are the influences of free and forced convection on mass burn rate. One bases the answers on semi-empirical approaches as of now, since the problem will be two-dimensional (unlike spherical symmetry leading to one-dimension) and the solution quite involved.

Studies indicate that

$$\dot{m}_{\text{free con}}/\dot{m}_{0g} = (1 + 0.2B_c^{-0.44}Gr^{0.3}), \tag{10.18}$$

where

$$Gr = \text{Grashof number} = 8r_{s0}^3 g(T_f - T_0)/v^2 T_0 \tag{10.19}$$

is the ratio of gravitational to viscous forces.

The extent of increase in the mass burn rate because of free convection can be as large as 20–40% compared to those under zero-g conditions, depending on the initial drop radius. This is the value of burn rate observed if one conducts experiments on droplets in a laboratory without any special equipment for zero-g application.

In the case of forced convection (laminar),

$$\dot{m}_{\text{forced con}}/\dot{m}_{0g} = (1 + 0.3Pr^{1/3}Re^{1/2}), \tag{10.20}$$

where $Re = 2\rho_g V r_{s0}/\mu_g$ is the Reynolds number.

Whenever forced convection dominates the flow, Reynolds number becomes the parameter characterising the flow features and it will appear as a principal variable (more like $Re^{1/2}$ for laminar flows).

The enhancement of burn rate due to flow can be also as large as in free convection, But if one causes a large flow past the droplet, extinction will occur. (This was discussed in Chapter 9.)

10.3 Boundary layer combustion

We shall be concerning ourselves with diffusion flames in boundary layers here. This does not mean that premixed flame combustion cannot occur in the boundary layers. They do occur and can be treated similarly. What are boundary layers?

Whenever fluid flows past sheets and plates, flat or curved, the fluid velocity at the surface of the plate is zero because non-zero fluid viscosity demands that there can be no difference in velocity between the plate and the fluid next to it. Consequently, the fluid velocity varies from zero at the surface to free stream value away from the surface. This zone over which variation in velocity takes place is called boundary layer (Fig. 10.3 (a)).

One might wonder why there are no gradients in the free stream even though every fluid has viscosity. In fact, it is precisely because of viscosity that there are no differences in velocity in the free stream. Viscosity acts as a great equaliser. It comes into action when there are differences in velocities and acts to smoothen the differences. In the case of flow past a wall, viscosity acts as a smoothening effect, taking the stream speed from zero at the surface to non-zero finite value in the free stream.

The usual descriptions of boundary layer show a fluid moving past a fixed body. One could equally well consider a moving body in a quiescent fluid. The velocity of the fluid near the surface is close to that of the surface. It reduces to zero away from the surface (Fig. 10.3 (b)). The region over which the variation takes place, again, is the boundary layer.

It is important to recognise that the idea of boundary layer is not restricted to velocity alone. It can be for temperature as well as for species mass (or mole) fractions. In fact, *just as viscosity is to velocity gradients, thermal conductivity is to temperature gradients and mass diffusivity is to species mass fraction gradients.*

Flow gradients need not always be next to a wall; one could have gradients in the flow regions as well. For instance, take the case of injection of a hot fluid into a cold flowing stream. There will be temperature difference between the two fluids in the flow which will be smoothened by thermal conductivity in a narrow region between the bulk of the cold and hot fluids. This layer is called mixing layer as it does not involve a wall. In the case of

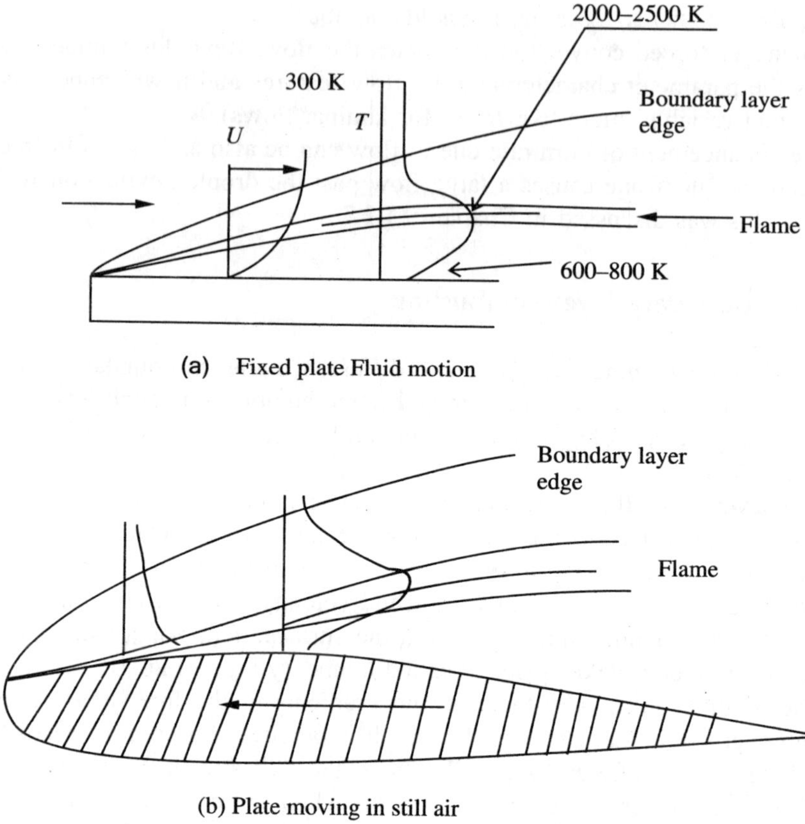

Figure 10.3 *Boundary layer combustion modes*

wall, the terminology of boundary layer is used. Another example would be that of the injection of one miscible fluid into another in a flowing system. Here the mass diffusivity plays a role of smoothening the differences in concentration between the two fluids.

Boundary layer thickness depends on the speed of the fluid, the distance from the front end of the surface and the viscosity of the fluid. These quantities can be combined to form Reynolds number ($Re = \rho U x/\mu$). The thickness of boundary layer (δ_v) can be shown to vary with Reynolds number as

$$\delta_v/x \sim Re^{-1/2}. \tag{10.21}$$

The exponent $-1/2$ on Reynolds number is typical of all laminar flows.

At very high speeds of the fluid flow, or large distances from the front edge, the flow no longer remains laminar, but becomes turbulent. Though they are not understood at the fundamental level, yet much is known about

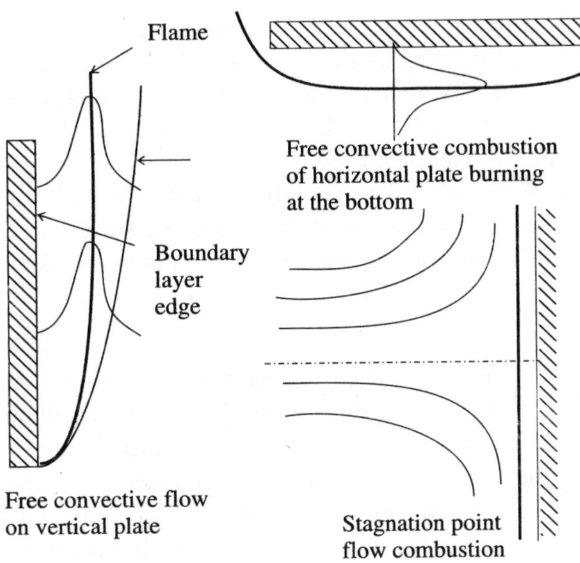

Figure 10.4 *Free convective and forced convective combustion modes*

their overall behaviour—certainly enough for engineers to carry out their designs pretty well. For these flows, the boundary layer thickness varies with Reynolds number as

$$\delta_v / x \sim Re^{-0.2}. \tag{10.22}$$

Combustion in the boundary layer occurs when the oxidiser flows past a solid surface or a surface supplied with liquid fuel or a large liquid fuel mass.

Figure 10.3 indicates the features of laminar boundary layer combustion. The temperature profile shows a peak temperature at the flame (2000–2500 K) dropping to ambient temperature on one side and to relatively high surface temperatures (600–800 K) on the other side. The zone between the fuel surface and the flame has fuel vapour and products diffusing towards this side from the flame. The zone above the flame has oxidiser and products. Fuel and oxidiser do not coexist under conditions of thin flame. This approximation is quite good in reality in so far as the estimation of various properties are concerned.

One could have problems of combustion in free convective conditions–something which happens in fire problems. This problem of combustion in free convective boundary layer is not different from what happens in forced convection (as shown in Fig. 10.4).

The question in such a situation is this: how will the mass burn rate of the fuel block depend on the mass flow rate of the oxidiser (forced convection), oxidiser mass fraction in free stream, pressure, and thermodynamic and transport properties of the fuel and the oxidiser? For this, one needs to have information on the velocity, temperature and mass fraction profiles to obtain the result. However, one has some shortcuts from a knowledge of similarity of these profiles and related features.

In order to solve boundary layer combustion problems, a simple way of starting the solution is to strike a heat balance at the surface of the burning fuel. It appears similar to the one written earlier and reads like

$$\dot{q}_g'' = k_g \left[\partial T/\partial y\right]_{y=0} = \rho_p \dot{r} L. \tag{10.23}$$

In (10.23), k_g is the gas phase thermal conductivity and $\dot{q}_g''$ is the heat flux to the surface, the expression given by the product of conductivity of the gas and partial derivative of temperature with distance normal to the local surface. The right-hand side is the product of the density of the solid/liquid fuel, $\dot{r}$ the linear regression rate and L the heat of phase change at the surface. The product $\rho_p \dot{r}$ is the mass flux from the fuel surface.

$$\rho_p \dot{r} L = \dot{q}_g'' \tag{10.24}$$

The expression for heat flux $\dot{q}_g''$ from the gas phase depends on the nature of the flow (free or forced convection) and boundary conditions (free stream temperature, for instance). Curiously, it also depends on $\rho_p \dot{r}$. This effect is called the blocking effect. It comes about in the following manner. If the heat flux from the gas phase increases, then one expects the mass flux from the surface (mass burn rate per unit area) to increase. This causes the boundary layer to thicken causing reduction in gradients. Thus, any effort to raise the burn rate by increasing heat flux will not happen in a linear manner as seen from (10.24) but will be lower. This modification is to be estimated from a rigorous analysis specific to the flow geometry.

We shall follow a general scheme for solving a variety of combustion problems. The heat flux to the surface is taken as a product of heat transfer coefficient and temperature difference between the flame and the surface. This gives

$$\rho_p \dot{r} = \frac{\dot{q}_g''}{L} = \frac{h_g(T_f - T_s)}{L} = B\,\frac{h_g}{c_p}, \tag{10.25}$$

where $B = c_p(T_f - T_s)/L$ represents the transfer number discussed earlier. The heat transfer coefficient is expressed in terms of a non-dimensional number called Nusselt number, defined by $h_g = Nu k_g/x$, where x is the characteristic length scale. In the case of a flat plate, vertical or horizontal, it implies the distance from the leading edge. In the case of a cylinder or sphere, it could refer to its diameter. Thus,

$$\rho_p \dot{r} = B\,\frac{k_g}{x c_p}\,Nu. \tag{10.26}$$

In order to account for the blocking effect, the Nusselt number is first evaluated without blocking effect and then corrected for this effect through the ratio (Nu/Nu_0). We therefore get

$$\rho_p \dot{r} = B\,\frac{k_g}{x c_p}\,\frac{Nu}{Nu_0}\,Nu_0.$$

Non-dimensionalising both sides by dividing by $(\rho V)_\infty$, the free stream mass flux, we get

$$\frac{\rho_p \dot{r}}{(\rho V)_\infty} = B\,\frac{k_g}{c_p \mu_g}\,\frac{\mu_g}{\rho V_\infty x} Nu_0 \frac{Nu}{Nu_0}$$

$$= B\,(Pr Re)^{-1} Nu_0 \frac{Nu}{Nu_0}. \tag{10.27}$$

The quantity $(\mu_g c_{pg}/k_g)$ is the Prandtl number with a value of 0.75–0.8 for combustible gas mixtures. (Nu/Nu_0), the blocking effect, can be calculated exactly for several laminar flows. For turbulent flows, it can be calculated only empirically. It goes like $\ln(1+B)/B$ for small values of B. Typical values of B for some liquid and solid fuels are shown in Table 10.1. For larger values, typically $B \sim 5$ or more, the expression (Nu/Nu_0) can be written as $C_0 B^{(m-1)}$. This form is curve fitted to compute values of (Nu/Nu_0) and C_0 and m are estimated.

The final result in several situations can therefore be written as

$$\frac{\rho_p \dot{r}}{(\rho V)_\infty} = C_0 B^m \frac{Nu_0}{Re_x Pr}. \tag{10.28}$$

In the case of free convective flows,

$$\rho_p \dot{r} = C_0 B^m Nu_0 \frac{k_g}{x c_p}. \tag{10.29}$$

The expression for Nu_0 for the situations identified earlier are set out in Table 10.2. One can take a typical case. For flat plate, stagnation point flows (flows in which fluid impinges normal to a flat plate, for instance) at low Reynolds number,

$$\rho_p \dot{r}/(\rho V)_\infty = C_0 B^m Pr^{-2/3} Re_x^{-1/2}, \tag{10.30}$$

where x is the distance from the leading edge or stagnation point.

For turbulent flows it varies as

$$\rho_p \dot{r}/(\rho V)_\infty = C_0 B^m Pr^{-2/3} Re_x^{-0/2}. \tag{10.31}$$

Table 10.1 *B and other parameters for some fuels with air (*polymers have no fixed phase transition temperature, c_p= 1.2 kJ/kg K; T_0 = 300 K; $c_p = 1.0$ kJ/kg K)*

Fuel	Boiling point °C	Latent heat kJ/kg	Flame temperature K	B
Acetone	56.7	523.0	2120	3.9
Gasoline	155.0	349.0	2200	4.5
Kerosene	250.0	290.0	2250	6.2
n-Pentane	36.0	364.0	2250	5.2
Iso-Octane	125.0	328.0	2250	5.2
PMMA*	~250–350	600.0	2200	2.0–2.5
PS*	~300–400	800.0	2350	1.5–2.1

For laminar free convective flows the mass burn rate will vary like

$$\rho_p \dot{r} = C_0 B^m (k_g/c_{pg}x)(GrPr)^{1/4}. \tag{10.32}$$

For turbulent free convective flows it varies as

$$\rho_p \dot{r} = C_0 B^m (k_g/c_{pg}x)(GrPr)^{1/3}. \tag{10.33}$$

The constant C_0 may take different values in each of the above cases. The dependence on Reynolds number and Grashoff number shown above are observed in several complex situations where flows are laminar or turbulent. The value of the exponent m on B was thought to be about 0.25 till the nineties. This small value for the exponent coupled with the variation of B by a factor of 1.5 over the fuels gave rise to the conclusion that the regression rate is about the same no matter what fuel you choose. Experiments showed otherwise—differences in regression rate between different fuels were much higher. This was explained in the nineties when the blocking effect was examined more carefully. It was discovered that the blocking effect depended on the density profile through the boundary layer. For instance, injecting carbon dioxide (molecular weight of 44) or gaseous species with even higher molecular weight differed the results of experiments from that conducted with air. In boundary layer combustion, most fuels have much higher molecular weight, more particularly polymeric fuels whose fragments in the gas phase have a molecular weight of several hundred. Consequently, a theory that was developed accounting for these effects showed a complex expression that could be approximated to $m = 0.5$ in most cases. This explained the observed dependence of regression rate on fuels.

The above relations explain an interesting fact which one experiences in every-day life. Take firewood logs burning in stoves. The varieties of firewood available differ in density (ρ_p over a wide range 300 to 1000 kg/m^3).

Table 10.2 *Nusselt numbers ($Re=\rho Vx/\mu$, $Gr=gx^3(T_f-T_0)/T_0\nu^2$; $\nu=\mu/\rho$)*

No. Situation	Relationship for Nu_0
1. Flat plate, laminar	$Nu_0 = 0.332\ Re^{1/2} Pr^{1/3}$
2. Turbulent($Re > 10^5$)	$= 0.036\ Re^{0.8}\ Pr^{0.3}$
3. Stagnation zone (plane) laminar	$= 0.57\ Re^{1/2} Pr^{2/3}$
4. Stagnation zone, laminar (Axisymmetric)	$= 0.93\ Re_x^{1/2} Pr^{2/3}$
5. Flow around a sphere, laminar ($Re < 10^{-4}$)	$= 0.37 Re_d^{0.6}$
6. Flow around a cylinder, laminar	$= 0.891\ Re^{1/2}$
$Re > 40,000$ turbulent	$= 0.024\ Re^{0.3}$
7. Vertical plate. free convection, $Gr < 10^9$(laminar) $Gr > 10^9$(turbulent)	$= 0.59\ (GrPr)^{1/4}$
8. Horizontal Fuel plate burning face up	
$Gr < 10^7$ laminar	$= 0.54(GrPr)^{1/4}$
$Gr > 10^7$ turbulent	$= 0.14(GrPr)^{1/3}$
9. Horizontal fuel plate face down turbulent	$= 0.27(GrPr)^{1/4}$
10. Horizontal cylinder (free convection)$Gr > 10^9$	$= 0.525(GrPr)^{1/4}$
11. Sphere	$= 2 + 0.6\ Gr^{1/4} Pr^{1/3}$

It is observed that lighter woods burn faster. This is consistent with the equation above, which expresses the mass flux of fuel (density times linear burn rate) in terms of flow, thermodynamic and transport properties. The other parameters remaining the same (as they usually do for similar sized logs), lighter fuels must burn proportionately faster. This also explains the observed 'long' combustion times for coal. Coal has a high density (1300 kg/m^3) and much lower volatile content ($\sim$ 30 %). Hence, if one used a wood burning stove to operate on coal, one would find that coal would burn for nearly twice as long or more after the coal had started burning — the effects of higher density and larger fraction of char in coal.

Typical regression rates vary from 0.02–0.4 mm/s for most solid/ liquid fuels with air, the precise value depending on the fuel, flow rates and size. These regression rates are very small and are essentially due to the diffusion nature of the flame.

10.4 Overview

Diffusion flames have been described as the largest class of flames encountered in nature. These flames usually appear yellow in colour. They are also tall because their heights depends on diffusion, and diffusion rates are small. Laminar gas diffusion flame heights increase with velocity. Turbulent flames scale with the diameter of the jet. Diffusion flame heights and heat transfer are relatively independent of pressure.

Liquid fuel droplet combustion in oxidising environment occupies a premier position in industrial and automotive engine combustion situations. Droplet combustion times scale with the square of initial diameter in zero-g conditions. Usually, d^2-law, as the basic relation is called, is obeyed even with free convection or moderately forced convection. The thermal properties of the liquid fuel do not have a significant influence on the burn rate. Drop combustion times are two to ten times smaller than vaporisation times under similar ambient conditions. Corrections to the burn rate because of the velocity of oxidiser or free convection are made by semi-empirical means through the use of $Re^{1/2}$ or $Gr^{1/4}$ as appropriate (in the laminar range).

Boundary layer diffusive combustion is another major combustion mode. It is relevant in hybrid rockets and fire in a variety of situations. A general analysis technique shows that the mass burn rate (or mass flux to be precise) varies with transfer number (to account for thermodynamic effects) and Nusselt number (to account for flow effects). The inter-relation between flow and thermodynamic effects occurs because of the blocking effect—the effect of reduction of heat transfer due to enhancement of mass efflux from the surface. A general statement of these relations is possible so that a variety of physical flow conditions can be accounted for. Laminar flow situations can be analysed exactly—sometimes using a computer. Turbulent flow situations need modelling of turbulence–reaction interactions. This area is not fully understood yet. For engineering needs, correlations can be developed and these are indeed satisfactory in many cases.

11 Flames—Premixed or Diffusion

Most natural flames are diffusion flames while most arranged combustions are premixed. This describes one essential difference between the two. One is naturally provoked to ask: why should arranged devices be premixed? One answer is that premixing leads to lesser pollutants and combustion can be expected to be completed better in much smaller volumes. This is indeed true. Premixing of fuel and oxidiser, in gaseous/condensed phase, would help the cause of combustion better since the elements do not have to look for each other. They are available in the immediate vicinity.

11.1 Premixed substances

It has been said that gaseous/ condensed phases can be premixed. Yes, one understands gaseous media being premixed. It happens all the time in a gas stove where fuel gas entrains air before coming out of the hundred odd holes of the burner to burn up. Or in a kerosene stove where, by an ingenious method, the kerosene vapour and air are mixed in the annular space between the perforated sheets before combustion takes place.

But does premixing occur in liquids? Well, if one uses chemicals which have both fuel and oxidiser elements in a single molecule, then one could treat the substance as having premixedness. Hydrogen peroxide is a case in point. It has both the elements in a single molecule (H_2O_2) and is of course very reactive by itself (it is also very corrosive). There are other liquid solutions which have both oxidiser and fuel elements almost of right proportions. These are explosive in nature and wait for the smallest opportunity to be triggered into exothermic reactions and gasify so fast that usually explosions result. One example is nitroglycerine (liquid), used extensively in solid propellant industry.

In solids too there are several cases where molecules have both oxidiser and fuel elements. Ammonium perchlorate (NH_4ClO_4) is oxidiser rich but has both elements in it. It burns up by itself at relatively high pressures (on ignition). HMX is another example.

All solid propellants are instances of premixing of fuel and oxidiser. When they burn at not too high a pressure, they act as though they were premixed. Premixed flames are affected by pressure and initial temperature significantly. This is because chemistry plays a strong role in their combustion schemes. The final temperature they attain on combustion depends on the mixture ratio. The flame speed depends on the mixture ratio, pressure and initial temperature. They can be quenched and are flammable over a relatively narrow range of mixture ratios.

Because pressure and initial temperature play an more important role in premixed flames, combustion of solid propellants depends strongly on these factors. The burning rate of a solid propellant varies with pressure as p^{m_2}, with m_2 varying from 0.3 to 0.8 and with initial temperature as 0.2–1% per degree centgrade.

11.2 Diffusion flames

Diffusion flames are generally more pollutant-generating, for the fuel does not get enough oxidant in the right place. Not all flames soot alike though. Candle flame for instance, does not soot most of the time. Surely, if you introduce a relatively cold surface into the flame, you can collect some soot. But most soot burns off inside the flame. In a kerosene wick flame (meant for lighting), being slightly larger in size and hence with taller flames, one finds heavy sooting. Yet in a kerosene stove one gets a blue flame. This is because the oxidant gets mixed with the fuel vapour in the right place, i.e., before any possible decomposition of the fuel takes place.

It is quite generally thought that peak temperatures in a diffusion flame must be lower than premixed because the combustion is not complete. One can measure the peak temperature of a candle flame by using a fine (thin) thermocouple and find that it is 1600°C (1873 K), just about 100°C lower than its adiabatic temperature. In fact, in the thin flame approximation, which is close to reality, the temperature of the flame is related to adiabatic flame temperature but is a little short of it, depending on the fluid mechanics of the flow. In the case of droplet combustion, the temperature is the same as adiabatic flame temperature. In others like stagnation point diffusion flame (same as opposed jet diffusion flame discussed in Chapter 9, section 9.3), it is lower.

In the case of diffusion flame, there is no well-recognised quantity like flame speed to define the reactivity of the fuel-oxidiser mixtures. A quantity called apparent flame strength, the mass flux of oxidiser or fuel in an opposed jet/stagnation point flow at the condition of extinction is defined. This quantity, again, defines the reactivity of the fuel–oxidiser system.

One of the most important aspects of diffusion flames is the dominance of fluid mechanics over kinetics with the result that the calculation of burn rates in diffusion flames is a lot less uncertain. This is because kinetic dominated phenomena depend on the parameters A_f, the frequency factor and E, the activation energy which are not known very accurately. Consequently, accurate predictions of features like ignition, flammability limits in premixed flows are dependent on some experimentally determined features more than in diffusion flames.

Though the simple results presented in the case of droplet combustion or laminar/ turbulent boundary layer combustion and free convective combustion contain such factors like $(k/c_p)_g$ which vary with temperature and composition, it is possible to analyse and make predictions which are quite accurate and representative of what is experimentally observed. In fact, such analyses have been completed in recent times in most of such instances.

An interesting feature of diffusion flames is their wide range of stability. If a burner is to be built and one seeks a diffusion/premixed solution to the device, the aspect of stability plays a critical role which might prevent the choice of a premixed alternative. In diffusion flames, the flame locates itself at stoichiometric flux ratio location and hence poses less restriction on its existence in the burner. In the case of premixed flame, one must locate regions where the speed of the flow is nearly equal to the flame speed. If the flow conditions are changed then the flame is likely to blow off.

This problem does not look so serious if one considers a gas stove. In a gas stove, the additional 'flame holding' effect is provided by the body through which premixed gas issues out. This enhances the stability of the stove flame. The flow rates are about 0.1 to 0.2 g/s, and the flow velocities through the holes are about 0.1 m/s. If one were to conceive a similar design for an industrial application with a power of the order of several hundred kilowatts to a few megawatts, the size of the burner would become too large. For instance, if one wishes to scale up the cooking stove designed for 2 kW power to 100 kW power, a top burner of diameter 0.35 m would be required instead of 0.05 m. But then in 0.35 m dia space one can push about 4 MW of thermal power, excepting that in such a case the combustion is largely in the diffusive mode.

In free flames (non-material bounded), premixed flames are indeed very unstable while diffusion flames provide much greater stability. But, clean combustion (producing minimum pollutants) demands premixed flame; greater stability calls for diffusion flame.

12 Combustion in Rocket Motors

One of the common subjects associated with the development of solid propellant rocket engine concerns the burn rate of the propellant and mechanical integrity of the propellant grain, as it is called. Figure 12.1 shows the way a propellant is arranged in an engine and how the burning takes place. Most motors need to pack the propellant in as small a volume as possible and yet generate a high burning surface to obtain the desired thrust. An n-pointed internal star (see figure) is a familiar configuration to achieve this. It is instructive to see the relationship between the thrust produced and the parameters of combustion. The thrust produced is a product of the mass flow rate through the nozzle and the exit speed (following Newton's laws). The mass flow rate is that which is produced by the combustion of the propellant and we can write,

$$F = \dot{m} V_e = \rho_p \dot{r} A_b V_e,$$

where ρ_p = density of the propellant, A_b the burning surface area and $\dot{r}$, the

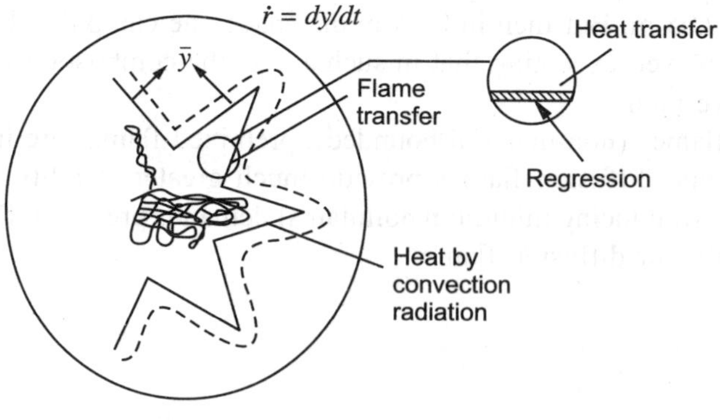

Figure 12.1 *How does a propellant burn?*

linear burn rate (the variation of the movement of the surface along a local normal, y, with time; see Fig. 12.1). The exit velocity, V_e can be shown to be a product of c^*, the characteristic velocity, and the thrust coefficient (c_F), which indicates the amount by which the characteristic velocity is amplified by expansion through the nozzle (typically 1.2 to 1.6). Thus,

$$F = \rho_p \dot{r} A_b c^* c_F.$$

Noting that the thrust varies as the burning area and burn rate, we can examine the linear burn rate $\dot{r}$ as a function of pressure and initial temperature. It is typically represented as

$$\dot{r} = a p_c^n \exp[\alpha(T_0 - T_0^\circ)],$$

where a, n and α are constants and T_0° indicates a reference temperature. For double base propellants, $n \simeq 0.6$–0.8 and $a = 0.5$–2 mm/s and $\alpha = 0.4$–0.6 % per °C. For composite propellants, $n \simeq 0.2$–0.4 and $a = 1$–2 mm/s and $\alpha = 0.2$–0.4 % per °C. The chamber pressure, p_c, is indicated in units of sea level pressure. For example, $p_c = 10$ atm implies 10 times the sea level pressure (0.1013 MPa). These are just facts derived from experiments.

These experimental data need explanation–why is it that burn rate increases with pressure much more for double-base than for composite propellants? Why is there a dependence on initial temperature? And so on.

Propellant combustion has essentially a premixed flame structure for double-base propellants and also for composite propellants at relatively low pressures. The last fact is so because at low pressures the flame thickness is large compared to the characteristic size of heterogeneity of the composite propellant (particle size of the oxidiser, say, AP). The way to understand propellant combustion is to recall the one-dimensional laminar flame propagation treated earlier. Figure 10.1 showed the many features of propellant combustion. The flame is about y^* away from the surface of the propellant. The burn rate can be determined from (10.24), which is rewritten:

$$\dot{q}_g'' = \rho_p \dot{r} L. \tag{12.1}$$

The heat flux from the flame, $\dot{q}_g''$, is composed of contributions from conduction and radiation. The radiation component is about 10–20% of that due to conduction in many situations; in a few cases it is as high as 30%. The conductive flux can be set out using y^*, the height of flame, which is related to chemical reaction rates as in laminar flame theory as

$$\dot{q}_g'' = k\frac{dT}{dy} = k\frac{(T_f - T_s)}{y^*}, \tag{12.2}$$

$$y^* = \frac{k}{c_p}\frac{1}{\bar{\dot{w}}_f'''}. \tag{12.3}$$

In the above equation, $\bar{\dot{w}}_f'''$ is the average reaction rate. Using the expression for reaction rate gives

$$\rho_p \dot{r} = B\sqrt{\frac{k}{c_p}\bar{\dot{w}}_f'''}. \tag{12.4}$$

The dependence of $\dot{r}$ on B (the transfer number) as above is not correct because it lacks the blocking effect (see Chapter 10, section 3 on boundary layer combustion for a discussion on this). The blocking effect can be determined after the conservation equations are solved completely to obtain

$$\rho_p \dot{r} = \sqrt{\frac{k}{c_p}\bar{\dot{w}}_f''' \ln(1+B)}. \tag{12.5}$$

The average of the reaction rate is taken from the surface to infinity, where the conditions are adiabatic. The behaviour of $\bar{\dot{w}}_f'''$ can be written as

$$\bar{\dot{w}}_f''' \simeq A_f p^n e^{-E/2RT_f}.$$

and

$$\rho_p \dot{r} \simeq \sqrt{A_f \frac{k}{c_p} \ln(1+B)} \quad p^{n/2}\, e^{-E/2RT_f}. \tag{12.6}$$

This shows that the burn rate increases with pressure like $p^{n/2}$. For bimolecular collisions, $n \simeq 2$. But for overall reactions it varies as $n \simeq 1.6$–2. Thus,

$$\rho_p \dot{r} \simeq p^{(0.8-1.0)},$$

a result consistent with experimental observations on double-base propellants. That the burn rate increases with pressure can be understood in one of two equivalent ways. An increase in pressure brings the flame thickness down and, hence, enhances the heat transfer to the surface of the burn propellant, thus increasing the burn rate. Alternatively, increase in pressure implies an increase in the average density of molecules, which need smaller physical distance for reactive collisions and hence the flame is brought closer to the surface resulting in increased heat transfer rate and increased burn rate.

In the case of heterogeneous propellants like ammonium-perchlorate-based composite propellants, the solid particles of ammonium are embedded in a matrix of binder and when the burning takes place, the flame structure is as shown in Fig. 12.2. There will be a diffusion flame between the oxidiser and the binder at the interface. Above the oxidiser particle, there will

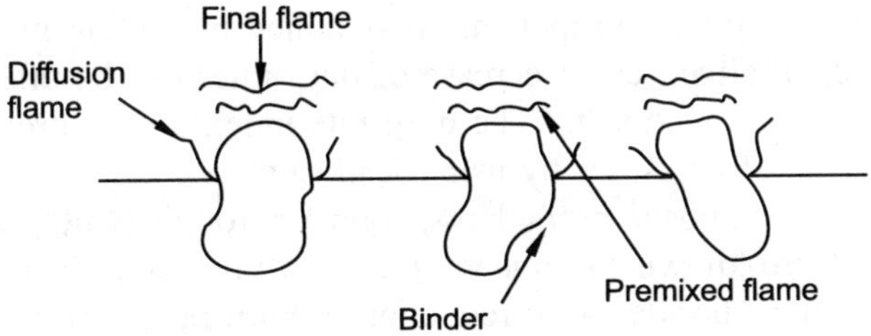

Figure 12.2 *Composite propellant combustion*

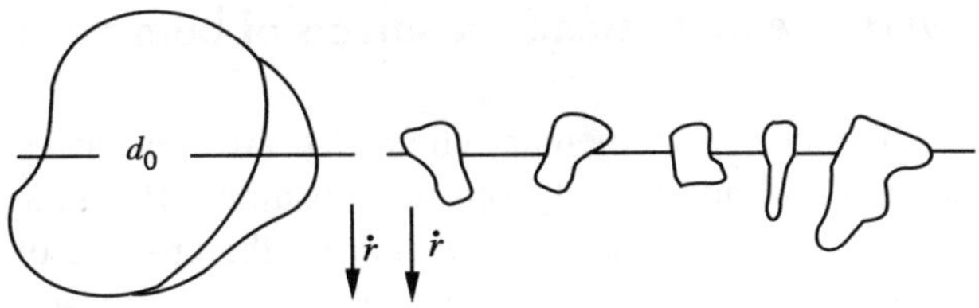

Figure 12.3 *Particle size effect*

be a premixed flame due to the fact that ammonium perchlorate (AP) can self-deflagrate (monopropellant) at high pressures (above 19 atm). The diffusion flame has a typical temperature of $\simeq$ 2800 K and the premixed flame above the AP particle about 1400–1500 K. The products of these flames are locally either fuel-rich or oxidiser-rich. They mix above the surface and burn up generating temperatures of 2800–3200 K, depending on the propellant composition and pressure. An approximate but complex mathematical model for the burning of the propellant and the burn rate as a function of pressure, particle size and other compositional variables has been worked out. This shows that as pressure increases, the diffusion flame effects dominate simply because the flame heights become comparable to the particle size of the oxidiser. And in a diffusion flame, the burn rate depends little on pressure. Thus the combined effects of premixed flame dominance at low pressure and diffusion flame effects at high pressure lead to an average dependence of the burn rate on pressure like $\rho_p \dot{r} \simeq a p_c^{0.2-0.4}$, as observed experimentally. One can similarly argue the effect of particle size on the burn rate. If one conceives of large particle sizes, then the same oxidiser is to be shared by the binder with these particles in comparison to the larger number of smaller particles being made available to the binder otherwise during combustion. This causes a better flame temperature distribution over the surface, and the flame moves closer to the surface (Fig. 12.3). Consequently, the heat transferred back to the condensed phase is higher and so the burn rate is higher as well.

Burn rate control is an important aspect of propellant design. Increase of burn rates in double-base propellants is obtained by adding metal powders of cobalt, copper, silver, etc. Decrease of burn rates can be effected by the addition of lead and lead salts. The burn rate index can be brought to zero over some range of pressures by using lead salts.

In the case of composite propellants, copper chromite ($CuCr_2O_4$) and iron oxide (Fe_2O_3) are known to enhance the burn rates significantly. Lithium oxide and lithium fluoride cause reduction in burn rates, and in some cases reduction of burn rate index as well.

12.1 How do we understand the effects of burn rate modifiers?

Catalysts, as understood in elementary chemistry, are substances which alter the rate of reaction without actually getting consumed. But in a combustion processes the catalysts get consumed, yet serving the purpose of altering the rates of reaction. Hence, it is more appropriate to call these catalyst-like substances burn rate modifiers.

Burn rate modifiers affect both gas phase and condensed phase reaction paths and also cause physical changes near the burning surface. There are many inorganic compounds that produce certain products which melt and spread over the surface and reduce heat transfer to the surface. Some will enhance the rate of reaction in the gas phase near the surface so that the flame is drawn nearer to the surface, causing added heat transfer. In a few cases, it may be a combination of events which leads to the changes in the burn rate vs. pressure behaviour. A remarkable feature of these burn rate modifiers is that even small amounts, typically 0.5% or less, affect the burn rates by more than 10–50%. These features are difficult to model and as yet not much progress has been made in understanding these dramatic effects.

The pressure in the chamber of a rocket engine is due to the balance between mass production rate and mass flow rate through the nozzle. While the former has already been described, the latter can be calculated from fundamentals of gas dynamics to be

$$\dot{m}_{\text{nozzle}} = (p_c A_t)/c^*, \quad c^* = \sqrt{(RT_f/\mathcal{M})/\Gamma(\gamma)}, \tag{12.7}$$

where c^* is the characteristic velocity, a function of flame temperature T_f, molecular weights of products of combustion and a function $\Gamma(\gamma)$ (0.6-0.64) which depends on ratio of specific heats, γ (~1.1–1.25). Equating the mass production rate and mass outflow rate through nozzle, we get:

$$\dot{m}_{\text{production}} = \rho_p A_b \dot{r} = \dot{m}_{\text{nozzle}} = p_c A_t/c^* \tag{12.8}$$

with $\dot{r} = a_1 p_c^n$, $a_1 = a \exp(T_0 - T_0^\circ)$. Here T_0° is the reference ambient temperature. From this equation, we get

$$p_c = \left[\rho_p \frac{A_b}{A_t} a c^*\right]^{1/(1-n)}. \tag{12.9}$$

This is a very revealing result. If you take a double-base propellant with $n = 0.8$, then

$$p_c \sim (A_b/A_t)^{5.0}. \tag{12.10}$$

If the mechanical integrity of the propellant (it implies the ability of the solid propellant as a structural entity to withstand the pressures and loads) is not satisfactory or the preparation of the propellant with the rocket motor is such that some portions not expected to burn initially are exposed (even tiny spacings of 0.1–0.2 mm are sufficient for gases to penetrate and cause combustion in unexpected places), then the burning area, A_b, increases beyond what the system is designed for. Even a 20 % rise in burning area implies that the pressure goes up by 248 %, i.e., if the rocket motor had been designed for 2.0 MPa (20 atmospheres), the local pressure goes up to 5.6 MPa (56 atmospheres). Surely, the motor designed for 20 atmospheres (qualified for 40 atmospheres as per the standard design code) will not withstand higher pressures and the motor would explode, consequently.

The problem is much less serious in the case of composite propellants which have n between 0.2 and 0.4.

12.2 Liquid rocket engines

Combustion in bipropellant liquid rocket engines has a character which is vastly different from solid rocket engines. The injectors atomise the liquid fuel and the oxidiser into tiny drops and these undergo vaporisation first and combustion next. The gases can recirculate inside the combustion chamber and therefore, the temperature of the gases in large part of the chamber, particularly toward the nozzle end, will be near adiabatic flame temperature. The time taken for completion of the combustion process as the atomised propellants move through the chamber is composed of that for the vaporisation and for the chemical reaction. Since the gas temperatures in the chamber are high, the time for chemical reaction will be quite small. It is only the vaporisation which takes substantial time ($\sim$ 2–3 ms). Hence the chambers are designed based on estimated vaporisation times. The vaporisation time is dependent on the drop diameter and relatively weakly on thermodynamic properties (B). The combustion chamber volume, therefore, is not strongly dependent on pressure. The volume of the chamber is estimated from a quantity called $L^* = v_c/A_t$, where v_c is the volume of the combustion chamber (up to the throat) and A_t the throat area. Its typical value is 0.8–1.2 m or so. From this statement it looks as though L^* is a

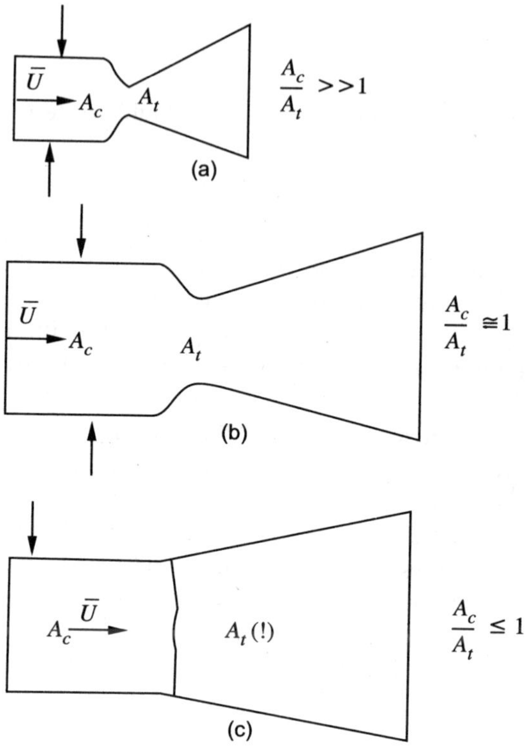

Figure 12.4 *Shapes of liquid rocket engine combustion chambers*

fundamental constant. This is not true. At the fundamental level, L^* should be non-dimensionalised with respect to characteristic length for vaporisation/reaction to be complete. This is essentially equal to $\bar{U}t_{vr}$, where $\bar{U}$ is the mean speed of the liquid droplets, t_{vr} is the time for vaporisation and reaction. Thus, the appropriate parameter is $L^*/\bar{U}t_{vr}$ or

$$L^*/\int_0^{t_{vr}} V dt.$$

But it turns out that $\bar{U}t_{vr}$ is a value not easily calculable because of the complexity of droplet size distribution and the nature of flow, and hence one works with a value of L^* directly in practice. One notices from Fig. 12.4 that the ratio A_c/A_t gets lowered from case (a) to case (c). It is known from gas dynamics that as long as the chamber pressure is larger than about twice the ambient pressure, the velocity at the throat is equal to the speed of sound at the local temperature (which is about 900–1000 m/s corresponding to throat temperature of 2700–3000 K). The speeds of fluid flow in the combustion chamber will be larger as we move from case (a) to case (c) since the combustion chamber cross-section becomes comparable to the throat area.

Higher speeds cause larger heat transfer to the walls and also increase the possibility of combustion instability.

'Combustion instability' refers to high frequency oscillations of the chamber pressure around the steady pressure resulting in extraordinary heat transfer to specific locations of the chamber, as a result of which a burn-through occurs almost always. This is a result of the coupling between the fluid flow and the acoustic oscillations. The acoustic oscillations, which are always present in any chamber, interact with the fluid flow and the heat generation mechanisms. The acoustic oscillations are accompanied by those of the heat generation as well. If these oscillations are in phase, then one gets amplification of the wave and quite often a detonation wave results. The travelling detonation wave causes a large rise in local heat flux to the engine walls, and hence the burn-through.

The frequency of oscillations (ω) can be obtained from an analysis of the acoustics in a given geometry. This leads to ω = const (a/d_c), where a is the local acoustic speed and d_c the chamber diameter. The ratio a/d_c is the inverse of acoustic travel time and hence represents acoustic frequency. At d_c = 0.2 m (for 30–50 kN thrust engines), ω = 3.0 kHz and for d_c = 0.5 m (for 500–700 kN thrust engines), ω = 1.2 kHz (constant$\sim$ 0.6, a = 1000 m/s).

Since acoustic energy varies as (frequency)^2, it is more difficult to excite high frequencies since the energy required is large. Thus, smaller thrust engines (using smaller combustion chamber diameter) are less prone to instability than higher thrust engines. In fact, engines of 500–700 kN thrust are almost always beset with the deadly high frequency instability problem. One of the best known examples of high frequency instability affecting the performance of the engine in recent times is the ARIANE launch vehicle programme of European Space Agency. The first stage used engines called Viking (built by French agency) which produced 700 kN vacuum thrust which had frequent occurrence of instability during its development. Though the team of designers was aware of the problems of instability when it first struck terror during the development of ATLAS engine in USA in the sixties, the Viking engine was deployed in the flight programme without specifically overcoming the problem in a clean manner. Alas! the second flight of the vehicle was struck by instability in one of the engines and the vehicle ended up in sea a short while after take-off. Hectic research and development efforts to overcome the problem have made the engine somewhat safe though not completely so.

Well then, how does one overcome instability? What one needs to do is to arrange for the acoustic oscillations and the energy release oscillations to be out of phase. One way of achieving this is to distribute the energy release over a wider region physically—not make it too concentrated. This will cause the energy to be put into other regions of the oscillating wave such

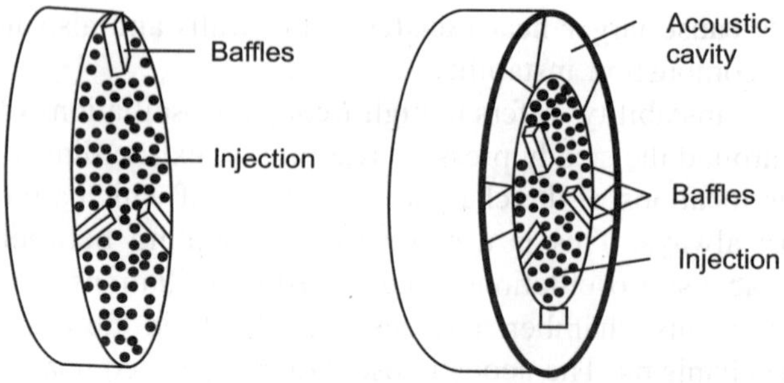

Figure 12.5 *Liquid rocket stabilisation device*

that the amplification factor due to in-phase energy addition decreases. The injector holes are made little larger, pressure drop is reduced so that the drop size distribution is made more coarse, and thus combustion energy release is made broader. This method is adopted for overcoming the oscillations in a few cases. Another method used raises the natural frequency of excitable oscillations. For this purpose the injector is provided with radial and/or circular baffles (see Fig. 12.5). Acoustic cavities are also provided so that the resonant frequency oscillations of the chamber are absorbed and instability is avoided. The last two techniques are used in many American liquid engines. These methods are proved to work well by testing by what is known as bombing technique. When the engine is running normally, a small bomb is exploded into the chamber so that a small pressure spike is caused. The resulting pressure oscillations are observed. If they die down, the engine is stable. Depending on the rate of decay of pressure, the stability of engine is rated.

It sounds a bit strange; we have talked so much about stability of liquid engine but very little of solid rocket engine. Why?

The essential elements of instability discussed above do occur in solid rocket engines also. But then propellants usually have a high metal loading (~17% aluminium). When these particles get into gas phase and combust, they provide acoustic damping. The damping is to such an extent that most instabilities are suppressed even in large engines. This does not mean, however, that instabilities are absent in solid rocket engines; they are present to a lesser extent and with lesser intensity.

12.3 Hybrid rocket engines

Hybrid rocket engines generally use a solid polymeric fuel and a liquid oxidiser. The feed system containing a tank, pressurisation unit, a valve and an injector resembles a liquid rocket engine and the combustion chamber

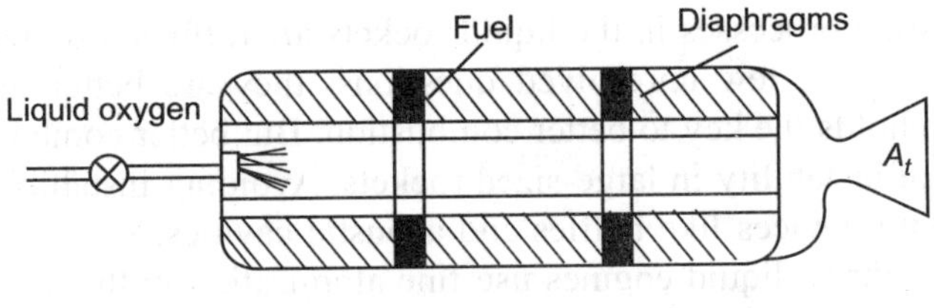

Figure 12.6 *A hybrid rocket engine*

containing the fuel block is configured like a solid rocket engine (Fig.12.6). During steady operation, combustion has to proceed close to the surface in a boundary layer. The principle of combustion in this engine is similar to the boundary layer combustion discussed earlier. Because the fuel vapours and gaseous oxidiser (obtained from the vaporisation of liquid droplets) mix and burn near the boundary, it takes a long distance for the entire oxidiser to be properly consumed. If the lengths are smaller, as they usually are, one gets a mixture of gases with oxidiser-rich and fuel-rich pockets passing through. To enable good mixing between these two, circular protuberances called diaphragms are provided. These produce recirculation zone downstream and up-stream of their location and result in better mixing. In moderately-sized engines, one needs as many as three diaphragms to achieve the complete mixing necessary for obtaining good combustion efficiency.

12.4 Overview

This chapter has discussed the details of how propellants burn, at what rates, and what factors affect them. Solid propellant combustion is more chemistry-dominated. Double-base propellants show substantial effects of chemistry. Composite propellants are affected by diffusional flame structure as well. As regards heat released or flame temperatures, the influence of additives is essentially linear, i.e., a small amount of additive causes a small change while a large amount, a larger change. This is because thermodynamic (or more truly thermostatic) effects are different from chemical kinetics or rate effects. In chemical kinetics the rate processes can be altered significantly by relatively small amounts of additive that influence the burn rate by altering the rate of only the key steps in a large number of elementary reactions occurring in the system.

Controlling the propellant burn rate is thus an unenviable task. The classical understanding that solid propellant rocket is simple is not true. Solid propellant rocket looks simple; but propellant making is a very complex task and has to be carried out very carefully.

Liquid propellant rockets in comparison look complex indeed. But a large part of it is mechanical-engineering based and is generally better understood.

The combustion processes in the liquid rockets are diffusion dominated and though there are a few unresolved questions, they are better understood. Atomisation holds the key to better combustion. But better combustion leads to problem of instability in large-sized rockets. Avoiding instability calls for using damping devices like baffles and acoustic cavities.

Most high-thrust liquid engines use fine atomisation in the injection process for achieving high combustion efficiency and baffles and other stabilisation devices for avoiding instability.

The combustion mechanism of hybrid rocket engines is embedded in boundary layer combustion and because of this, mixing is a serious problem. In order to facilitate efficient mixing of the fuel vapours and the oxidiser, devices like diaphragms are provided in the combustion chamber. Combustion in these engines is less prone to instability because of the damping provided by the fuel surface.

13

Stoves, Burners, Combustors and their Efficiency

Stoves are a part of domestic scene anywhere in the world. Burners are used in industries as well. Those used to produce heat in furnaces to melt metals and conduct special purpose heating operations on large scale—like preheating before the welding operation in an industry—belong to this category. Combustors are indeed the same as burners in the technical sense. In the generally understood sense, combustors are compact devices used for generating hot gases from fuels and oxidiser to perform some task, say run a gas turbine to generate electrical power, propel an aeroplane, run pumps in a liquid rocket engine and so on.

All these combustion devices are designed considering the following issues.

High combustion efficiency and high utilisation efficiency

These are two different aspects. In the first, one examines how much of the chemical energy that can be converted to thermal energy (or heat) has been actually converted. In the second, one examines how much of the heat released is utilised by the device into which the heat is being transferred. While the first is a function of combustion detail, the second is a part of heat transfer scheme. In some cases only the first part is important, e.g., gas turbine combustion. Subsequently, the hot gases go to a turbine and the phenomenology is different—it is the flow through a rotating machinery that does the work.

Stability and turn-down ratio

The operation of the combusting device must be stable over the operating range. The operating range is described by what is classically known as turn-down ratio. It is the ratio of the peak to the lowest acceptable power. The lower limit of the power level is decided by stability, pollution level and efficiency, depending on the device.

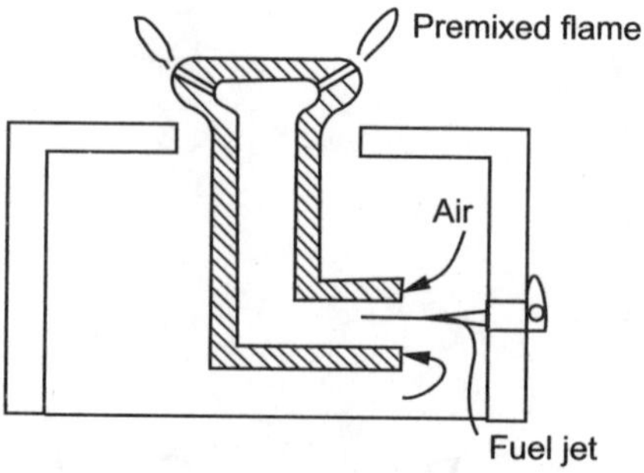

Figure 13.1 LPG gas stove combustion design

Compactness

The device for combusting the fuel must be as compact as can be accomplished. In some cases like aircraft gas turbines, an increase in compactness by a factor of two (volume of combustion has been reduced by a factor of two) has made possible tremendous advances in aircraft operational performance, which in turn has brought about a reduction in the operating costs of fleets of aircraft. In other areas like domestic stoves or industrial burners, one would like compactness but not at a high premium in relation to other factors like cost.

Cost

It is important that one does not ignore the cost of the system. Be it an aircraft gas turbine engine or a domestic stove, the cost factor drives the designer while making choices from the available options.

13.1 The devices

The combustion devices commonly in use are gas stoves, kerosene stoves, wood burning stoves, gas burners, liquid fuel burners for furnaces, special purpose burners, coal combustion devices and gas turbine combustors.

Some of these have been discussed in earlier chapters, but we will examine them briefly here.

Gas stove

In gas stoves, the jet of the fuel issuing from the tiny holes entrains air and moves up, comes out of the head where it is ignited (Fig. 13.1). Once ignited, the flame is stable and largely bluish over the range of flow rates permitted by the valve. The process of entrainment is not complete or satisfactory if the internal passage carrying the fuel-air mixture is somewhat blocked. In such a case the fuel flow rate is not affected but the flow rate of air entrained will not be adequate. In this case, the fuel–air mixture will be slightly fuel-rich and one may end up with yellow-tongued flames. One will also have the problem of sooting locally if the mixture is largely fuel-rich. Combustion efficiencies in these stoves is close to 96–98% in most situations. The efficiency of energy utilisation controlled by heat transfer efficiency is about 75% in the best situation. This efficiency is dependent on vessel shape and size. Flat bottomed vessels of diameter of about three times the diameter of the flame give the highest possible efficiency.

Kerosene stove

In the case of kerosene stove, it must be said that the design using perforated cylindrical sheets is ingenious and deceptively simple, as stated earlier. It might be possible for one to configure other methods of burning kerosene. But none that the author has seen or able to conceive is as good as the original design. The performance of the stove without and with perforated cylindrical sheets makes immense difference to combustion. Without any one of them, the flames surround each wick and will be yellowish, sooty and tall. A few moments after both the sheets are placed, (and wicks ignited, of course), the flame turns bluish, and flame height reduces significantly. The perforated sheet quenches the diffusion flame because air is getting inducted through the perforations and heat is taken away from the base region by the surrounding metal parts. Hence, the vapours mix with air and the flame gets converted to a premixed flame. The precise mechanics of such a transformation has not been satisfactorily worked out yet.

Wood stove

Wood stoves belong to a class of devices used extensively but not understood much. Most designs that one sees around the world have been developed without adequate scientific input.

A typical wood stove used in cooking is shown in Fig. 13.2. It has been observed that the efficiency obtainable with such stoves having three supports for keeping the vessel is about 10%. It is true that the efficiency of a stove operating in an open area does not exceed this range. But it is incorrect to assume that efficiencies of single pan stoves is limited to 10%. The simplest of the types shown in Fig. 13.2 can give efficiencies of about 12% even though sooting is a significant problem. Slight tuning of the heights of vessel vis-à-vis grate reduces soot as well. Efficiencies up to 25% can be obtained by providing a grate and a confined metal surrounding to the combustion zone. To obtain efficiencies better than this and to lower emissions, one needs greater care in the design of the elements. (Smoke and soot are serious problems in such stoves.) Two designs shown in Figs. 13.3 and 13.4 (discussed later) use fan based staged air supply to ensure clean combustion leading to high utilisation efficiency ($\sim$ 50%) with minimal smoking and sooting tendencies. The key aspects are prepared fuel with little moisture and controlled air–fuel ratio. Now that we have mentioned

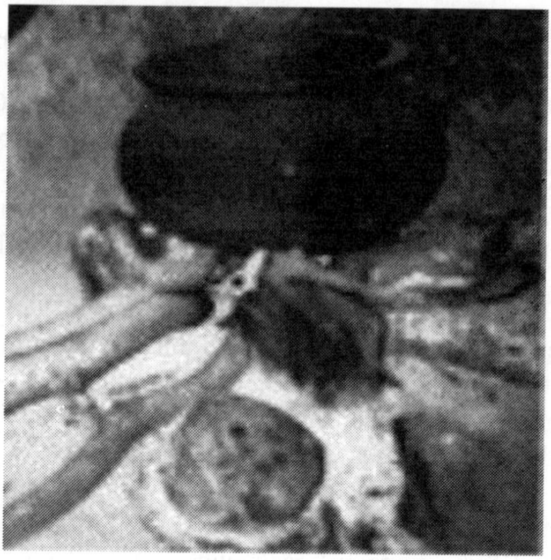

Figure 13.2 *The classical wood stove – vessel on three stones*

smoke and soot, let us discuss what they are, how they are generated and what can be done to eliminate them.

Smoke consists of a number of gaseous species that are intermediate products of combustion and some volatiles from wood. Smoke is a problem in the case of kerosene combustion devices as well. It gets generated if gaseous fuel elements mixed with air are such that the mixture is beyond the flammability limits at the local temperature of the gases. This is why one finds smoke issuing from a weakly burning wood stove having some pieces of wood which have suddenly been quenched or have not been ignited. This implies the operating power of the stove is low compared to its nominal capacity. Since open stoves (stoves which do not have chimney and have fuel entry area wide open) generally smoke considerably when slightly wet wood is used or when the used dry-wood is not tended properly, it is often misconstrued that chimney-less stoves always smoke. This again is untrue. If the region around the combustion zone is confined and is kept reasonably hot ($\sim$ 400°C, say) with the amount of air entering the combustion zone restricted to a value a little above that dictated by stoichiometry (which is about 6.5 with dry wood), the smoking tendencies reduce ubstantially. In fact, it is possible to run such wood stoves, with some attention, with no smoke at all.

Sooting is a phenomenon in which, due to lack of sufficient oxidant at the right place, the fuel breaks down to smaller fragments till fine carbon atoms agglomerate along with hydrogen and form clusters to produce soot. A lot of research has gone into the origin of soot in the combustion of hydrocarbon or biomass. Soot is formed largely in diffusion flames or fuel-rich premixed flames. It is a kinetic process starting with ions like $C_nH_m^*$ reacting sequentially with acetylene and other hydrocarbon compounds, much like polymerisation reactions; one of the asymptotic soot compositions is C_8H. The soot crystallites form spherical nodules of diameter 0.01 to 0.05 μm. Soot is generally undesirable in cooking stoves, diesel engines and similar situations. But its presence is beneficial in furnaces because the presence of soot enhances the emissivity of flames and hence the transfer of heat by radiation.

In a stove, sooting occurs when the combustion rate is high. Combustion rate is measured in terms of fuel burnt per unit time. Another way of specifying combustion rate is power. The mass consumption rate multiplied by the heat of combustion gives power. Typically, consumptions of 1 kg/h of kerosene implies 12 kWth, i.e., 12 kilowatts of thermal power, and 1 kg/h of sun-dried wood implies 4.5 kWth. If a stove is designed for a nominal power (2 kWth), sooting may become significant at a power level 10–15% above the nominal value (2.2 to 2.3 kWth). In contrast, the problem of smoking discussed earlier is important (for wood stove) at lower power levels, typically one quarter of nominal power (0.5 kWth). Thus, the range of operation of a stove is 0.5–2.2 kWth, bounded by smoking and sooting tendencies respectively. This range is expressed by the turn down ratio, it being the rate of peak-to-minimum power levels (4.4 in this case).

One of the problems in designing fuel-wood stoves is that the feed stock does not have fixed geometric and physical properties. The same stove may burn at a time ten logs of 10 mm dia or two logs of 30 mm dia. In the latter case, the fuel flow rate is 40% lower. This gives less power. On the other hand, if one has packed 30 pieces of 5 mm dia during combustion, one would have 50% higher power. When using a wood stove, the user cannot be expected to keep track of surface area permitted for combustion (!) and therefore, a minimum level of sooting and possibly smoking as well is to be expected. These issues are taken care of in gasification-based stoves discussed subsequently.

Let us look at the question of stability. Anybody who has worked with wood stoves would know that once in a while, a well-mixed non-sooty flame is obtained a little (or much) above the wood pieces, whereas over a large part of the time the flame is confined around the wood pieces on the grate. It is also seen from experience that the non-sooty, good flame above the wood pieces is somewhat finicky. It will be blown off easily, either by a slight wind or a readjustment of the wood pieces. It may also turn out that occasionally the flame around the wood pieces on the grate is re-established. Whenever the non-sooty flame above the pieces blows off, smoke issues. In this case, what is happening in the non-sooty flame is that the volatiles from the fuel wood and air taken in from various holes or fuel inlet are mixed together before the flame is created. Hence, it is a premixed flame. The

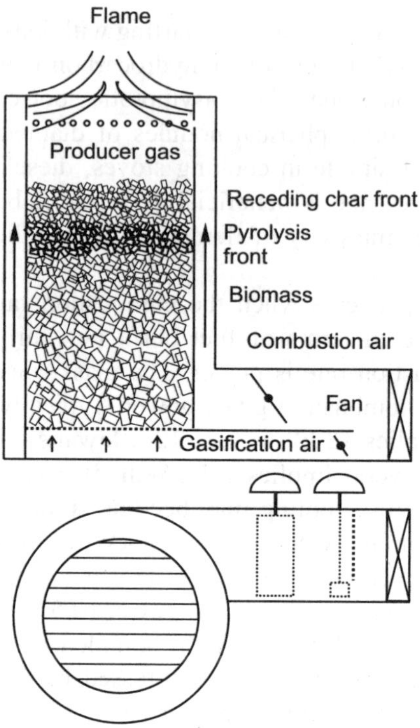

Figure 13.3 *A fire and forget gasification stove for a fixed amount of solid fuels - biomass or coal*

premixed flame requires good conditions for it to be anchored. It is difficult to anchor it in a fluid stream of non-constant velocity and so it tends to blow off easily. This is not so with the diffusion flame around the wood pieces on the grate. It is indeed difficult to extinguish it once a few pieces start burning. This discussion implies that premixed flame, though more efficient, is more unstable. Hence one needs premixed flame for good combustion and diffusion flame for stability. A good design therefore combines both kinds of flame structures for optimal performance.

Several of these issues are addressed by using what is known as gasifier stove. Figure 13.3 shows the sketch of such a stove. The key point in this approach is to convert the solid fuel to a gaseous fuel and then burn the gaseous fuel. The process of converting the solid fuel to gaseous fuel is called gasification. It is also a combustion process, but conducted at sub-stoichiometric conditions at an equivalence ratio of about 0.25 to 0.3 corresponding to an air-to-fuel ratio of 1.7 to 1.8. In this procedure the fuel bed is *not ignited or burnt from the bottom* as is done classically (by adding fuel pieces periodically) . Instead, a prepared fuel bed of finer pieces of biomass in a packed bed is lit from the top with some air flowing from the bottom through the bed. This leads to the flame front moving through the bed from top to the bottom, consuming the fuel rather uniformly. A hot surface at the top transfers heat to lower layers which causes ignition when the temperature crosses the critical temperature of 580–620 K for biomass and 700–850 K for coal. At this time the solid mass releases some volatiles which get ignited with air flowing around. This raises the gas temperature enabling the transfer of heat to the solid material. Hence, the temperature of the solid mass also goes up after all the volatiles are released and the material becomes char. The flame front will move down to the bottom converting all the material to char first and then consuming the char as well. There are two stages of reaction here. The flaming sub-stoichiometric combustion leads to products CO, H_2, CO_2, H_2O, and higher hydrocarbons. These pass through the char bed above the flaming pyrolysis zone where the char reacts with H_2O and CO_2 at high temperatures to produce additional CO and H_2. The higher hydrocarbons crack down to smaller fragments and also react with surrounding gases.

This process is self-regulating: changes in air flow rate (+ /–) change the gasification rate likewise (+ / –). One needs air beyond this region to burn up the *fuel gases.* Since the gasification process is self-regulating, the power can be controlled by controlling the flow rate through the bed, this air being typically called the *primary air.* The gaseous combustion process that occurs above the bed is facilitated by the supply of air called the *secondary air.* At power levels of 2 to 3 kWth meant for domestic applications, the primary and secondary air can be supplied using a single fan of the type used in computer industry; there is very little pressure drop to be negotiated through the bed. Use of such fans helps to reduce the cost of the stove. The design shown in Fig. 13.3 is a fire and forget type. Once loaded, it will burn though till all the fuel is used up. Reuse implies cooling down the stove and reloading the combustion space with pieces of biomass or pellets.

Another form of stove, called ejector induced gasifier stove, is meant for long stocks of wood, usually called firewood. Figure 13.4 shows such a stove schematically. Air from a fan is blown into the combustion chamber through holes in a centrally placed circular tube or specifically arranged tubes with holes. These holes are so sized and located that air comes out vertically in the form of jets at velocities between 5 to 15 m/s. The high velocity jet causes an ejector action and draws fluid from the bottom region. This region is connected to the horizontal chamber containing the firewood. After the system is lit by turning on the air flow, a small air stream is caused to flow through the horizontal chamber containing the fuel. This flow causes gasification by providing enough heat to cause pyrolysis. The char that is produced gets pushed on to the grate in the bottom section of the combustion chamber. The pyrolysis gases flow through the hot char bed and the gasification reactions proceed significantly in this region. These gases move up by the ejector action (also aided by free convection due to the hot combustor wall) and burn with air to produce clean combustion gases and high temperatures at the exit region. The ash tray at the bottom plays an interesting role in addition to helping extract ash. If some space is provided for air to be drawn into the combustion chamber, the air will oxidise the char and generate hot gases with products of char gasification. If the ash tray is closed ensuring that there is no air flow from the bottom, the char conversion does not take place and the char gets accumulated on the grate. After it is noticed that firewood can no longer be pushed into the system because the char bed on the grate is filled up, the char can all be extracted out, quenched with a ceramic material (or water, if such a material is unavailable) and stored for use as charcoal. By controlling the bottom tray spacing, one can consume all the charcoal and create excellent combustion with peak efficiency. The difference between the ejector stove and fixed biomass stove described earlier is that the ejctor stove allows continuous operation. Both efficiency and emission performance are slightly inferior to the the fixed biomass stove.

One of the key features of the above process is the ability it provides to control undesired emissions with fixed supplies of primary and secondary air. Since the throughput of the biomass and the gases is in a narrow range, the air-to-fuel ratio can be controlled to be in a narrow range to ensure uniform performance. It is possible to obtain high combustion efficiencies through this control. Keeping the excess air at no more than 10%, high flame temperatures of around 1500 K can be obtained over most of the time as also high heat transfer efficiencies. Practically realised efficiencies are between 40 to 55%, depending on the vessel shape and size and the use of dry high density biomass (pellets).

Biomass stoves used world over allow combustion process to occur in free convective mode. The performance of the stove in terms of sooting and to a lesser extent smoking, would be compromised because it would be very difficult to assure a fixed air-to-fuel ratio. Small wind currents can create significant deviations in the stoichiometry and lead to sooting or smoking. If a fan is used to drive a fixed amount of air, then the deviations of stoichiometry due to ambient air currents can be reduced substantially for ensuring excellent thermal and emission performance.

13.2 Burners

Burners are devices used for burning gaseous, liquid or solid fuels in furnaces or combustion chambers. While conventional stoves usually depend on natural draft for the intake of air, the more modern designs of stoves and burners have a forced draft using fans and blowers. All such combustion devices operate on the principles of : (i) swirling air or fuel gas to help cause stable combustion in a short distance from the burner, (ii) a swirling spray

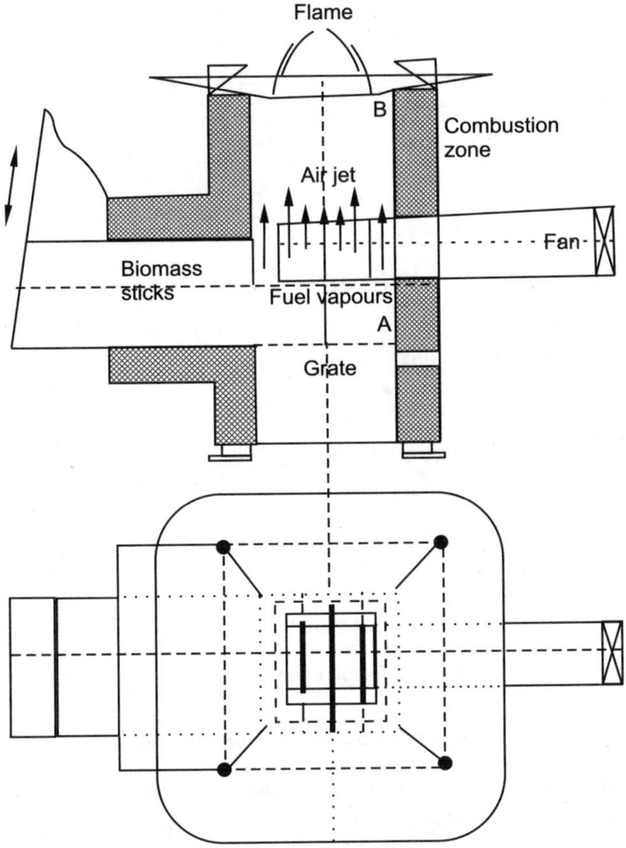

Figure 13.4 *A continuously operating, high efficiency ejector induced gasification stove for solid fuels - biomass or coal*

to atomise the liquid fuel to very fine droplets. This is done by raising the pressure of the liquid to as high as 70–100 atm and making it issue through a specific device, (iii) creating a recirculation zone to complete the reaction in a smaller volume and stabilising the combustion process. Figure 13.4 shows the typical details of swirl combustion process.

In the case of swirl burner, air is introduced in the tangential direction so that the flow has a very large tangential component. This causes the flow to stay close to the outer wall because of the centrifugal force component. Fluid particles take a helical path so that for the same axial distance the total distance covered is much larger depending on the extent of tangential component. Gaseous fuel may be injected into the chamber through a number of holes. If the fuel is in a liquid form, it will need atomising as well. This is done by one of the several means available. A method called pressure atomisation introduces the liquid in a tangential direction at certain

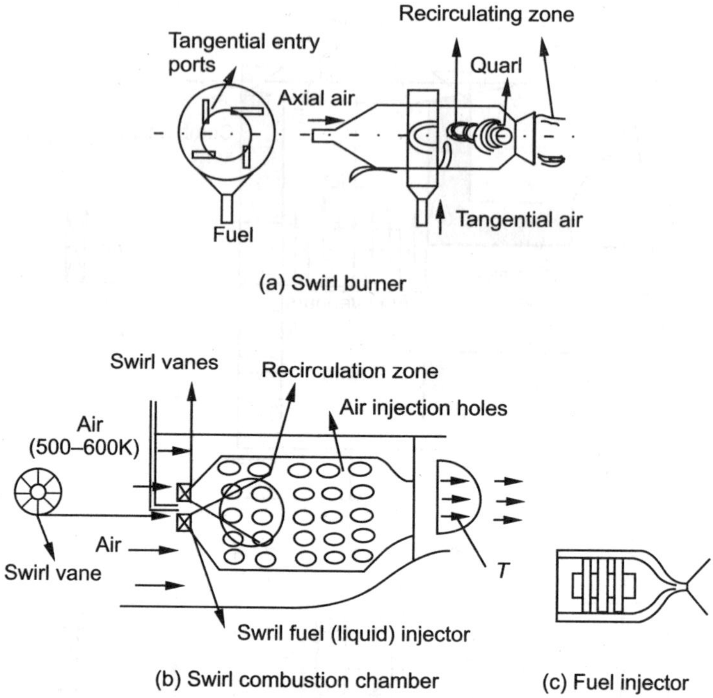

Figure 13.5 Swirl combustion devices

radius. The design seen in Fig. 13.5 (c) uses a helical screw-cut rod-in-a-tube configuration. The tube is reduced to a tiny orifice at the exit through a smooth conical shape. The tangential velocity of the liquid increases and when it comes out of the orifice, and a thin conical sheet emerges. This causes early atomisation, to form fine droplets. The swirl injector is used in gas turbine combustors, liquid rocket engines, burners for furnaces and even in the spray used by a hairdresser.

In case (a), the flame is stabilised as a cylindrical flame. It appears bluish in the case of LPG at some flow rates. The flame is stable over a wide range of air-to-fuel ratios, typically a factor of four. This factor is also called the turn-down ratio. The interpretation of this term is somewhat similar to the one stated earlier. For a fixed air flow rate, the lowest flow rate is the one at which the flame blows off and the highest flow rate the one at which the flame occurs significantly outside the burner (or incomplete combustion occurs inside the burner). The ratio of highest-to-lowest fuel rates then becomes the turn-down ratio.

13.3 Combustion chambers

The swirl combustion chamber shown in Fig. 13.5 (b) corresponds typically to a gas turbine combustor. The fuel and air injection regions are similar to the burner used in a furnace—only the holes present in the casing of the gas turbine combustor is different. Why does the gas turbine combustor need a casing with holes? The story has to begin backwards. Every gas turbine has a compressor rotated and powered by a turbine. Between the compressor and turbine is the combustion chamber. The hot gases from the combustion chamber are expanded through blades in the turbine running at speeds of 9000–30,000 rpm, depending on the size of the engine (larger engines running at lower speeds). The turbine blades face a very hostile environment–high temperature and high speed of the gases flowing past them. To add to these problems, the conditions imposed are periodic because of the large number of steady runs and shutdowns. In order to help preserve the structural integrity of the turbine blades, the temperature of the gases impinging the blades of turbine is limited to about 1000–1600 K. It is to be noted that stoichiometric flame temperature is 2300 K; consequently, the combustion process has to be conducted under fuel lean conditions, typically 1:50 or 1:100 (stoichiometry is 1:15).

The fuel-lean conditions in many cases may be outside the inflammability limit. One may also note slight amelioration because the air coming into the chamber is at higher temperatures ($\sim$ 600 K) and this widens the inflammability limit. How can combustion be made stable at such lean fuel-air ratios? The combustion chamber is so designed that for the given fuel flow, the air flow is split into several fractions and introduced through holes meant for the purpose. The first fraction is controlled at a fuel–air ratio near stoichiometry to ensure good combustion conditions. The remaining portion of the air is introduced later to dilute the gas to bring it to the designed exit temperature. The positions of holes and the size of the chamber are decided by semi-empirical correlations based on stirred reactor studies which give the maximum heat release rates (per unit volume) for any fuel–air ratio. This is the upper limit beyond which reactions cannot proceed and the flame gets extinguished.

For LPG–air combination, the maximum heat release rate is about 10^4 MW/m^3. For LPG–oxygen, it is 4.5×10^6 MW/m^3. Typical heat release rate in a domestic kerosene stove is about 4.0 MW/m^3 while in a rocket engine it is about 10^5 MW/m^3. These values can be used in the preliminary design of the combustion chamber of gas turbine or similar engines to arrive at the size of the combustor.

The efficiency of the combustion chamber of a gas turbine engine is close to 99% at take off or nominal operating conditions. It decreases at high loadings, implying higher flow rates, lower pressures and relatively

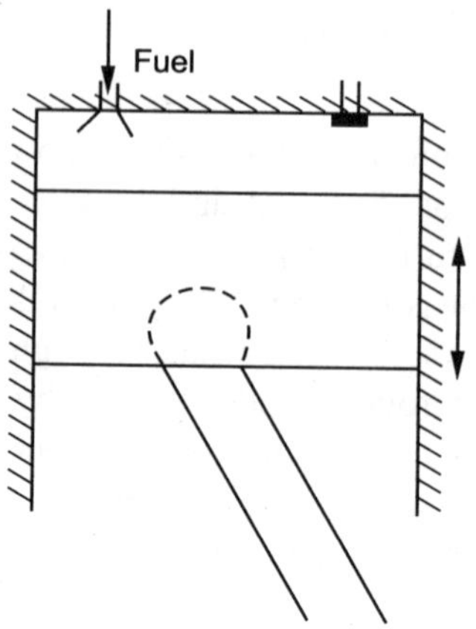

Figure 13.6 *Diesel engine combustion chamber*

smaller volumes of the chamber (put together by m/p^2v in Chapter 9). The efficiency goes down to as low as 65% at high loadings, close to blow off.

Figure 13.6 shows the combustion chamber of a reciprocating diesel engine. The fuel is sprayed into the combustion chamber even as the piston is moving upward and compressing the air. This occurs at about 20°–25° of crank angle before the top dead centre.

The liquid diesel is injected at pressures upward of 50–70 MPa through extremely tiny orifices so that the liquid is atomised to very fine droplets as early in its path as possible. The droplets ignite by themselves because the surrounding air is hot (~ 500–600 K). The droplets burn up raising the pressure in the chamber (which peaks slightly after the piston crosses the top dead centre), and the expansion process extracts the energy released. The whole process takes place under highly transient conditions. The time available for combustion is about 4–5 ms for a 1500 rpm four-stroke engine. Higher speed engines permit even lesser time for combustion.

The mechanics of combustion is slightly different in the case of spark ignition engines. The carburettor mixes the fuel in the form of vapour or very fine droplets with air and this is inducted into the combustion chamber. After it is inducted, the spark is fired causing ignition. During this process the gas is also being compressed. After ignition, the flame travels and consumes the entire reactant mixture. Again, the peak pressure is attained after the piston recedes from the top dead centre. Many two-wheelers have two-stroke spark ignition engines. These engines, because they have to be compact, run at high speeds, as much as 4500–5000 rpm. The time available for combustion in such cases is about 2–3 ms. That is why the pollutant emission per unit power of such engines is higher as compared to that in four stroke engines.

13.4 Overview

This chapter has considered the application of combustion in devices. Stoves, as conventionally understood, are burners which burn gas, liquid fuel or solid fuel with natural draft. Use of forced draft helps improve the combustion process, with the possibility of outstanding efficiency and emission performance. Industrial devices like burners have to burn at high flow rates of fuel (and so high power) and employ forced draft fan which keeps the pressure inside the system higher than the ambient or use an induced draft fan which draws the air through the combustion device so that the pressure inside the combustion unit is below the ambient. Combustion is also carried out at higher pressures (2 to 20 atm) so that the device can be made more compact. This is because higher pressures imply higher volumetric reaction rates ($\simeq p^2$) so that the volume of the chambers for burning up at the same fuel flow rates can be reduced approximately as p^{-2}.

Swirl is another artifice for reducing the length of the combustion chambers. Swirling the flow implies causing tangential entry of the fluid into a cylindrical chamber. This reduces the axial length of the chamber even though the path length for combustion remains the same. Most combustion devices use this process to great advantage.

The turn-down ratio is typically about 4 for many combustion devices—stoves, burners and gas turbine combustion chambers.

The knowledge of combustion processes in high thrust/power gas turbine engines has led to benefits in terms of reducing the combustor size and therefore, its weight to almost half in about a decade and a half.

The combustion chambers of reciprocating engines have also undergone a sea change in the last three decades through the use of high pressure turbo-superchargers and electronics for sensing and controlling the combustion parameters.

14 Fire Spread and Fire Prevention

जामिः सिन्धूनां भ्रातोय स्वस्रामिभन्न राजा वनान्यंति ।
यहातजूतो वनं व्यास्यादग्निर्ह दाति रामा पुतिव्याः ।।४।।

He is the close comrade of the rivers as is a brother of his sisters. He devours the earth's forests as a king his enemies. When driven by the breath of the wind he rages around the forests, the Flame tears asunder the hairs of Earth's body.

Rig Veda

Let us take a few instances of fire in our environment.

(a) Suppose there is a fire in a location where wooden furniture, e.g., tables and chairs of various shapes and sizes are present. Can it be estimated how much time is available before the fire can be controlled?
(b) A large grassland with a dry stack catches fire at one end. Would this lead to a total loss of material? At what rate would the fire propagate? How can one combat the fire?
(c) Most present day clothing is made of synthetic fibres like nylon and polyester which are prone to catch fire to an extent greater than cotton. Can the clothing be made fire resistant?

These are questions that need careful analysis on the basis of principles discussed till now.

14.1 Fire spread rates on thin and thick sheets

Let us consider a thin sheet of paper in horizontal position being ignited at one end. It is known that flame will propagate at a uniform rate called flame spread rate. The mechanics of flame spreading is as follows (Fig. 14.1).

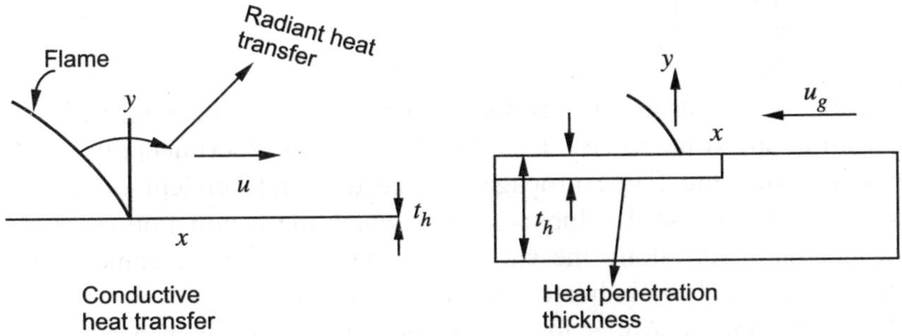

Figure 14.1 *Flame spreading mechanism*

The flame transfers heat to the surface of the sheet by conduction and/or radiation. The heat has to be transferred ahead by conduction so that some regions ahead will volatalise and thus enable ignition. This helps continued propagation of the flame. The flame spread rate can be estimated by first writing the heat balance equation on the surface of the sheet at a point closest to the flame (we can identify such a location by $x = 0$; see Fig. 14.1),

$$k_g \left[\frac{\partial T}{\partial y}\right]_{y=0} = \rho_p V_g t_h c_p \left[\frac{\partial T}{\partial x}\right] (x = y = 0). \tag{14.1}$$

The left-hand side is the heat flux transferred from the flame. The right-hand side is the heat received at the surface ahead of the flame. It is obtained by multiplying the convective flux per unit distance by the thickness of the sheet across which the temperature is taken to be uniform.

It is important to estimate the gradients $(\partial T/\partial y)$ and $(\partial T/\partial x)$ at $y = 0$.

$$\frac{\partial T}{\partial y} = \frac{(T_f - T_v)}{\Delta y}; \quad \frac{\partial T}{\partial x} = \frac{(T_v - T_0)}{\Delta x},$$

where T_f, T_v and T_0 are the flame, surface vaporisation and ambient temperatures respectively. The characteristic distance Δy and Δx are identified with distance for heat to be transferred from the flame to the surface and along the sheet from the flame to the point of ignition. The characteristic physical features describing the distance are thermal diffusivity (k_g) and velocity of the gas phase (of the local wind, say). Thus, $\Delta y = \Delta x = k_g/\rho_g c_p u_g$, where u_g is the speed of the wind against which the flame may be spreading. With these we get

$$\rho_p V_s t_h c_p = k_g \frac{(T_f - T_v)}{(T_v - T_0)}$$

or

$$V_s = \frac{k_g}{\rho_p c_p} \frac{l}{t_h} \frac{(T_f - T_v)}{(T_v - T_0)}. \qquad (14.2)$$

This equation indicates that as the thickness of the sheet increases, the propagation speed decreases. This has been found experimentally valid. It also shows that the flame propagation speed is independent of the wind speed. This is because the thickness over which the conduction takes place from the flame and along the sheet are taken to be of the same scale. A more rigorous analysis indicates this to be correct.

As an example, consider the combustion rate of a thin paper kept horizontally. Typically, for bond paper and its combustion, we can set T_f = 1800 K, T_0 = 300 K, T_v = 600 K, t_h= 0.001 m. Introducing these into the expressiona above, we get V_s = 21 m/h (~ 6 mm/s). The experimentally measured value of the same is 18 m/h (you can do it yourself at your home and find the value to be around this).

If the fire spreading is occurring over a thick sheet, then it is not correct to assume that temperature is uniform across the whole section. The extent of penetration of the heat wave can be estimated from

$$t_h = \sqrt{2\alpha_s t},$$

where α_s is the thermal diffusivity of the solid and t is the time where $t = \Delta x/V_s = k_g/\rho_g c_p V_s$. Substituting the value of t_h in (14.2), we get

$$V_s = V_g(\Gamma_g \Gamma_s)^2((T_f - T_0)/(T_v - T_o))^2, \qquad (14.3)$$

where $\Gamma_g = \rho_g c_p k_g$, $\Gamma_s = \rho_p c_p k_s$. These are the thermal responsivity or thermal inertia of the gas and the solid fuel respectively.

Thus, in the case of a thick fuel the propagation speed is proportional to wind speed and does not depend on the thickness. This result is also confirmed by experiments. The dependence on pressure appears largely through the term ρ_g in Γ_g^2, a result again supported by experiments.

The result obtained earlier can be used for estimating the rate of spread of the flame down thick sheets, as may happen in a situation of fire. The velocity V_g, which would be a known velocity in case of a wind flowing past, is now identified as free convective driven velocity and is obtained as follows.

The balance between convective term and the body-force related acceleration due to free convection gives

$$V_a^2/2 = L\, g\, \frac{\rho_\infty - \rho_f}{\rho_{f\infty}} = L\, g\, \frac{(T_f - T_0)}{T_0}, \qquad (14.4)$$

where L is the characteristic distance producing free convection. This is identified as $L = k_g/\rho_g c_{pg} V_a$, and it leads to

$$V_a^3 = 2\frac{k_g}{\rho_g c_p}\, g\, \frac{(T_f - T_o)}{T_0} = 2\alpha_s g \frac{(T_f - T_0)}{T_0}. \tag{14.5}$$

Thus,

$$V_a = \left[2\alpha_g \frac{(T_f - T_0)}{T_0}\right]^{1/3}. \tag{14.6}$$

Using this, one can get the flame speed for downward propagating flame over thick sheets. In the case of thin sheets the earlier result, which is independent of buoyancy force, holds good.

In the case of an upward propagating flame, the flame accelerates over the sheet because heat transfer occurs from the upper regions of the flame and the flame gets initiated at several points even before the material is burnt up at the lower regions.

14.2 Bush and grassland fire

In the case of bush and grassland fire, the elements concerning the fire spread are the same as discussed above. In large fires, radiation plays a significant role in heat transfer. It may turn out that 50–70% of the heat transferred to regions surrounding the fire is due to radiation in the case of fires larger than about a metre in size. One of the additional features responsible for fire movement concerns fire brands. These are objects which are burning, but get separated from the main material and move downstream due to wind and fall farther down and ignite new materials. This can be a serious problem in large forest fires, particularly during summer. One of the methods of overcoming forest fires started this way would be to create a reasonably wide strip of cleared land in close viscinity and ignite the material at the edges all round. This ensures that the material inside will burn out, thereby, limiting further damage. One of the features which helps such an outcome is that the wind always moves towards the flame in the case of a large fire. This is because the fires produce high enough plumes which draw air from all around to 'feed themselves'.

Preventing fires is indeed an important task in domestic and industrial environments. Fire hazard in materials like fabric, wood panels and panels made of synthetic materials are handled by introducing fire retardants in the materials by impregnation or coating. This leads us to the question: what reduces the propagation of fires and flames? Large number of studies show that phosphorous and halogen (Cl, Br, I) compounds are very effective in reducing the propagation of fire. Some of these materials (listed in Table (14.1) absorb large amount of heat and form char and thus prevent further transfer of heat and active radicals promoting combustion. Others interact chemically to reduce the rates of reaction. The latter effect is particularly true of halogen-based compounds.

Fire prevention techniques have been, by and large, an art rather than a science, and it is only in the last two decades that systematic attempts to understand the origin of fire and its spread have led to effective measures for reducing the damages caused by fire. While the development of fire science is complicated due to a whole variety of factors involved, the understanding obtained through it helps in better judgement and planning of strategies for fire fighting.

Table 14.1 *Flame inhibitors/retardants*

Ammonium chloride	$NH_4\ Cl$
Ammonium sulphate	$(NH_4)_2\ SO_4$
Mono-ammonium phosphate	$NH_4\ H_2\ PO_4$
Tri-sodium phosphate	$Na_3\ PO_4$
Methyl bromide	$CH_3\ Br$
Methyl chloride	$CH_3\ Cl$
Sodium tetraborate	$Na_2\ B_4\ O_7$

14.3 Overview

This chapter discussed briefly the mechanics of fire spread and fire prevention. Simple theoretical models are possible for predicting fire spread rate on thin and thick sheets, in horizontal or vertical modes, with or without wind. More is possible in terms of predictions for larger fires where radiation is important (not discussed here).

Fire prevention methods, while involving common sense concepts of keeping fuel away from oxidant or not having fire or ignition sources close to fuels and so on, also involve the design of materials less inflammable and chemicals which discourage specific fire types.

The last two decades have led to considerable understanding of the mechanisms of fire spread and prevention, driven as it were by the need to transport large number of special chemicals in large quantities by rail or road. There have been serious disasters in the past in the transportation of inframmable goods.

15 Solid Fuels: Combustion and Gasification

Solid fuels appear in various forms: biomass, coal and synthetic polymeric solids. Municipal solid wastes consist of bio-residues and synthetic polymeric solids. Most of this matter has volatiles as well as fixed carbon (excepting non-charring synthetic polymers like polyethylene). Combustion of these fuels involves two stages — devolatilisation with gas phase combustion and char combustion. Devolatilisation is also a gasification process, called pyrolysis. However, gasification in the true sense implies conversion of solid fuels into gaseous fuels capable of being transported for combustion over a distance, something not possible in direct combustion process.

Solid fuels are characterised by varying shapes and sizes, moisture fraction and ash content. Bio-residues like wood chips, coconut shells, corn cobs, bagasse and shells of seeds generally have low ash content of about 1%. Rice husk and hay have ash contents up to 20%. Australian coals have an ash content of about 5%. The ash content of Indian coals could be as high as 50%. Most green biomass has a moisture fraction up to 60%. Thin-walled biomass like sugarcane leaves loose their moisture quickly. Thick-walled biomass like bio-stock takes weeks to loose their moisture naturally. If they need to be used for thermal conversion purposes, drying needs to be a part of the system. Thus, sizing and drying are prerequisites of an efficient conversion process for these solid fuels. The ash resulting from the combustion process could be in a fine form, which requires proper handling as well.

Combustion of solid fuels has been discussed in Chapter 13 in connection with stoves and combustors. One can raise a question now: if we can burn solid fuels efficiently with little emissions, why should there be a need for converting solid fuels to gaseous fuels? If solid fuels are burnt, then it is imperative that the heat be extracted at the location of heat release. This is performed classically by burning fuels on the grate of a combustion system or a fluid bed combustion system built along with a high pressure steam boiler. The steam is subsequently used in a steam turbine to generate electricity. One of the limitations of this approach is that whereas the hot gases of combustion are typically at 1500–1700 K, the superheated high temperature steam would reach only about 650 K. Since the peak cycle temperature at which work is done will be lower, the conversion efficiency will be limited because of thermodynamic considerations. The peak conversion efficiency from solid fuels to electricity in this process is about 36–38% at large throughputs (hundreds of tonnes per hour). The expectation is that if one uses a high pressure combustion process as a part of the system, one can extract higher efficiency from the conversion process. One can then ask a question: why not use the hot gases directly in a reciprocating engine or a gas turbine? Reciprocating engines are essentially internal combustion engines that induct fuel gas and air from the atmosphere and generate heat inside the cylinder at high pressure. They cannot induct the burnt gases, for, no purpose would be served.

Gas turbine engines can utilise hot gases from a combustion system separately located. In this case, however, the combustion system needs to be operated at high pressures as indicated earlier. This would need a high pressure fuel feed and ash extraction systems. Further, the hot gases will need to be cleaned for fine particulate matter to ensure that they do not cause erosion of the highly stressed hot blades of the turbine. These additional systems will occupy space and there will be heat loss from the bounding surface. One way of reducing the size of the clean up problem would be to convert the solids to gas and clean-up the gas before being used in the combustion system. This would reduce the volume of the gas to be handled to about *a third* of that for a completely burnt condition. This makes the gasification process attractive. There are several other benefits of the gasification process as discussed below. The gasification process can be conducted with air or oxygen. When the intention is to use the gas for power generation, air can be used as the oxidant. In this case, one generates a gas that has about 20% each of CO and H_2, 1–2% CH_4, 10–12% CO_2 and the remaining nitrogen. The combustibles in this case are CO, H_2 and CH_4, with CO:H_2 in the ratio of 1:1. This gas is called producer gas in literature.

If one needs to generate a synthesised gas to be used subsequently to produce a liquid fuel, one uses oxygen and in this case the specific process design leads to a gas with about 45% CO, 22% H_2, 6% CH_4, about 2% of higher hydrocarbons and 25% CO_2. A CO:H_2 ratio of 2:1 is needed for producing methanol from this gas through a catalytic process. The several benefits of the gasification process are as follows.

(a) In the case of gas turbines used at high power levels (several hundreds of megawatt electric, MWe), the hot combustible gas from the high pressure reactor is passed through a high pressure, high temperature candle filter to separate the particulate matter before being used in the combustion chamber of the gas turbine engine. A high temperature valve (~ 600°C) controls the flow rate into the combustor. The open cycle efficiency of the gas turbine engine is about 35%. The hot gases from the gas turbine are typically at 600 K and would in turn be used in a boiler to generate high pressure steam that would be used in a steam turbine to generate electricity. Thus, electricity is generated in two locations – gas turbine as well as steam turbine, typically in 3:1 ratio. Such a strategy of using a fuel leads to conversion efficiency of 45 to 48%. This operation is called integrated gasification combined cycle (IGCC).

(b) It is possible to operate an ambient pressure gasifier, cool and clean the gas to take it through a separate compressor and inject it into the gas turbine combustion chamber, with the other elements remaining the same. This scheme entails some loss in efficiency because of the need for compressing the gaseous fuel—something not required when mined natural gas (usually available at high pressures) is used directly.

(c) It is also possible to take the cooled and cleaned gas into a reciprocating engine, the exhaust of which can be used in a steam cycle. The open cycle efficiency of the reciprocating engine will itself be close to 40%, leaving behind exhaust of 350 to 400°C, which is not as energetic as in the case of a gas turbine. However, if the power of the exhaust is adequate to generate at least a few MWe, it is possible to construct an IGCC system via this route. One of the advantages is that reciprocating engines are far more tolerant to the quality of maintenance than gas turbines. The combination of atmospheric pressure gasifier and the more rugged reciprocating engine offers a lower-cost option for power generation at lower power levels (~ 30 MWe).

(d) Smaller power systems down to even 10 kWe can benefit from gasification process. Its use in reciprocating engines promises a solid fuel-to-electricity conversion efficiency of at least 20%. A well designed 100 kWe engine-alternator system can promise a conversion efficiency of 25%. Higher power engines offer even higher efficiencies, exceeding 40%.

(e) Several thermal applications needing gaseous fuel in a distributed gas arrangement for multi-furnace operation in an industry can benefit from piped clean gas from one gasification system that can run any or all systems.

(f) Where a reduction operation is to be conducted in a metallurgical industry, particularly with CO, one can use gas directly in the operation.

Usually, mined natural gas which is processed and piped is the normal fuel. With the option of biomass-based producer gas as an alternative to natural gas, it is possible to generate an equivalent gas locally.

(g) If we interpret the gasification process itself as a staged combustion process under sub-stoichiometric conditions (involving homogeneous combustion and heterogeneous reaction with char as the two steps) with further processing either in a burner or an internal combustion system, one has more options for emission control.

15.1 Pyrolysis, combustion and gasification process

Biomass has about 75% volatiles and coal about 30%. The processes that occur in the conversion are described as follows:

1. Solid (with moisture) $\rightarrow$ dry solid $\rightarrow$ char (at $\sim$ 350°C) + volatiles
2. Solid (with moisture) + air $\rightarrow$ char + products of flaming combustion at sub-stoichiometric conditions $\rightarrow$ ash + some unconverted carbon (with oxidant, like air)

If the aim is to obtain liquid fuel from the solids, one needs to heat the solids in the absence of air like in option 1 above. When this is done, the biomass will release moisture including bound moisture at a temperature less than 150°C and volatiles at temperatures of about 350°C. After the devolatilisation process is complete, one obtains solid char (up to 30 %), some liquid components (3 to 50%) and non-condensable gases like CO, CO_2, H_2, CH_4 and higher hydrocarbons as the remaining fraction. If the heating rate is low, there is enough time for reactions between various volatilised components, which lead to a small fraction of liquid components (about 3 to 5 %). If the heating rate is very high (about 1000°C per second), a large fraction is liquid and if this is condensed immediately, one gets what is known as *pyrolytic oil* which contains combustibles with 20% water, which forms azeotropic mixtures with other liquids. High heating rates demand that the solid be pulverized to a fine size. The liquid obtained from this process has a calorific value about half of liquid fossil fuels. This liquid is difficult to ignite and its use is therefore limited to continuous combustion systems. While combustors meant for stationary applications can accept the fuel without difficulty, to operate internal combustion engines like gas turbines, a higher degree of purification to eliminate the fine char in the liquid is required.

The thermal conversion process of coal or biomass with air to lead to a combustible gas (gasification process) can be arranged in one of the several ways—fixed bed, moving bed or fluid bed. In fixed bed, one can have relative movement of the air and solids in co-current, counter-current and cross-draft mode. The fuel in a fixed bed moves down by gravity.

In combustion systems with a moving grate, solids are transported at the required rate over the grate and air is passed from the underside of the grate partly and over the grate partly. Air can be blown into the combustion system or drawn by induction through a induced-draft fan located downstream, close to the chimney.

At relatively large throughputs, one uses a fluid bed combustion system. In this system, the fuel is fed into a bed of sand that is maintained in a *suspended* condition with bubbles of air moving up in a random way. The fuel is fed in the specified size range into the bed. The fuel constitutes no more than 15% of the bed material. Because of the intense movement of the solids and air, the bed temperature becomes uniform and it is possible to maintain it in a narrow range by a suitable control of the air-to-fuel ratio for a fixed fuel feed rate. Fluidisation velocities are typically between 0.8 to 1.5 m/s. It is the sand bed that determines the fluidisation velocity, largely. Fluid bed combustion systems allow for strategies to control the emissions of oxides of sulphur and chlorine-based compounds nicely, and are therefore a preferred option for combusting coals.

When the fuel throughput is very large, the demand for minimising the size of the combustor for a given throughput leads to the use of circulating fluid beds. In these systems, the air flowing at relatively large velocities—7 to 10 m/s—carries the bed material and the fuel feed through a vertical reactor. The bed material with partly processed fuel is returned to the bottom from another section that separates the gas from particulate matter.

Both fluid bed and circulating fluid bed combustors can be altered in their geometrical construction to function as gasifiers by altering the air-to-fuel ratio to 25 to 30% of the stoichiometric value. Since they operate at a fixed temperature and the residence times are usually insufficient for complete conversion, the condensable fraction of the gas (tars) is substantive ($\sim$ 10 g/nm^3). One needs to introduce separate tar cracking systems (using dolomite or nickel-based high temperature catalytic bed) before the gas becomes acceptable to gas turbines.

In a fixed bed operating in counter-current mode (called updraft systems), the air moves up in a porous bed of solid fuel that is moving down (see Fig.15.1). A high temperature zone is created at the stage where air first meets with the fuel. The fuel would have lost moisture and volatiles in the upper stages and hence it is the hot char that reacts with air to generate combustible gases which are rich in CO_2. This gas moves up, mixes with the volatiles and moisture, generating a gas that has a high fraction of condensable. The gas taken out of the system has to be used in a combustion system very close to the gasification system lest the condensable choke the connecting piping. One of the advantages of such a system is that one can use

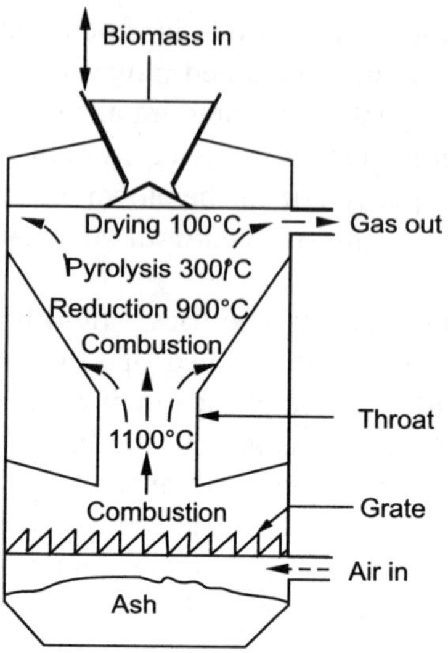

Figure 15.1 *Updraft gasification system*

a variety of biomass or coal or material with high moisture fraction. The ruggedness of operation however brings down its efficiency, for allowing significant moisture in the feed stock is thermodynamically inappropriate. One can dry the biomass by a low grade heat – from the waste heat, for instance. This kind of approach is common in European countries where the gas is burnt in boilers to help service heating applications in districts. The liquid content in the gas is about 5 to 20 g/nm^3, too low to treat as a liquid fuel, too high to be ignored in the system design for clean operations.

In fixed bed co-current systems, also called downdraft gasification systems (see Fig. 15.2), the air is drawn through the solid fuel as it moves down. In one system design called the closed-top system (Fig. 15.2) which originated in Europe during World War II period and is meant largely for wood chips, the air is drawn from tuyeres surrounding the chamber carrying the fuel. During the operation, air burns up the biomass or coal to char and then reacts with the char to generate a gas. The gas when cooled contains about 35% to 38% combustibles and 15% inerts (13% CO_2, and 2% H_2O) and some higher hydrocarbons ($\sim$ 100 to 500 mg/nm^3). The temperature distribution in the high temperature zone is punctuated with lower values in the zones between the air injection nozzles. This leads to enhanced tar generation, particularly at throughputs lower than the nominal.

The open-top design (Fig. 15.3) is more recent and allows a better char participation in tar conversion. Even so, some tar finds its way through the system at lower throughputs, as described earlier. Hence, to run the open-top system in a closed-top mode without a throat would not be a proper strategy.

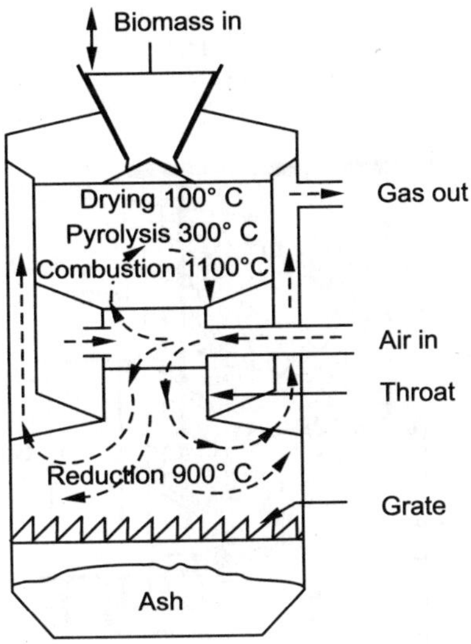

Figure 15.2 *Downdraft gasification system–closed top World War II class design*

If the air is drawn only from the top, the flaming pyrolysis front keeps moving up continuously (typically at a rate of 150 to 180 mm/hr). Since the depth of the entire reaction zone is about 0.5 to 0.75 m, this reactor will operate in the gasification mode leaving behind about 15% to 20% char continuously. Thus, when the flame front reaches the top, the reactor would be full of char. Beyond this point it will act like a charcoal reactor. This makes the operation of the reactor non-steady and is undesirable for long, continuous operations.

By introducing air in stages, one part at the top and another via the air nozzles, one can stabilise the flame front at some zone above the side air nozzles. The gasification that occurs in the flame zone much above the side air nozzles allows the gas to be re-burnt in the air nozzle area, thus raising the temperature of the char bed again. This allows the higher hydrocarbons (tar) to be cracked substantially, leading to a better tar reduction and also carbon conversion. An interesting feature is that the tar fraction in the hot gas changes little with the throughput, even at one-third of the nominal throughput. The technical reason for this observation is that the tar fraction is a combination of two factors—temperature and residence time. At higher throughputs the thermal profile is much better but the gas residence time is small, while at lower throughputs the temperature profile is poorer but the residence time is higher. Measured tar levels with dry biomass are less than 50 mg/nm^3 over a range of throughputs, implying lower turn-down ratio (see Chapter 13). The other advantage of such a system design is that it is possible to control the peak temperature while still managing to provide a broader, high-temperature environment to enable tar cracking.

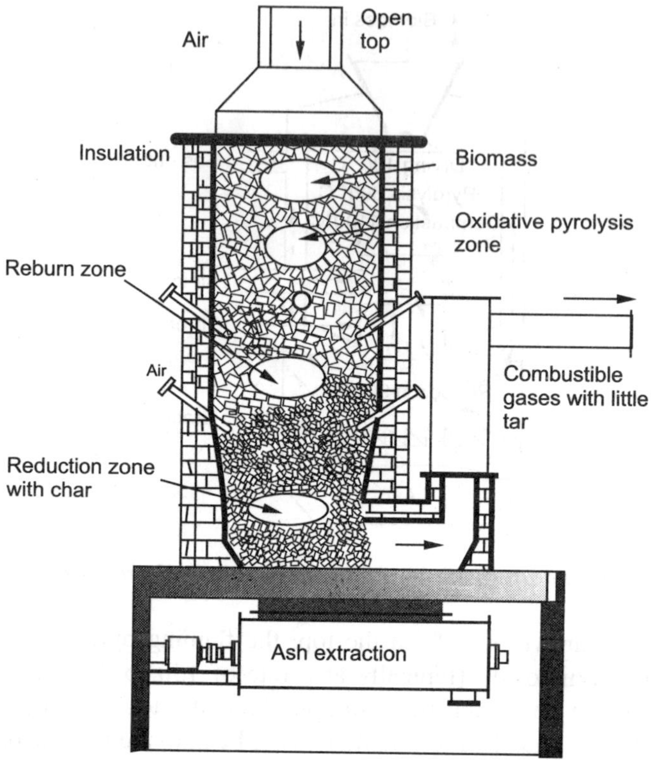

Figure 15.3 *Open top reburn downdraft gasification system—IISc design*

Peak temperature control is essential to ensure that ash fusion does not occur. This is particularly important when handling feedstock like urban solid waste, where one can expect an inorganic content of up to 20% with all the preprocessing scheme in position. With this system design one can capture nearly 80% of the energy of the raw feedstock in the gas. The gas composition containing higher fraction of hydrogen is favoured in this design (by 2 to 3%). This is helpful in obtaining higher conversion efficiency in internal combustion devices that depend on flame propagation process. The presence of higher hydrogen enhances the flame propagation speed and helps more complete combustion and better realisation of energy in the gas.

There is an important and essential difference between fixed bed downdraft design and fluid bed design. In the former case any change in throughput can be demanded and the *gasification process picks up by itself.* The char bed responds to the increased flow rate of air and the conversion process stabilises to the required demand. In the case of fluid bed design, one has the freedom to fix the flow rates of fuel and air independently. This may look like an advantage, but actually is not. If one is operating in the gasification mode, the performance of the system in terms of composition including tar is a strong function of the air-to-fuel ratio. Changes toward richer or leaner condition alter the composition significantly. The system elements downstream of the reactor will need to be designed to deal with these variations. Problems of tar generation are far more serious with bio-fuels compared to coal since the volatile content in bio-fuels is very much higher.

The hot gas has to be cooled and cleaned for use in advanced combustion systems and engines. The typical demand of high throughput engines in terms of tar and particulate matter is that they should be less than a few ppm in order that the engines operate on producer gas just as well as with natural gas.

15.2 Overview

This chapter has considered the thermal conversion processes for solid fuels. The recognition that solid fuels are generally of varying shapes and sizes with different moisture and ash content is important for designing a combustion system expected to be efficient with minimum gaseous emissions. One general principle is to convert the solid fuels into gaseous fuels so that combustion control is better exercised. Also, when the solid fuels are converted to clean gaseous fuels, it is possible to use them for mechanical power generation (and thereby, electricity) as well as for high grade heat.

Combustion devices looked at in this chapter are the moving grate system and the bubbling and circulating fluid beds. Fluid bed systems allow better thermal and emission control.

Gasification devices include fixed bed systems and bubbling and circulating fluid bed systems. Fixed bed gasifiers can be updraft or downdraft.

Updraft gasifier is tolerant to variations in fuel quality but generates a combustible gas with high levels of tar. It is usually used for raising steam or other thermal applications. Fluid bed gasification systems also generate gas with substantial amounts of tar. Downdraft gasifiers, on the other hand, provide good performance including very low levels of tar, but the feedstock must be better prepared in terms of size and with minimum moisture (sun-dry condition usually implies 8 to 12 % moisture). This burden on fuel preparation for use in downdraft gasifiers pays off by reduction in maintenance of end-use devices like engines. Fixed bed systems respond to change on demand at the downstream end (through the opening of a valve in the pipe carrying the gas, say) without any additional action. Fluid bed systems, however, need to control the fuel feed and air flow rates as soon as a change in demand is sensed.

16 Emissions from Combustion Systems

16.1 The pollutants

In discussing emissions from combustion systems, we will need to consider the emissions from furnaces of power plants, process industry and others, and from light and heavy-duty motor vehicles. We will exclude the emissions from rocket engines even though these are not environment friendly (because exotic chemicals are used), since these occur infrequently and do not constitute a significant fraction of the emissions on an average.

All fuels that are used in combustion devices are based principally on elements C, and H, with oxidant being O and the 'inert' N. Apart from these, there are other elements like S and Cl present in the 'fuels' in a small quantity that participate in the conversion process. High temperature chemical reactions are dominated by C and H with O and the chemical pathways inevitably involve elements N, S and Cl when these are present. The principal products of combustion are CO_2 and H_2O. The other products of the combustion process are (a) UHC, unburnt hydrocarbons including soot, (b) CO, carbon monoxide, (c) NO, NO_2, N_2O, (oxides of nitrogen, generally termed NOX referring to NO_x, where x can be 0.5, 1 or 2), (d) SO_2 and SO_3, (oxides of sulfur) which emanate from sulphur present in some fossil fuels (some oils and coal) and to a very tiny extent from biomass, and (d) HCl and dioxins, the compounds of C, H, Cl, and O.

The emissions are quantified usually in terms of ppm in the exhaust at a certain oxygen fraction (different people use different levels: 3, 5 or 10 %) and g/MJ of heat input. The emission index is best characterised by g/MJ because it relates to the amount of energy used in the process and hence energy efficiency is embedded in the index. It also rationalises the fuel because fuels of different calorific values can be conceived by users depending on the local fuel prices and the index will still be a true indication of the emission. In the case of motor vehicles, the emission indices are expressed in terms of g/km since it is this quantity that needs to be minimised.

16.2 Why are they the pollutants and what are their health hazards?

16.2.1 Carbon dioxide

CO_2 is a major product of combustion. Every kg of methane, gasoline and diesel burnt produces 2.8, 3.1, 3.3 kg of CO_2 respectively. In India, about a hundred million tonnes of liquid fossil fuels and five hundred million tonnes of coal are used every year and these amount to the emission of CO_2 of about a billion tonnes.

CO_2 is called a greenhouse gas as it absorbs the long wavelength radiation reflected by earth at 300 K into space (at 0 K). It is now established that the emission of CO_2 leads to global warming, and in recent times. substantial evidence has been brought out by the international agency, IPCC (Intergovernmental Panel on Climate Change). The problems of global warming are brought out vividly by the changes noted in the surface temperature of earth, which had not changed for a thousand years till about 1900 after which there has been a sharp rise by a degree in the next hundred years. This change has been very clearly related to industrialisation. Increasing concentrations of greenhouse gases are likely to further accelerate the phenomenon of climate change. It is expected that the average global surface temperature could rise by 2.5°C in the next fifty years, and by 6°C in the next century, with of course, some regional variations. Evaporation will increase as the climate warms, which will increase the average global precipitation. Soil moisture is likely to decline in many regions, and intense rainstorms are likely to become more frequent. Sea level is likely to rise by as much as 0.6 m, which will lead to inundation of coastal cities and possibly of tsunami-like activity.

16.2.2 Unburnt hydrocarbons, soot and solid particulate matter (SPM)

These are connected pollutants and are generally found in emissions from light motor vehicles running on gasoline as well as heavy motor vehicles running on diesel. Particulate matter or suspended particles are a complex mix of organic and inorganic substances in suspension in air. Some of these are produced through the combustion process. Oxidation of gaseous emissions such as sulphur dioxide and nitrogen dioxide form acids in air, which then combine with ammonia to form ammonium salts such as ammonium sulphate and ammonium nitrate. Both these particular salts exist as solid particles at low humidity or as solution droplets at higher humidity. Airborne particulate matter is usually described as SPM (suspended particulate matter) and TSP (total suspended particulate matter). The particulate matter which exists in the air as a result of combustion, though smaller in concentration as a proportion of TSP, is of greater consequence to human and environmental health. The fine particulate matter emitted from engines is capable of penetrating deep into the lungs as it is generally too small to be filtered by the system of nose and throat. The fine black particles of diesel engines (soot) may be impregnated with complex organic compounds like polycyclic aromatic hydrocarbons (PAHs) which are suspected carcinogens. In fact, it is increasingly being recognised that a greater part is played by the particle size and less by the total suspended particulate matter itself. Even at relatively low concentrations, fine particulate matter seem to cause changes in lung function and increase in cardiovascular and respiratory diseases (including asthma attacks). What is of most concern is that there appears to be no safe limit for this type of air pollution, and hence reducing the emissions from vehicles is sought through continuous reduction in the limits of several undesirable gases like carbon monoxide, oxides of nitrogen, sulphur dioxide and halogens. We will now examine each of these pollutants in some detail.

16.2.3 Oxides of nitrogen

Nitric oxide constitutes more than 90% of the oxides of nitrogen. It is a reactive gas, considered undesirable in automobile exhaust because of the role it plays in the formation of photochemical smog. However, it has also many valuable physiological functions in the human body.

NO is synthesised within human cells by an enzyme called NO synthase (NOS) found in the neurons of the brain, in the cells that line the blood vessels and in macrophages. It diffuses freely across cell membranes. It relaxes the smooth muscle in the walls of the arterioles. It also inhibits the aggregation of platelets and thus keeps inappropriate clotting from interfering with blood flow. There are many more positive functions for NO in the human, animal and plant life cycle when they are synthesized in the system. Nitroglycerine, which is often prescribed to reduce the pain of angina, does so by generating nitric oxide, which relaxes the walls of the coronary arteries and arterioles. (It is good to note that the Nobel prize to one of the three winners, Ferid Murad, was thought particularly appropriate because he showed how nitroglycerine works by releasing NO. Alfred Nobel's fortune came from his invention of dynamite, made from nitroglycerine!)

However, when freely found in the atmosphere, the oxides of nitrogen are irritant gases and their effects on the human respiratory system are observed in the lower airways and the lungs since the aqueous surfaces of the upper airways retain only small amounts of the inhaled oxides of nitrogen. Studies have shown that concentrations of oxides of nitrogen more than 1300 micrograms per normal cubic metre causes functional changes in healthy subjects – particularly an increase in the resistance offered by the airways. Inadvertent exposure to high concentrations of oxides of nitrogen is expected to result in pneumonia, bronchitis and pulmonary oedema.

Nitric oxide reacts with ozone (O_3) in the atmosphere in the presence of ultraviolet light from the sun and generates nitrogen dioxide.

$$NO + O_3 \leftrightarrow NO_2 + O_2 \tag{16.1}$$

In the presence of certain hydrocarbons (complex oxygenated hydrocarbons produced because of incomplete combustion in vehicles) the equilibrium that would be established as per the relation (16.1) would be disturbed and more of NO_2 and O_3 would be found in the near-earth atmosphere.

Because ozone has limited solubility in water, the upper respiratory tract is not as effective in scrubbing ozone from inhaled air. Consequently, majority of the inhaled ozone reaches the lower respiratory tract and dissolves in the thin layer of epithelial lining fluid (ELF) throughout the conducting airways of the lung. In the lungs, ozone reacts rapidly with a number of biomolecules following an exposure up to 8 hours, leading to reductions in forced expiratory volume in one second (FEV1) and some or all of the following respiratory symptoms like cough, pain on deep inspiration, and shortness of breath. These effects are reversible, with improvement and recovery time varying from a few hours to 48 hours.

At high altitudes there is a protective ozone layer that filters harmful high energy radiation which includes ultraviolet radiation, limiting its penetration to the surface layers of the earth. When an aircraft flying at a high altitude (e.g., Concorde during its service) releases oxides of nitrogen into the atmosphere, the reactions noted above will work the other way and lead to reduction in the ozone fraction and thereby to conditions where more harmful radiation reaches the earth's surface.

The release of these gases as well as those containing chlorine and bromine through various human activities, particularly chlorofluorocarbons in aerosols, has caused a gradual depletion of the ozone layer over North America, a large part of South America and Asia, nearly the whole of Europe, Australia and New Zealand. Consequently, harmful UV radiation that impinge these regions is known to cause dryness and wrinkling of skin and an increase in the incidence of skin cancer.

16.2.4 Sulphur dioxide and halogens

The main sources of sulphur contaminated fuel are coal, lignite and heavy fuel oils. From an automotive point of view, high speed diesel is the largest contributor of sulphur dioxide to the atmosphere. For petrol vehicles the quantity is around 0.02% by mass sulphur, whereas it is more like 0.2% by mass for diesel fuel. Oxides of sulphur are known to be so corrosive that its undesirable effects were known earlier than those posed by oxides of nitrogen. Inhaled sulphur dioxide is highly soluble in the aqueous surfaces of the respiratory tract, much more than oxides of nitrogen, and is therefore absorbed in the nose and the upper airways where it exerts irritant effects; little of it reaches the lungs. Sulphuric acid mist and some sulphates are more powerful respiratory irritants than sulphur dioxide and produce similar but more severe effects. The emission of oxides of sulphur into the atmosphere is the cause of acid rain, due largely to the formation of sulphuric acid (H_2SO_4) (and nitric acid (HNO_3) from the oxides of nitrogen); these have several impacts. Acidic aerosols or tiny solid or liquid atmospheric particles with a high acid content, when inhaled, lead to respiratory diseases. Acid rain can also lead to the reduction in visibility due to sulphate aerosols. Impaired visibility is a safety issue for airport traffic control. In addition, acid rain and acidifying pollutants can accelerate corrosion of building materials such as stone, brick, concrete and metal.

Dioxins are compounds of chlorine, oxygen, carbon and hydrogen. The presence of chlorine is essential for the formation of a series of chlorinated compounds, the most toxic of which is dioxin. This is largely produced in municipal waste incineration systems which is usually coupled to high pressure boiler-steam turbine system for power generation. It is also produced due to improper burning of household trash, and in very limited amounts from natural processes like forest fires. Municipal wastes often contain PVC (polyvinyl chloride) articles like footwear and waste rubber items, the combustion of which is the principal reason for dioxin. The melting point of dioxin is 305°C and its boiling point 412°C. It gets carried through the boiler system and is deposited in varying amounts along the way; a small fraction of it gets emitted into the atmosphere. The behaviour of the emissions do not appear to be straightforward; on occasions the emissions can become excessive because of the pealing off of the collected material. Dioxins are extremely persistent compounds, and they exist in the environment from both man-made and natural sources. Studies have shown that while all humans have some dioxins in their system due to their natural distribution in the environment, significant exposure to dioxins at higher doses may cause chloracne, which is a severe skin disease with acne-like lesions that occur mainly on the face and upper body. Other effects of exposure to large amounts of dioxin include skin rashes, skin discoloration, excessive body hair, and possibly mild liver damage. One of the other health effects is the risk of cancer in adults, particularly with long term exposure. While dioxin emission has been a matter of considerable international concern, significant research effort has isolated the problems and found solutions to limiting its emission in power generation systems using urban solid waste.

16.3 How are the pollutants generated?

16.3.1 Unburnt hydrocarbons (UHC), carbon monoxide and soot

The generation of these pollutants depends on whether the combustion process is premixed or diffusion limited. It also depends on the combustion device which may allow only a certain residence time for the combustion process.

Most furnaces/stoves using gaseous fuels can be relatively easily designed and be operated at slightly lean mixture ratios for obtaining high combustion efficiency while ensuring very low emissions of UHC, CO and soot. If more emissions than optimum is observed, then it is usually due to a defect in the equipment or its management.

The emission of the above components from a carburetted, gasoline-based engine is due to a few reasons. There is a quench layer next to the walls where the fuel will collect along with the thin layer of lubricant. This will get scraped occasionally and will get into the gas phase where the conversion remains incomplete and one could get some unreacted gasoline, some intermediate products of combustion including CO and some soot as well. Under low operating loads, it may also lead to incomplete flame propagation. Two-stroke engines are greater culprits compared to four-stroke engines.

Even when UHC emissions are negligible, it is possible to have significant CO emissions. CO is a slowly oxidising fuel. The burning velocity of CO in *dry air* is pitifully low — about 0.1 m/s. Addition of water vapour will raise the burning velocity to about 0.25 m/s, still lower than the burning velocity of natural gas. The key reaction step responsible for the change is $CO + OH \leftrightarrow CO_2 + H$. A less important, but relevant reaction is $CO + HO_2 \leftrightarrow CO + OH$. The OH and HO_2 (peroxide) radicals get generated in the presence of H_2O along other classical pathways. Because the reactivity of CO is lower, it takes longer time for its conversion compared to other hydrocarbon fragments (that take other paths to complete conversion) and hence, it ends up in the exhaust.

Soot has been discussed briefly in Chapter 13 in connection with wood stoves. It is a product of rich combustion with a set of compounds called polycyclic aromatic hydrocarbons (PAHs) acting as precursors. These PAHs coagulate into larger structures which condense into clear, tarry substances thought as nascent soot particles. Over time, surface growth kinetics convert these particles into black, spherical, primary soot particles with diameters of approximately forty nanometres. The particles collide with each other, conglomerate or agglomerate into larger particles. Newly-formed soot particles are especially hazardous because they have very high PAH loadings. Part of the overall concern about soot as a carcinogen is that PAHs remain attached to the soot particles and are transported into the lungs along with the soot.

The important parameters that influence the formation of soot in such flames are the parent fuel molecular structure, the flame temperature, the amount and nature of diluents either in the fuel or in the oxidiser, pressure, and the flame—premixed or diffusion. Diffusion flames have a greater tendency to soot, and higher the flame temperature, greater is the soot fraction. Experiments have shown that in terms of sooting tendency the ordering for diffusion and premixed flames as follows.

$$\text{Aromatics (Benzene, etc.)} > \text{Alkynes (Benzene, etc.)}$$
$$> \text{Alkenes (Acetylene, etc.)} > \text{Alkanes (Ethylene, etc.)} \quad \text{(Diffusion flames)}$$
$$\text{Aromatics} > \text{Alkanes} > \text{Alkenes} > \text{Alkynes} \quad \text{(Premixed flame)}$$

The ordering seems unsurprising with diffusion flames. However, the ordering in the case of premixed flames is different and seems not easy to justify. For instance, acetylene with a triple bond on C with a high C:H ratio, like benzene, should be expected to soot more than ethane. However, reverse is the case. The critical *equivalence ratio* beyond which sooting tendency is strong for acetylene (C_2H_2) occurs at 2.0, while for a straight chain hydrocarbon like ethane (C_2H_6), it occurs at 1.7 and for n-octane (C_8H_{18}) it is 1.4. This has made the investigation into the fundamental mechanisms of sooting very interesting. Many well-designed experiments have been conducted to elucidate the mechanisms. In premixed flames there are two competing processes: (a) the oxidiser (O_2 in air) and some radicals like the hydroxyl (OH) reacting with the intermediates from the pyrolysis, and (b) the pyrolysis process itself. The principal reactant goes through the chain reaction and generates acetylene and some cyclic compounds including ring compounds. The poly-aromatic hydrocarbons continue to react with acetylene, producing many complex compounds that react with atomic hydrogen. This takes away hydrogen from the compounds till a large soot particle emerges (C_8H). The two processes, (a) and (b) identified above, are temperature-dependent; however, increased temperature enhances the oxidation rate more than the pyrolysis rate. Hence increased temperature leads to reduced sooting tendency. If we recognise that the flame temperature of acetylene is much higher than ethane or n-octane (see Table 4.8), it is clear why acetylene has a higher equivalence ratio for sooting compared to ethane or n-octane. An interesting correlation has been developed between the sooting equivalence ratio and the number of carbon bonds in the fuel molecule. Ethane has one bond and n-octane has 7 bonds. It is expected that n-octane should have greater sooting tendency compared to ethane, a fact that is consistent with experimental result.

Soot in a flame is not always *undesirable*. The multi-billion dollar carbon black industry spends a considerable amount of research money investigating ways to produce more soot with better specified characteristics. This soot eventually finds its way into tires, toner cartridges, and many paints. In addition, continuum radiation from soot produces the better radiant heat transfer from many non-premixed flames. This helps increased heat transfer to the walls in a boiler. Thus, soot is desirable under some conditions, and at other times, very undesirable.

Diffusion dominated situations—fuel oil burners, diesel and fuel oil combustion in reciprocating engine cylinders and kerosene combustion in gas turbine combustor—are characterised by a combustion process where fuel rich regions and oxidiser-rich regions are inevitable. Thus, the combustion process is characterised by a whole range of stoichiometries. Hence there is no escape from the production of several of the undesired intermediate compounds. What is pertinent is whether enough mixing takes place subsequently and whether the mixed conditions provide the temperature and composition structure and residence time for the burn-out of these undesired species. Usually, at full throughput conditions the thermal environment is favourable for the reduction of these pollutants to low levels. At part loads and accelerating conditions, however, the conditions can be severe. In reciprocating engines the air flow rate into the cylinder is always constant and the fuel flow rate is varied depending on the load. Thus, the air-to-fuel ratio varies from a very large value at no-load condition to values little above stoichiometry at full load. In fact, the full load is determined by the criterion that a specified air-to-fuel ratio be maintained to limit the emissions — UHC in the form of smoke and perhaps, oxides of nitrogen.

There are several instances where a standard equipment like a burner which would initially be using lighter oil as a fuel with acceptable emissions would turn out to generate significant emissions subsequently essentially because, the costly lighter oil would have been replaced by a cheaper, heavier one. The C:H ratio would be more adverse (becoming higher), making it difficult for the combustion process to cope with the 'more difficult' fuel. In such a case, it may be necessary to alter the equipment designed for the lighter fuel substantially or even abandon it.

16.3.2 Oxides of nitrogen, NO_x

Of the oxides of nitrogen, the principal pollutant is NO. Other oxides of nitrogen form a very small fraction of NO_x. Even so, nitric oxide is a necessary ingredient of our life cycle.

The oxides of nitrogen get generated through three routes: (i) thermal route leading to 'thermal NO', (ii) hydrocarbon-fragment related route leading to 'prompt NO', and (iii) fue-bound nitrogen leading to 'fuel-bound NO'. The thermal route is by far the most important route. About 90% of NO is captured by it. It involves the reactions as follows.

$$O + N_2 \leftrightarrow NO + N \tag{16.2}$$

$$N + O_2 \leftrightarrow NO + O \tag{16.3}$$

$$N + OH \leftrightarrow NO + H \tag{16.4}$$

The first two reversible reactions are the Zeldovich mechanism. When the last reversible reaction is included, the reaction set is termed extended Zeldovich mechanism. The two principal controlling factors that affect the formation of NO are temperature and oxygen fraction. Staying in the oxidiser-rich region of the stoichiometry, close to the highest temperature generates the largest NO. Allowing first part of the combustion to occur on the rich side and providing small residence time toward the oxidiser-rich side helps limit the NO generation. A simple correlation that delineates the role of the residence time and flame temperature reads as

$$NO_x(\text{g-mole/cm}^3) \sim \tau_r^{(0.26)} \exp(-16400/T_f), \tag{16.5}$$

where NO_x is the emission at stoichiometric conditions and T_f is the adiabatic flame temperature at stoichiometry. τ_r is the residence time interpreted as the volumetric throughput divided by the volume of the combustion chamber.

16.4 Allowed emissions

The allowed emissions depend on the legislative measures adopted by a country. While it is true that in some instances the adoption of a newer, more environmentally-benign technology has had accompanying economic benefits, in many cases, new investments are called for. Hence, apart from the availability of the technology, it is the preparedness for adopting the clean up process that matters most. In most advanced countries the emission norms are set up after the government goes through an extensive consultative process. The norms are revised after periodic review and are variously expressed depending on the specific application in each country. Some countries have more stringent norms than others. In recent times these differences have been narrowing due to greater awareness. Over the last 25 years, when the environmental load has increased due to the increased population and industrialisation, more and more stringent norms have been imposed using newer technologies that have resulted from greater understanding of the pollutant formation in systems. The allowed emissions depend on the application – light motor vehicles using gasoline or diesel, heavy transport vehicles using diesel, stationary power generation systems, stationary thermal systems (furnaces, stoves, etc.). The emissions for motor vehicles are expressed in terms of g/km. For stationary applications it is expressed in terms of g/MJ (or g/kWh, g/bhp hr). For light motor vehicles, a simple equivalence may be obtained by taking, say, a 15 km/litre fuel performance. This implies that 1 g/km is about 0.36 g/MJ. For a heavy transport vehicle, one can take 4 km/litre fuel performance, implying that 1 g/km is about 0.09 g/MJ.

For light motor vehicles the allowed emissions of CO, NO_x and UHC were set at 50, 2.5, and 6.1 g/km in 1960. In 2004, these have been brought down to 1, 0.12 and 0.08 g/km respectively. For heavy transport vehicles it is 6, 1.5 and 1.5 g/MJ respectively. Smoke should be limited to 0.02 g/MJ for heavy vehicles.

The emissions from an engine as measured at the exhaust pipe with a range of fuels varies from 2 to 10 g/MJ for CO, 0.05 to 0.2 g/MJ for NO_x and 0.01 to 0.1 g/MJ for UHC. The measured levels can exceed the allowed values in specific cases and in such cases the engines need an exhaust treatment using a three-way catalyst or a similar system to limit the emissions to allowed levels.

Limits for dioxin in various western countries expressed as tolerable daily intake are typically, 1 to 10 pg per kg bodyweight (1 pg $=10^{-12}$ g). Because the toxicity is high even at low levels, and all improvements are related to bringing the magnitude to very low levels. Fine measurement systems are required to be designed to obtain these values accurately.

16.5 Strategies for emission reduction

16.5.1 Carbon dioxide

The emission of CO_2 can be brought down only by improving the efficiency of the process that uses any of the fuels (reducing kg fuel per unit product output; the output could be electricity, a certain distance moved or a physical product). Replacing fossil fuels by renewable fuels (that can be generated at least at the same rate as its use) so that neutrality of CO_2 production is achieved is another approach actively being pursued in recent times. The argument that if we replace fossil fuels by biomass the effort would be sufficient to meet the obligation of CO_2 reduction has some subtle aspects. Biomass is used as the primary fuel in stoves for domestic applications. In most parts of the world, the stove is operated with inadequate air-to-fuel ratio control, leading to emissions of UHC and CO. This is partly due to the use of stoves in regions with no availability of electric supply, which makes the inflow of ever-varying and fluctuating air into the combustion space due to buoyancy a certainty. The greenhouse effect of some of these gases is substantive and it is argued that a well-managed fossil fuel stove would produce lesser green house gas effect in comparison to poorly burning biomass stove. The key requirement then is to ensure a biomass stove design that delivers high combustion efficiency, something that is consistent with the burning of pollutants as completely as possible.

16.5.2 Carbon monoxide

The CO emission from industrial sources is minimised by ensuring some excess air and a good mixing of the fuel and the air. Increased excess air implies larger in-house power consumption for delivering this air. Hence, careful optimisation is needed to allow a minimum of excess air. In the case of automobiles, one needs to use a catalyst to burn off the more-than-prescribed CO.

16.5.3 Sulphur oxides

Current emission standards on sulphur oxide emissions are very strict and are met by post-combustion treatment of the exhaust gases. In coal-based power stations, this is achieved by scrubbing, i.e., mixing the exhaust gases with water droplets that contain limestone, which reacts with the oxide according to $CaCO_3 + SO_2 + 0.5O_2 \rightarrow CaSO_4 + CO_2$. The scrubbers are expensive and constitute a significant fraction of the cost of a modern coal power station.

In fluid bed systems, the addition of limestone to the feed ensures the absorption of sulphur oxides into the condensed phase. Sulphur is also a problem with diesel and residual oil. Specifications on diesel ensure that sulphur fraction is very low—less than 0.3%. Residual oil that is used for combustion in industries generates significant sulphur oxides. These gases need to be scrubbed to ensure that the oxides are not emitted into the stack. A dilute alkaline spray wash helps in retaining the oxides within the industry for offline treatment.

16.5.4 Oxides of nitrogen

Reducing NO in combustion systems has been a major preoccupation of the combustion scientists and industry for the past two decades (and continues to be so even now). It is recognised that its production is low in fuel rich regions, lower flame temperature and with shorter residence times. All these factors are used for reducing the NO emission. The following schemes describe the alternatives.

Lean burn scheme Wherever it is possible, one can use lean, premixed combustion with a low flame temperature. This is however thermodynamically inefficient and usually not adopted.

Rich-quench-lean This is a technique generally adopted in gas turbines, where a rich flame is used in the primary zone of the combustor (for stability); rapid mixing with air lowers the temperature to reasonable levels quickly, and then, the extra fuel burns under lean conditions. Various variants of the scheme are used in all low NO_x burners. The aim always is to minimise the residence time in the high-temperature region.

Ammonia injection The NO emitted from coal combustion is controlled by reacting it with a reducing agent like ammonia.

Reburn This technique employs the inverse of prompt mechanism. Extra fuel is injected after the first flame for extra power and for transforming the NO back to N_2.

Use of catalyst The NO emitted from gasoline engines is reduced by a catalyst in the exhaust.

EGR The use of exhaust gas recirculation (EGR) reduces the flame temperature for both premixed and non-premixed flames. There are ways of arranging EGR in combustion chambers in which the oxidiser and fuel jets are introduced separately at high velocity (50 to 100 m/s) from a base so that the burnt gases are entrained into the fuel and oxidiser streams. This process allows the mixing to occur without reaction till a stage when the fuel and the oxidiser fractions have been brought down to low levels while the temperature has risen to about 1200 K. In this condition the entire system works almost like a stirred reactor. This process reduces the peak temperature by about 100 to 150 K and helps reduce the emission of thermal NO_x.

Air preheat Use of preheated air for the same flame temperature allows very lean operation and hence decrease in prompt NO generation.

16.5.5 UHC

Release of UHC from industrial burners is not a very serious issue because ample residence time can usually be given to the reactants inside the combustion chamber. Meeting the UHC emission standards for diesel engines calls for fine atomisation of diesel and good mixing of it with air inside the cylinders. In the case of spark-ignition engines the emission standard is met by fitting a catalyst, generally a three-way catalyst, which achieves simultaneously the oxidation of UHC, CO and the reduction of NO. For this to be possible, the mixture has to be very close to stoichiometric condition, which motivates partly the use of complex electronic engine management control systems in modern cars.

The exhaust is passed over a usually precious metal surface of platinum, nickel, rhodium, etc, that has a very high surface area. The action of the metal is to catalyse the particular reactions related to oxidation of UHC and CO and the reduction of NO to N_2, so that its rate is high even at low temperatures ($\sim$ 400–900 K). The mechanism of catalysis involves the diffusion of the reactants towards the surface, their adsorption by the metal surface, particularly in the active sites where the reactants meet to form the product. This product is then desorbed back to the gas phase, to be removed by mass transfer (diffusion) into the bulk stream (adsorption means a chemical bonding between the reactant molecule and the atom (s) on the metal and desorption implies the breaking of this bond). The rate of the overall process depends on the nature of the catalyst, the temperature, and the fluxes of the gas inside the catalytic bed. Catalyst can degrade with time due to impurities and poisoning, particularly from sulphur compounds. Hence the fuel is processed to remove all the sulphur in catalyst-fitted cars.

Table 16.1 sets out many of the above observations to enable a quick appreciation.

Table 16.1 *Pollutant control strategies for various combustion systems*

System	CO	SO_x For coal and liquid fuel	NO_x For coal and liquid fuel	UHC
Incinerators	Excess air	Switch to low S fuel, scrub with limestone or Use Low S fuel	Lean burn mixing scheme Reburn, EGR, React with Ammonia	Excess air ensure high temperature (T)
Industrial burners	Excess air	Same as above	Same as above	-
Coal power stations	-			- -
Spark-ignition engines	use catalyst avoid misfire		Catalyst, lean burn, EGR	Catalyst, avoid misfire
Diesel engines	Good mixing fine drops	Remove S from fuel	Good mixing fine droplets EGR	Good mixing
Gas turbines	Good mixing fine drops	-	Lean burn mixing strategy	Good mixing ensure high T

16.6 Overview

This chapter has considered the aspects related to gaseous emissions from combustion devices – why they are pollutants, how they are generated and how to reduce them. Excepting CO_2 which is a major product of combustion (constituting about 15% by volume of the products of combustion cooled to ambient conditions), most others are found at very low levels (parts per billion as in the case of dioxins, parts per million for nitric oxides, unburnt hydrocarbons and carbon monoxide). The aim is to reduce the total magnitude of emissions by consuming a smaller amount of fuel for the same job, be it a furnace or an engine and next, by reducing the pollutant per unit magnitude of the fuel. Both aspects are interesting, but the second one is more challenging. The pathways by which these small amounts of irritants are generated are subtly arranged by nature and uncovering them is a fulfilling task – the formation of soot in these systems is a case in point.

In many practical systems, turbulence in the flow becomes an important feature to be accounted for in the calculation of the emissions. In many systems, combining the chemical pathways with fluid flow provides ways of predicting the pollutants by computational procedures when such predictive procedures are combined with data from selected prototype systems.

Emission reduction procedures are developed by understanding the way in which emissions are generated. Combating the emissions in ground-based systems like combustion systems for boilers and other chemical processes can be accomplished with relatively greater ease. Providing larger residence time, better mixing and specific inorganic treatment procedures help to reduce the emissions. Reciprocating engines and gas turbines for transport applications have to be more compact devices and hence call for greater ingenuity in reducing the pollutants. The fuel itself has to be cleaned up before use in these engines — sulphur is a major element that is reduced substantially by chemical processing before the fuel is considered acceptable. In addition, spark ignition engines use catalysts to reduce the other pollutants. Compression ignition engines need to evolve in-cylinder handling of fuel through better atomisation to reduce the emissions. In recent times, diesel engines have begun adopting exhaust treatment before being released into the atmosphere. Filtration of particles less than 10 micrometers is one such treatment.

Several, more stringent standards are being set to reduce the emissions from stationary sources, moving vehicles, both terretrial and arial. Compliance with there will call for intelligent ways of fuel processing and design of combustion systems.

17 Explosives – Solid and Liquid

17.1 Propellants and explosives

Propellants and explosives are substances containing fuel and oxidiser in a single molecule (or mixed together), or those which are in an unstable molecular configuration such that on appropriate initiation they burn slowly (a few to about a hundred mm/s), or they burn up very fast (at speeds of about a few to ten km/s). This ratio of a million in terms of regression rate distinguishes propellants from explosives. Propellants burn slowly or deflagrate while the explosives explode or detonate. Quite often, the word explosion is used cause connote situations where pressure rise in a confined chamber occurs very fast, sometimes leading to its rupture. Such situations *do not constitute detonation.* It is deflagration coupled with confinement that causes the pressure to rise and hence, an explosion. Thus, all explosions are not detonations, whereas all detonations are surely explosions.

17.2 Deflagration and detonation

Deflagration occurs in premixed gases and solid propellants, subjects discussed in Chapters 6 and 12 respectively. Typical speeds of solid regression rates (or deflagration rates) are 0.2 to 10 m/s (note that this is highly subsonic), and the flame thickness is about 0.2 to 5 mm—smaller the thickness, larger the propagation speed.

Detonations can occur in gaseous mixtures. reactive liquids and solids. Detonations, as a rule, propagate at supersonic speeds. Detonation speeds can vary between 2 to 10 km/s and the thickness over which the structure spreads varies between 0.02 to 20 mm depending on whether the propagation is occurring in a gaseous mixture at high or low pressure, or in a liquid, or a solid. The mechanism of the detonation is the same in all cases. It gets initiated with a supersonic wave passing through the unburnt material. Just upstream of the supersonic wave (in the case of a gas phase, within a few mean free paths, or in the case of condensed phase, molecules in close proximity), reactions occur and heat is released and the wave propagation is sustained as a detonation wave.

In a typical one-dimensional view, the mass conservation relations are the same across the waves (deflagration and detonation). The pressure is nearly constant and momentum equation plays a marginal role in deflagration, whereas in the case of detonation, pressure varies significantly and the momentum equation plays a significant role. This is also consistent with the momentum carried by the fluid in the two cases. In the case of deflagration, the magnitude of ρU^2 is about 0.2 Pa (= 2×10^{-6} atm) for most fuel–oxidant mixtures; it is 100 Pa for H_2–O_2 mixture at its highest propagational speed. For a typical detonation in a solid explosive, the difference in pressure would be 1000 to 10000 MPa! In the case of deflagration, the energy and species conservation equations play a major role with the rate of chemical reaction as the important feature while in the case of detonation, the energy equation plays an important role and species conservation a minor role. One can obtain the approximate detonation speeds without having to write the differential form of the conservation equations in the case of gaseous mixtures. This approach is known as Chapman–Jouguet treatment. In this treatment it is taken that the critical speed of propagation causes the burnt zone to reach acoustic speed, a feature that is the limiting condition for supersonic flows with heat addition (in this case, chemical heat release). Only if one needs the structure of the detonation does one need to treat differential form of conservation equations. In the case of liquids or solids, even though the phenomenology is the same as that of gaseous mixtures, it is not possible to compute the detonation speeds because the equation of state for the burnt gases is not known at the extreme conditions that prevail in this zone: pressures in the range of hundreds of thousands of atmospheres even though temperatures of 5000 K are obtained. In the case of deflagration, one needs to treat the differential form of equations to obtain speeds of propagation; simultaneously, the structure of the flame gets determined.

Detonation can be caused in a transition from deflagration, even in the case of a gaseous flame propagating in a duct. More frequently, it gets generated by a shock wave which itself could be triggered by a hammer blow, a pistol shot through a material or by friction (particularly with a rusted knife) or when the size of the material is large enough for thermal runaway reactions to proceed in the condensed phase. Detonation speed is largely independent of the reaction rate though reaction is an important ingredient of the mechanism for sustaining the detonation. It is strongly dependent on the magnitude of the heat release. Detonations in condensed phase are affected by two- and three-dimensional effects significantly. Even so, the departure of the observed speeds from the calculated detonation speeds is not large and can be explained, at least qualitatively. There are also limits in terms of mixture ratio for the propagation of detonation in gases. These limits usually fall between the composition limits of propagation for deflagration (see flammability limits, Chapter 7).

17.3 The substances

Detonating substances have been known to humankind for nearly 600 years. The first substance that was developed was the gunpowder with a typical composition of 75% KNO_3, 15% C and 10% S, which held sway till about a hundred and fifty years ago when gun-cotton or nitrocellulose was discovered. Further discoveries were that of nitroglycerine followed by trinitrotoluene, all within few decades. Alfred Nobel is credited with establishing of the field by systematic work on methods of handling these dangerous substances in addition to inventing other additives – oxidising salts like nitrates and other combustibles to make ordinary blasting explosives. It was in 1920 that the explosive property of RDX was discovered even though this compound was synthesised in 1899. These substances dominated the field till about fifty years ago when ammonium nitrate, sensitised by fuel oil as a cheap commercial explosive, and other variants of the same were explored. There are a variety of compositions available today to meet the objective, commercial or military, constructive or destructive, with the desired precision at a minimum cost! In military applications, one needs to store sensitive materials in a not-too-benign an environment, sometimes subject to hazards of heat and shock. Therefore, safety demands that less sensitive explosives be deployed. If a more sensitive material needs to be used, it has to be appropriately desensitised with the addition of binders. Such a requirement has led to the development of what are known as plastic-bonded explosives. Explosives are designed mainly to serve the following roles: (i) anti-personnel device (like grenade) which calls for fragmentation leading to high speed of the fragments, (ii) blasting devices for inflicting structural damage over an area and (iii) penetration device to perform armour-piercing action. The more recently developed fuel-air explosives may be used as an anti-personnel device. In missile applications, where the explosive material is to be carried as a payload, one would like to carry the minimum mass to achieve the desired destructive result (an extension of this concept leads to the use of nuclear warheads instead of conventional warheads of the kind discussed here).

In commercial use of explosives, minimisation of cost per unit output becomes important while making a choice. On the technical side, when used in underground mines, the safety of the mine itself has to be ensured. Most underground mines release methane as a consequence of long term biogenic activity. This gas can combine with air from the atmosphere to form combustible mixtures in some pockets, though the design of operation of the mine would aim at flushing these gases out. If the explosive were to release hot gases for a duration over which ignition of the gaseous mixture can occur, the entire gaseous mass can deflagrate and this can lead to deflagrative explosion. Hence, the design of the explosive should be such that on its operation, only a blast wave should be generated and very little gas or residual hot particles that can cause further ignition of the surrounding mixture should be generated.

When the explosives are used for blasting, as may happen in the building of tunnels, quarrying, and earthwork, fragmentation should be avoided and hence there is need to control the explosive intensity. One of the recent applications of explosives has been in the demolition of old and dilapidated buildings in a very short duration. In this technique explosives are located at several locations in the building and their explosion initiated with appropriate time delays—half to a few seconds—explosives in the interior portions being initiated earlier. This process enables complete containment of the explosion and even the nearest buildings do not experience any residual effects.

The measure of the intensity of an explosive is the detonation velocity which also implies the peak pressure developed during the explosion. Table 17.1 shows the data on several explosive compounds. The detonation velocities of HMX, RDX and PETN are so high that they can create a very high detonation pressure which is an indication of the destructive potential of the material. A smaller amount of these substances is adequate to create the same damage potential as a larger amount of other substances. TNT, on the other hand, is a not a powerful explosive. Power described this way is different from the sensitivity of the material to thermal or shock inputs. That HMX is very stable implies that unless the right input is provided, it will not detonate. On the other hand, the fact that PETN or NG is extremely sensitive implies that they are susceptible to some random input like friction, slight temperature rise or dropping of the container to the ground from a short height which can lead to explosion. They need extreme care in handling. To alleviate this problem, mixed compositions have been developed. They are listed in Table 17.2. In the list of explosives provided in Table 17.2, 'poly' refers to a polymer like HTPB and the class of explosives, 'PBXN' refer to plastic bonded explosives. These have been produced for safe storage and handling and would function with the right detonating input. There are many more compositions developed for specific missiles and applications including underwater warheads. For instance, PBXN-101 is used in a strike missile and PBXN–103 in Mk 46 torpedo.

When shock waves move through fluids/condensed phase of different densities, interface effects due to differing densities will be felt. A shock

Table 17.1 *Properties of explosive compounds (HMX: cyclo-tetra-methylene tetra-nitramine; RDX: cyclo-tri-methylene tri-nitramine; PETN: penta erythritol tetra nitrate: TNT: trinitrotoluene; AN: ammonium nitrate; NG: nitro-glycerine (L = liquid); NC: nitro-cellulose)*

Explosive	Density kg/m^3	Detonation velocity km/s	Detonation pressure /1000 atm	Comments
HMX	1900	9.1	387	Very stable
RDX	1810	8.9	341	Desensitising needed
PETN	1770	8.3	340	Sensitive, expensive
TNT	1640	6.9	189	Not sensitive
AN	900	2.0	-	Explosive in large amounts Used with other compounds
NG(L)	1600	7.0	-	Very sensitive used with other compounds
Lead azide	4000	5.2	156	Very sensitive, primary explosive

Table 17.2 *Some explosive mixtures*

Compound	Composition	Application
ANFO	AN 94, oil 6	Commercial
Blasting gelignite	NG 92, NC 7.6, chalk 0.4	Commercial
Pentolite	PETN 50, TNT 50	Military
Amatol	AN 80. TNT 20	Commercial/military
Ammonal	AN 65, TNT 15. Al 17, C 3	Commercial/Military
Cyclotol 75/25	RDX 75, TNT 25	Military
HTA -3	HMX 49, TNT 29, AI 22	Military
PBXN-101	HMX 82, poly 18	Military
PBXN- 103	AP 40, Al 27, NC 6, TMETN 27	Military

wave in air hitting a solid surface will get reflected as a shock; it also passes into the solid medium as shock. *If the shock wave in a solid medium hits the surface beyond which is air, say, then the shock wave gets reflected as an expansion wave which transmits the shock wave into the atmosphere.* It is this behaviour of the shock reflecting as an expansion wave that causes the breaking up of brittle materials like rock which can withstand very little tensile loads.

An interesting feature in Table 17.2 is the occurrence of TNT in many compositions even though it is a low-performing explosive. The reason for this is that it can be melted at 80°C, a value that is far from the decomposition temperature of 250–300°C, and hence one can integrate other compounds into it to produce explosives of desired detonating property. One useful and interesting property of detonation of mixtures is that the mixture detonation speed is a weighted mean of its components.

The detonation properties described in Table 17.1 are dependent on the density of the substance. It is possible to reduce the density of packing crystals and powders in containers to lower levels. In doing so, the detonation velocity will be lowered linearly, generally. Typically, a reduction in the density of RDX from 1800 to 800 kg/m^3 through packing arrangements leads to a reduction in detonation speed from 8.9 to 5.5 km/s.

There are many substances that deflagrate easily but do not detonate. There are many other substances which detonate easily but deflagrate with difficulty. Nitrocellulose, one of the main ingredients in propellants and explosives, deflagrates easily and does not detonate if the nitrogen content in it is much lower than 12 %. Beyond this value of nitrogen, it would detonate. Ammonium perchlorate (AP), the mainstay of composite solid propellants, does not even deflagrate at ambient conditions. It requires a minimum pressure (called low pressure deflagration limit, LPDL) before self-deflagration is possible. It is very difficult to detonate AP. Ammonium nitrate is both a propellant ingredient as well as an explosive. When mixed with a binder and made into a propellant or when stored in small amounts, it is 'docile'—it only deflagrates on initiation. However, when stored in large amounts as happens during transportation in ships (ammonium nitrate is also an industrially needed chemical for fertilisers), a small fire in the hold can transform into a detonation—a phenomenon known as deflagration-to-detonation transition already alluded to. Among substances which can be used both as propellants as well as explosives are RDX [cyclotrimethylene trinitramine, $C_3H_6N_3(NO_2)_3$] and HMX [cyclotetramethylene tetranitramine, $C_4H_8N_4(NO_2)_4$]. When these substances are made into a propellant, they can be ignited to deflagration and detonation-initiation procedures (like shocks) do not cause detonation since the propellants contain other materials which prevent excitation to detonation. However, when the substances are held pure, shock initiation leads to detonation (see later).

In the category of detonating substances which are difficult to initiate into deflagration, trinitrotoluene (TNT, $C_7H_5N_3O_6$) is a clear example. A blow from a detonator, or friction can initiate TNT into detonation. Further, when TNT is confined in a tube, a strong initiation by deflagration can transition itself into detonation. However, lighting TNT at ambient pressure is not easy, though possible.

Applications needing energetic substances usually demand only one feature—deflagration or detonation. All thrust generating propulsion systems for launch vehicles or missiles use propellants which deflagrate. In order to initiate combustion or ignition, heat sensitive explosive material is used. Detonating explosives used in military hardware like hand grenade, shrapnel shell, bomb, shaped charges for piercing armours and other applications like line mine clearing charge to clear the mine infested field; and in civilian requirements like underground coal mine operations, explosive forming for cladding vessels for industrial operations, quarrying, seismic prospecting and others. When the requirement is of detonation, one does not want the deflagration mode of functioning. An example of this requirement is in mining. In an underground mine, if a section of the material is to be dislodged through the use of explosives, one must only have detonation and no deflagration. The latter is unacceptable since the atmosphere may have combustible gas like methane–air mixture which might lead to propagation of deflagration, resulting in a gaseous explosion.

17.4 Structure of explosives and warheads

The structure of the explosive is generally as follows. The main charge that provides the destructive effect will be based on one of the several compositions described in Tables 17.1 and 17.2. These are triggered into detonation by a booster charge, which itself is triggered by what are known as initiating explosives. The initiating explosives are usually selected from heat sensitive compounds like lead azide, lead styphnate, mercuric fulminate, etc., in small quantities, usually deposited around a thin nichrome wire and covered with a thin plastic coat. Whenever detonation is desired, an electric current, typically, 0.7 to 1.0 amperes is passed through the wire. This leads to a tiny explosion and fire, which is caught up by the booster charge that converts the small outburst into definite small blast with sufficient shock strength to kick-start the detonation of the main charge. Typical primary initiating detonation charge is about 0.1 to 0.5 g. The booster charge is about 50 to 200 g. The main charge varies from as small as 100 g to as large as 500 kg depending on the application. Booster compositions are developed from the same materials but at different composition levels.

In hand grenades the shell is filled with explosive material, the amount of explosive depending on the desired damage potential. The surface of the shell is covered with grooves to enable fragmentation in an intended way, and at the centre is located a pin, initially held tight. When the grenade is to be operated, the safety catch is removed and the grenade is thrown. Once the top of the pin hits a hard surface, it hits a small cap filled with a primary explosive. This starts a delay segment booster for a few seconds and then the main charge is detonated. In the case of drop bombs. the design is somewhat similar, excepting that the fragmentation facility is not called for.

Two major concepts in warhead design aimed particularly at armour piercing capability are the shaped charge and the explosively formed penetrator (EFP). The fundamental principles of these are depicted in Fig. 17.1. In the case of shaped charge warhead, initiation takes place at the sharp cone

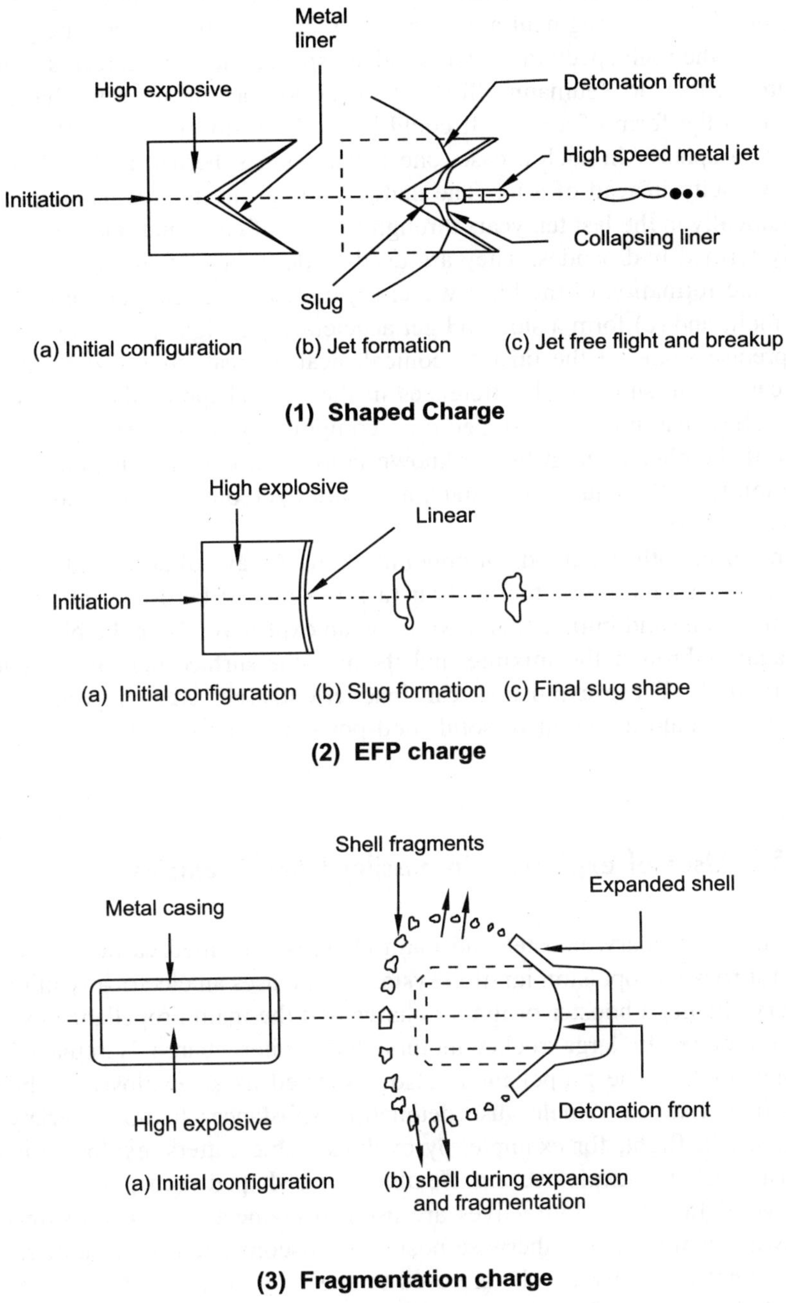

Figure 17.1 *Fundamental principles of warhead design*

end. This engulfs the cone, melts the metal outer sheath into high speed jet around the axis segment and directs the slug into the target. The performance of the high speed metal jet is indeed spectacular. The effect is termed Monroe effect or Neumann effect. There is no specific need to shape the charge in the form of a cone. It could be in the form of a hemisphere or a part of a sphere. In such a case, one generates a spherical melted blob of high velocity instead of a jet. The understanding in this area has improved dramatically in the last ten years through the use of computational tools, normally termed hydrocodes. They are used to describe various features such as (a) the formation of the blast wave; (b) movement such that the material will melt, and (c) form a slug and get accelerated to high speed. By varying the precise shape of the liner to conical, near-conical, spherical or others, one can create substantial differences in the final shape of the accelerated melt. These can now be designed on a computer quite accurately, since the basis of the phenomenon lies in known conservation equations, albeit with uncertainty in the equation of state, a feature overcome through calibration with detonation data.

One of the other methods of obtaining a blast wave of sufficient strength is to create a mixture of fuel and air (a fine spray of kerosene into a large volume of air) and initiate this mixture by an explosive. Then the blast wave propagates through the mixture and its over-the-surface damage potential is very high. These explosions can inadvertently get created even in fine pulverised coal-dust in air or solid food powder in air as well.

17.5 Uses of explosives in missiles/launch vehicles

The idea of primary, booster and main charges described earlier are valid even for rocket propulsion ignition systems. One uses an electrically initiated primary charge, a booster or igniter charge and the main propellant in small rocket motors. In large rocket motors, the igniter charge is replaced by pyrogen motor. The propellant is also respected as an explosive, albeit a weak one. Launch vehicles use detonating substances to do a variety of functions. In flight, for example, pyrovalves, cable cutters, explosive bolts, explosive latches, explosive zip, flexible linear shaped cords, etc., are used for several functions. Pyrovalves are used to connect a high pressure line to downstream element otherwise positively disconnected because of safety requirements. Explosive bolts are used to separate the elements on demand. Flexible linear-shaped cords are used for stage separation and also in vehicle destruct systems which need to get activated in case the vehicle deviates from the intended path. The principles used in the design of these systems are the same as described earlier.

17.6 Explosion and detonation–simple analysis

To understand the subject of explosives in condensed phase, it is useful to briefly review the phenomenon in gaseous mixtures. Gaseous mixtures of fuel and oxidiser can be detonated through the impingement of shock waves; some mixtures also have a tendency to move from deflagration to detonation. The understanding of which combination will detonate and which will not is still empirical, and the determination has to depend on experiments for gaseous or condensed phase substances; however, at what speed it will detonate and what will be the structure of the detonation are questions that have been answered to a significant extent, certainly for gaseous mixtures. One-dimensional conservation equations of mass, momentum and energy for a gaseous medium are analysed, with the energy equation having one term involving the amount of heat released due to exothermic chemical reaction.

$$\rho_1 U_1 = \rho_2 U_2 = \dot{m}'' \quad \text{(mass)} \tag{17.1}$$

$$p_1 + \rho_1 U_1^2 = p_2 + \rho_2 U_2^2 \quad \text{(momentum)} \tag{17.2}$$

$$h_1 + \frac{U_1^2}{2} = h_2 + \frac{U_2^2}{2} \quad \text{(energy)} \tag{17.3}$$

$$p = \rho R T \quad \text{(equation of state)} \tag{17.4}$$

The quantity $\dot{m}''$ is the mass flux through the wave. The enthalpy difference $(h_1 - h_2)$ is the heat released by the chemical reaction, Δh_r. The equation of state is still the ideal equation of state since the temperatures downstream of the shock are sufficiently high (5000 K) even though pressures are high (about 10 to 15 MPa). We use a simple treatment of the equations by transforming them into Mach numbers and requiring that $M_2 = 1$ to obtain the detonation velocity. We take note that $a_i = \sqrt{\gamma R T_i}$, where a_i is the acoustic speed (i= 1, 2) and γ is the ratio of specific heats at constant pressure to that at constant volume. We also treat $h_i = c_p T_i$ where c_p is the constant pressure specific heat taken as the same for both i = 1, 2. The mass, momentum and energy equations transform to

$$\frac{\gamma p_1^2 M_1^2}{T_1} = \frac{\gamma p_2^2 M_2^2}{T_2}, \tag{17.5}$$

$$p_1(1 + \gamma M_1^2) = p_2(1 + \gamma M_2^2), \tag{17.6}$$

$$c_p T_1 \left[1 + \frac{\gamma - 1}{2} M_1^2\right] + \Delta h_r = c_p T_2 \left[1 + \frac{\gamma - 1}{2} M_2^2\right]. \tag{17.7}$$

Substituting $M_2 = 1$ and after performing some algebra, one gets

$$\frac{(1+\gamma M_1^2)^2}{2M_1^2(1+\gamma)} - (1+\frac{\gamma-1}{2}M_1^2) = \frac{\Delta h_r}{c_p T_1}. \quad (17.8)$$

Since M_1 is likely to be large ($\sim$ 3 or more), one can simplify the equation by ignoring the constants to obtain

$$M_1 = \sqrt{2(\gamma+1)}\sqrt{\frac{\Delta h_r}{c_p T_1}}. \quad (17.9)$$

As can be seen, the detonation velocity is a direct function of the heat released in the combustion process. One of the principal approximations is that the specific heats are constant and the same; however, they depend strongly on the composition that itself depends on the calculated temperature under burnt conditions. Thus, if one adopts an iterative procedure, with the calculation of the composition depending on the procedure discussed in Chapter 4, one can get better estimate of the detonation Mach number and the detonation velocity. Such a calculation demonstrates that the results of calculation are close to experimental values.

The above theory assumes that a reaction occurs instantaneously when the shock sweeps the fluid. In reality, reactions do take time. This inevitably leads to the question of the determination of the structure of the detonation wave. This calls for the use of conservation equations written in differential form to include the reaction rates. A simple and very elegant theory has been explored by Zel'dovich, von Neumann. and Doring, in whose honour the structure is called the ZND structure of detonation. The essential content of the theory is that when shock propagates through a gas (or any substance), it heats up the gas to high temperature which initiates exothermic reactions behind the shock wave. The experimental observations generally follow the conclusions reached by the ZND theory. The shock thickness is an inverse function of the shock Mach number and is of the order of 3 to 6 molecular mean free paths. Since the chemistry depends on high energy collisions, if it occurs as it does, it must be accomplished with very high probability since the number of possible collisions itself is small. This implies that most reactions should occur at nearly peak temperature, which in turn implies that the details of the temperature profile are not very relevant. Hence, the predictions of the theory whose quality of prediction does not have to depend on the details of the profile turn out to be good when one considers situations where one-dimensional approximations are valid. Deviations occur because of the finite size of the duct containing the gas mixture. Detonation velocity varies inversely with pressure and diameter of the explosive. Both these have been explained as due to boundary layer behind the travelling detonation inside the tube. Many experimental results of the kind described above have been borne out by calculations quite satisfactorily. One of the contributory reasons for this is the equation of state which can be taken as ideal in a gaseous medium even though pressures are high because the temperatures are also high.

We now turn to detonations in condensed phases. Even though the broad principles of detonation are the same as in the gas phase, the aspect concerning the equation of state complicates the matter substantially in the condensed phase. To appreciate this, we need to look at some elementary facts. The acoustic speed in air at 300 K is 340 m/s. It is about 1600–2000 m/s in a solid. If a shock wave were to travel through a solid at a Mach number of 1.5, the pressure rise will be 10,000-15.000 atm. If the Mach number is 9, the pressure rise is in excess of 500,000 atm. The temperature rise is about the same—3000 to 5000 K. Under these pressures, even though temperatures are high, the fluid density is so high that non-ideal effects with respect to the equation of state become very important, which needs to be accounted for. Uncertainty in the parameters of the equation of state leads to the use of detonation data to fix these parameters, and hence the predictability of the theory is compromised.

We now take up the dependence of explosion (or otherwise) of reactive solids as a function of size and their chemical properties. Whenever reactive solids are transported, size becomes an important criterion. One should carry them in relatively small amounts and sizes. The basic reason is that beyond a particular size, the heat generated because of the auto-catalytic reactions cannot be dissipated into the surroundings at a rate matching its generation, and hence the temperature of the solid begins to rise. This leads to explosion. This phenomenon can be formulated as an unsteady conduction–reaction balance problem, with the initial conditions depending on the ambient temperature and boundary conditions depending on the heat lost into the atmosphere or to a set temperature at the outer surface. The solution to the problem will describe the behaviour of the temperature profiles in time. For some sizes, the ambient temperatures (= initial temperature) and reaction parameters (like the activation energy and frequency factor) of a particular solid and the peak temperature which occurs at the centre of the solid and will rise exponentially; this is interpreted as an explosion. Stated in this manner, the problem is complicated to handle analytically. Instead, it can be posed differently. Consider the steady state problem and ask the question whether a steady solution to the problem exists or not. If it exists, then there will be no explosion. If no solution exists, then it is a case of explosion. This approach is simple and works very well. Frank Kamenetskii, in his book *Diffusion and Chemical Kinetics*, has outlined the procedure and obtained results in delightfully simple and elegant manner for solids in plane two-dimensional, cylindrical and spherical configurations. The governing equation is

$$k\frac{d^2T}{dx^2} - \frac{n}{x}\frac{dT}{dx} = HA_jY_r exp(-E/RT), \qquad (17.10)$$

where Y_r is the mass fraction of the reactant. The mass fraction can be related to temperature using the Schvab–Zeldovich formalism as $Y_r = (T_f - T)/(T_f - T_0)$, where T_f and T_0 are the flame and ambient temperatures, respectively. The parameter n in the second term on the left-hand side is 0 for plane geometry, 1 for cylindrical geometry and 2 for spherical geometry. In the case of explosion, the deviation in temperature from the ambient value to that required to cause explosion will not be much and therefore, the amount of reactant which is consumed is small and hence Y_r can be treated as 1 in the analysis. One can non-dimensionalise various terms in the equation by

$\xi = x/L_e$, $\theta = \dfrac{E}{RT_0}\dfrac{(T - T_0)}{T_0}$. $\Omega = \dfrac{HA_jL_e^2}{kT_0}\dfrac{E}{RT_0}\exp(-E/RT_0)$, where L_e is the size of the explosive and T_0 represents both the initial and the boundary temperatures. The normalised equation assuming small departures of T from T_0 can be written as

$$\frac{d^2\theta}{d\xi^2} - \frac{n}{\xi}\frac{d\theta}{d\xi} = -\Omega\exp(\theta). \tag{17.11}$$

The boundary conditions can be set for θ as $\theta(1) = 0$. Symmetry condition gives $\theta = 0$. First, let us consider the case $n = 0$ (plane case). The fact that the second order differential equation does not have any term explicitly in ξ allows reduction of the problem to first order equation and its solution resulting in

$$\exp(\theta) = \frac{a}{\cosh^2(b \pm \Lambda\xi)}, \tag{17.12}$$

where $\Lambda = \sqrt{a\Omega/2}$. Invoking symmetry condition leads to $b = 0$.

These results, when combined with the boundary condition at $\xi = 1$, leads to

$$\frac{\cosh\Lambda}{\Lambda} = \frac{\sqrt{2}}{\Omega}. \tag{17.13}$$

One can show from this relation that no solutions are possible for $\Lambda < 1.2$ or $\Omega > 0.88$. This comes about due to the left-hand side having a minimum value because either the numerator or the denominator will contribute to an increase in the value of the function. This leads to $\ln a = 1.2$ and hence the maximum temperature, $T_{\max}$ as

$$T_{\max} = T_0\left[1 + 1.2\frac{RT_0}{E}\right]. \tag{17.14}$$

For typical values of E = 180 kJ/mole, T_0 = 300 K, the departure of the maximum temperature from the ambient will be 1.6 %, which is negligible.

All that this means is that a reactive solid at an ambient temperature will remain quiet until the temperature departs from its original value by only a few degrees. Beyond this change the reaction rate rises so fast that the temperature reaches runaway conditions and the result is an explosion.

For the case of cylindrical geometry ($n = 1$), the length scale L_e can be interpreted as the radius of the explosive. In this case a transformation, $y = \ln \xi$, converts the differential equation to

$$\frac{d^2\phi}{d\xi^2} = -\Lambda \exp(\phi), \tag{17.15}$$

where $\phi = \theta + 2y$. The solution technique is very elegant and simple and leads to the result that explosion occurs for all $\Lambda > 2$. This leads to the maximum temperature departing from the ambient by an expression similar to (17.15), but with the constant 1.2 replaced by 1.38.

For the spherical case, analytical solutions are not possible. Numerical solutions show that the coefficient 1.2 in (17.15) is replaced by 1.6 in this case. In all the cases, the fact that $\Omega > \Omega_{\text{crit}}$ (= 0.88, 2, 3.32 for plane, cylindrical and spherical geometries, respectively) leads to explosion implies that the same material shaped in one form or the other will explode.

It is not to be interpreted that spherical geometry is less sensitive compared to cylindrical, since, in the case of spherical geometry the total material is bounded, whereas in other cases the material can be semi-infinite. If one were to treat a cube of dimension L_e instead of a plane material of width L_e, one would get a different result, in fact, closer to the spherical geometry. The dimensions of the explosive, the kinetic parameters, thermal conductivity, are all contained in the definition of Ω and can be used to explain the dependencies of the explosive character on these parameters through the criterion of explosion indicated above. The proportionality with respect to L_e^2 and $\exp(-E/RT_0)$ will explain why larger sizes and those with higher activation energy will explode. It is for these reasons that in explosive industries, the material is transported using only small sizes of the explosive substances. As described earlier, major explosions of AN (ammonium nitrate) transported in large quantities on ships can be traced to the size effect described above.

17.7 Overview

This chapter has considered the subject of detonation that occurs in gases, liquids and solids. In the case of gases, the two limiting propagation features are deflagration and detonation. Deflagration is a subsonic flame propagation producing little pressure changes. Detonation is a supersonic propagation with substantial pressure changes. Since propagation is supersonic, such a propagation in condensed phase leads to very high velocities (because acoustic speeds in condensed phase are very high) and to extreme pressure changes that are catastrophic. There are substances that detonate easily and deflagrate with difficulty; others deflagrate easily but detonate with difficulty. There is use for each of these in a variety of applications, several of which are useful to society. Detonations in gaseous mixtures are understood better and can be predicted. Detonation in liquids and solids are far more difficult to understand. Hence, most of the developments in explosives is still in the realm of sophisticated art; yet, the current data collection and understanding are such that one can design weapons and explosives meant for specific applications using conservation equations that involves both fluid mechanics and solid mechanics.

18 Is There More to Understand?

The understanding of any field, including combustion, proceeds in stages. The understanding of complex interaction between fluid flow, combustion and heat transfer in one or multiple dimensions is not always direct, simple or straightforward. Sometimes very complex phenomena are amenable to one-dimensional concepts for the purpose of understanding the principal mechanisms; sometimes not. That is why the effort becomes challenging and interesting.

Can we identify a few problems whose solution is yet to be understood grossly and in detail?

Take the case of a candle. It is not possible to predict the burn rate of a candle so easily. Why is it so?

Firstly, the situation is complex even under simplified axisymmetric assumptions which make the problem two-dimensional. The physical phenomena to be accounted for are not simple. The heat transfer back to the candle wax makes it melt. The melted wax has to climb up the wick due to surface tension and vaporise on the wick to burn up in the flame. Yes, there is nothing spectacular in the elements. And, it is not solved.

What happens when oil is spilt on the surface of sea, something that happens when an oil tanker is involved in an accident? The danger the oil slick poses to sea birds, flora and fauna is very substantial. Is it possible to understand ignition and flame propagation of oil-on-water?

Chemistry-dominated phenomena like inflammability limits have already been mentioned as problems yet to be explored. Many such phenomena are being currently explored and much will be done by chemical kineticists in defining the reaction scheme and its parameters and by combustion scientists in solving 'realistic problems'. The combustion of some fuels like alkanes (heptane, octane, kerosene ...) in kinetic regime is affected by the lack of the chemical steps in pyrolysis and combustion, for these are very complex molecules indeed. The work towards revealing the basis for decomposition of such fuels has begun in recent times. More will be done in the future.

Combustion of composite propellants as far as their burn rate dependence on pressure is in concerned is yet to be satisfactorily modelled. The time is ripe for solving combustion problems of sandwiches, as they are called, where two-dimensional pieces of oxidiser are sandwiched between thin binders. One can then take on three-dimensional combustion problems.

These are a few samples of what is yet to be understood. The list is not exhaustive—several more problems remain to be resolved.

19 Further Reading

1. Fristrom R. A. and Westenberg A. A., *Flame Structure*, McGraw–Hill, New York (1965).

2. Gaydon, A. G and Wolfhard, H. G., *Flames, Their Structure, Radiation and Temperature*, Third edition, Chapman–Hall, London (1970).

3. Glassman, Irvin., *Combustion*, Academic Press, New York, Third edition, (1996).

4. Goodgar, C. M., *Combustion Calculations*, MacMillan, London (1977).

5. Gordon, S and McBride, B. L., *Methods of Calculating Equilibrium Composition, Adiabatic Flame Temperature, Rocket Performance and Detonation*, NASA SP 273 (1977).

6. Lewis, B. and von Elbe, G., *Combustion, Flames and Explosion of Gases*, Second edition, Academic Press, New York (1961).

7. Murthy, Kanury, A., *Introduction to Combustion Phenomena*, Gordon and Breach, New York (1975).

8. Spalding, D. B., *Combustion Fundamentals*, McGraw-Hill, New York (1985).

9. Williams, Forman, A., *Combustion Theory*, Second edition, Benjamin/Cummings, California (1985).

10. Turns, Stephen. R., *An Introduction to Combustion—Concepts and Applications*, Second edition, McGraw-Hill (2000).

11. Carleone, Joseph, *Tactical Missile Warheads*, v. 155, Progress in Astronautics and Aeronautics, AIAA Series (1993).

The major publications where most of the work on combustion is reported are:

(a) *Proceedings of Combustion Symposia* (international) held biannually; thirty volumes till 2005.

(b) Journals like *Combustion and Flame, Combustion Science and Technology, Fuel, Combustion, Explosion and Shockwaves, AIAA Journal of Propulsion and Power, Progress in Energy and Combustion Science* and others.

Index